"十三五"职业教育国家规划教材

国家示范性高职院校建设成果·职业英语系列

胡扬政 主编

酒店英语服务实训
（第3版）

English Practice for Hotel Service
(The Third Edition)

U0367278

清华大学出版社
北京

内 容 简 介

本书为北京市高等教育精品教材立项项目。本书根据酒店,特别是五星级酒店对酒店人才的需求特点而编写。本书以学习者的酒店英语职业技能发展为中心编写,将英语语言习得与岗位服务功能相结合,将相同岗位不同的英语服务技能构成若干实训项目,以不同的岗位服务功能构成若干酒店英语服务实训模块,通过这些模块的综合实践,提高酒店英语实用职业技能,包括用英语与客人有效沟通的能力、酒店英语礼仪服务得体的应用能力、酒店英语服务的实操能力、用英语销售酒店产品的能力、用英语进行销售策划的能力、用英语处理投诉的能力、用英语解决突发事件的应变能力、用英语进行个性化服务的能力、用英语解决问题的能力、用英语进行创新服务和创新工作的能力。通过酒店服务案例实训,"案例与提高"和"酒店经理点评"等栏目进一步培养学生的创新服务能力。

《现代酒店服务英语(第3版)》和《酒店英语服务实训(第3版)》为配套教材,前者供课堂教学使用,后者用于模拟实训和酒店岗位实训。本套教材获评"十二五"和"十三五"职业教育国家规划教材。

本书适用于高职高专、应用型本科及成人院校酒店管理专业、旅游管理专业及相关专业的教学,也可用于中职院校教学、酒店员工培训或自学。

本书封面贴有清华大学出版社防伪标签,无标签者不得销售。

版权所有,侵权必究。举报:010-62782989,beiqinquan@tup.tsinghua.edu.cn。

图书在版编目(CIP)数据

酒店英语服务实训/胡扬政主编. —3 版. —北京:清华大学出版社,2017(2024.1重印)
(国家示范性高职院校建设成果.职业英语系列)
ISBN 978-7-302-46250-7

Ⅰ. ①酒… Ⅱ. ①胡… Ⅲ. ①饭店－英语－高等职业教育－教材 Ⅳ. ①F719.2

中国版本图书馆 CIP 数据核字(2017)第 021103 号

责任编辑:吴梦佳
封面设计:常雪影
责任校对:袁 芳
责任印制:刘海龙

出版发行:清华大学出版社
    网　　　　　址:https://www.tup.com.cn,https://www.wqxuetang.com
    地　　　　　址:北京清华大学学研大厦 A 座　　邮　　编:100084
    社　总　　机:010-83470000　　　　　　　邮　　购:010-62786544
    投稿与读者服务:010-62776969,c-service@tup.tsinghua.edu.cn
    质　量　反　馈:010-62772015,zhiliang@tup.tsinghua.edu.cn
    课　件　下　载:https://www.tup.com.cn,010-83470410
印　装　者:北京嘉实印刷有限公司
经　　销:全国新华书店
开　　本:185mm×260mm　　　　印　张:19.5　　　　字　数:481 千字
    (附光盘 1 张)
版　　次:2008 年 8 月第 1 版　2017 年 4 月第 3 版　　印　次:2024 年 1 月第 8 次印刷
定　　价:58.00 元

产品编号:069544-03

丛书编写委员会

专业总策划：

王成荣　吕一中　李宇红　平若媛

总　主　编：

胡扬政　王莉莉

副　总　编：

刘　玥　周欣奕　胡冰冰　苑丽娟　胡　霞

王　艳

委　　　员：

Glenn L. Hyatt　Udo Schwarzboeck　Mariah J. Xu

郭远志　李作聚　苏　讠己　王海龙　宋　娜

冯茂芳　李维维　田志英　刘　莉　包　博

宋光辉　谷书霞　申　巍　杨明军　王金红

高亚妹　李　梅　高兰凤　苏玉刚　周其艳

徐庆颖

总　序

在经济全球化的今天,既具有专业能力又具有职业英语能力的毕业生已成为各行各业亟须的人才。在越来越多的工作岗位上,具有较强的职业英语能力已成为竞聘的重要条件甚至是首选条件。随着中国经济的迅猛发展,各行各业对新职业人的职业英语能力的需求和要求还会更加强烈。

因此,提升学生的职业英语素养与职业英语能力,实现学生高质量就业,成为北京财贸职业学院示范校建设的一项重要任务。该校坚持英语教学改革三原则,即:为专业建设服务,为特色人才培养服务,为示范校建设服务;以学生职业英语能力发展为中心,通过专业英语课程、普通商务英语课程等职业英语课程模块的建设,通过课堂教学和实践教学体系的建设,构建高职职业英语能力培养体系;以 DCPEA(Development-Centered in Professional English Ability)为高职专业英语课程建设新模式,以"6P"为知识载体,实现英语语言运用能力的培养与实际的英语工作技能养成的有机结合;把课程建设、教材建设和科研相结合,努力建设职业英语精品教材,实现专业英语教学内容、教学方法和训练方式的完全转变;探索高职双语课程的建设及其教材的开发;提高学生用英语"能财会商"的能力,提高学生在未来职业发展中的竞争能力,提升专业的综合实力,满足首都市场经济发展对财贸人才的新需求,满足社会对新职业人多变的需求。

我们的职业英语系列教材建设力求体现以下特色。

(1) 理念与目标:以学生职业英语能力发展为中心,建设财经专业类职业英语精品教材。

(2) 建设任务:以"6P"为知识载体,培养学生的职业英语素养与多种职业英语能力。"6P"知识载体具体如下。

- Profession(职业):以不同的职业英语工作为教材编写主线。
- Position(岗位):以不同岗位的英语工作任务构成教学模块,或以行业内对英语需求高的岗位的不同工作任务为教材编写重点或模块。
- Procedure(工作流程):以具体的英语工作任务为技能,以其工作过程为教学内容。
- Point(要点):以工作流程中的语言要求和工作注意事项为技能要点。
- Performance & Practice(演练与实训):通过模拟演练和(岗位)实训提高学生英语工作中的实际应用能力。

(3) 建设过程:以学生所学专业及其对应的未来职业为切入点开展调研,确定职业英语工作任务和职业英语能力;由行业专家和专业教师指导或策划,由一线专业英语教师任主编,多名英语教师及行业专家共同编写,努力体现教材的职业性、实用性、规范性、现代性和趣味性。

(4) 建设策略:英语语言运用能力的培养服务于职业英语的工作要求,并根据不同的职业英语工作需求,决定英语语用能力培养的侧重点;融入职业资格考试内容,教材内容和岗位英语工作任务努力配套,课堂教学教材和实训教材配套。在实训教材中引进案例教学和项目教学。教学栏目、教学情境、教学任务和教学实践的设计体现不同的职业英语能力培养的特色,使教材成为专业英语课程改革、实现职业英语工作能力培养的助推器。

前任院长王茹琴教授不仅为我院的英语教学改革指明了方向,还为职业英语教材的编写提出了宝贵的建议并给予了大力的支持;国际教育学院院长潘勇为职业英语课程的建设和为青年作者队伍成长积极铺路搭桥,出谋划策;清华大学出版社为本套丛书的策划出版付出了不懈努力,在此一并表示谢意。

胡扬政　王莉莉

2022 年 1 月

再版说明

《现代酒店服务英语(第 3 版)》和《酒店英语服务实训(第 3 版)》(以下简称《现代酒店服务英语》套书)互为配套的 DCPEA 模式的课堂和实训教材。其中的《酒店英语服务实训》为 2007 年北京市高等教育精品教材立项项目(项目编号 561)。这套书不仅是最早的高职专业英语工作过程导向教材,而且是北京财贸职业学院"国家示范性高职院校建设成果·职业英语系列"的范本,本套教材被评为"十二五"和"十三五"职业教育国家规划教材。

建设和不断完善《现代酒店服务英语》套书 DCPEA 模式研究型规划教材,旨在构建以"6P"为知识载体的高职酒店英语 DCPEA 新课程模式,实现学生五星级酒店实训和就业"零距离",并为高职高专及应用型本科的专业英语(ESP)教学改革、课程和教材建设提供系统、翔实、可供借鉴的模式、理念、经验和对策,为从根本上改变专业英语课程教材和教学严重滞后于专业人才培养需求的现状,实现专业英语课程职业英语能力培养的完全转变尽绵薄之力。

一、DCPEA 模式的《现代酒店服务英语》套书的建设过程

1. 第 1 版

DCPEA 是 Development-Centered in Professional English Ability 的缩写,意为"以职业英语能力发展为中心"。这个模式是主编带 2003 级和 2004 级学生参加酒店面试而引发的一系列思考和调研并结合酒店英语课程改革和建设提出来的,经过对 2005 级学生全方位的教学改革验证之后,被用在《现代酒店服务英语》套书中。2008 年 8 月出版了全套教材的第 1 版。

2. 第 2 版

(1) 美籍专家对每一篇对话进行仔细的修改并在美国录音;根据专家的意见,我们又认真修改了全书,以确保本书英语语言的质量,确保美国现代口语进课堂。

(2) 根据学生对教材使用的反馈要求,为全套教材配置了光盘和音频文件。

3. 第 3 版

(1) 在实训教材(主教材第 3 版)增加"再版说明",并引入高职专业英语 DCPEA 课程和教材建设模式,为任课教师教学改革、课程建设和科研提供借鉴。

(2) 根据社会发展及酒店自身的发展对酒店服务的新需求,全套教材第 3 版由专业英语教师重新编写"商务中心服务"等模块。在课堂教材中,作者把自己曾经在知名酒店商务中心的商务活动服务经历改写成教学内容,以提高学生的酒店英语综合服务能力和创新能力。在实训教材中,我们删掉了酒店现在实际上已不存在的服务,还删掉了学生在酒店实训中一直没有接触到的服务。

（3）为更好地提高学生的职业英语实用能力,结合语言学习的规律,在实训教材中增加"实训回望",并给出"部分参考答案"。

（4）增加教学附件。本书在修订中增加了二维码,手机扫描二维码可直接播放对话录音。

4. 第4版修订初步预期

（1）对课堂教材的部分模块和个别章节进行重写。

（2）酒店业人员流动性较强,进入酒店除了实训能力考核外,还有许多次的酒店英语面试,课堂教材第4版将补充酒店英语面试能力的培养。

二、酒店英语 DCPEA 课程与教材建设模式的构建

一个发展中心:以学生"职业英语能力发展为中心"为理念。

两个教学导向:以服务任务和服务过程为导向,并以服务任务为技能。

两种实践教学体系:建立课堂演练和酒店岗位实训或模拟实训相结合的实践体系。

"6P"知识载体(6P 模式):将"6P"知识载体渗透到酒店英语服务能力的培养中。

（1）Profession(职业):以酒店,特别是五星级酒店的英语服务内容为主线。

（2）Position(岗位):以不同服务岗位的工作组成教学模块;以相同岗位的不同服务为技能构成教学单元。

（3）Procedure(过程):以具体的服务任务和流程构成教学内容。

（4）Point(要点):以服务工作中的英语语言要求和实际操作注意事项为技能要点,并作为教学重难点。

（5）Performance & Practice (演练与实训):通过模拟服务演练和岗位实训来提高"新酒店人"的酒店英语职业素养和职业技能。

多种英语服务能力培养(十种):用英语与客人有效沟通的能力、酒店英语礼仪服务得体的应用能力、酒店英语服务的实操能力、用英语销售酒店产品的能力、用英语进行销售策划的能力、用英语处理投诉的能力、用英语解决突发事件的应变能力、用英语进行个性化服务的能力、用英语解决问题的能力、用英语进行创新服务和创新工作的能力。此外,还有用英语应对面试的能力(第十一种)。

五法运用:任务或情境教学、实践教学、项目教学、案例教学、讨论式教学等教学方法融入《现代酒店服务英语》全套教材。

两结合、两侧重、两设计的教学策略:"两结合"即将英语语言习得与酒店岗位服务功能结合,将英语语用能力的培养与英语服务技能养成结合并服务于职业能力的培养;"两侧重"即侧重听说;"两设计"即将服务要求和案例演练提高设计在酒店英语教学和职业英语技能的养成中,培养高职学生娴熟的英语服务应用能力。

三、DCPEA 模式的现代酒店服务英语配套教材的建设创新与特色

本书以多方位的调查与研究为依据,以全方位的课程改革为实证,首创高职酒店英语DCPEA新的课程和教材模式;建设以"6P"为知识载体的高职酒店英语精品教材和国家规划教材;创建以学生"职业英语能力发展为中心"的课堂教学和与岗位实践相结合的教学体系,培养学生英语礼仪的应用能力等十种酒店英语服务能力。课堂情境教学和岗位实训配

套,课堂教材与实训教材配套,相辅相成。引进旅游饭店职业英语证书的考试内容,提高酒店管理专业学生的酒店英语实用技能和职业素养,提高他们在未来职业发展中的创新能力和综合竞争实力。

富有创意的教材构架、根据教师实践经历改写的教学内容,这些教学栏目和融入不同教学方法的教学设计,以及受学生喜爱的由实训实例改写的案例故事,颠覆了传统的专业英语教材的编写模式和体例,实现了英语语用能力培养与酒店岗位英语服务能力培养的有机结合,不仅有助于教师进行课堂教学改革,还将对学生职业发展产生深远的影响。本书体现了职业性、实用性、时代性及语言的规范性。教材建设与课程建设和科学研究相结合,尽显DCPEA 职业英语培养的研究色彩。

好的专业英语(ESP)教材不能只是教学内容简单的输出器,更不能是公共英语教材的翻版。它需要作者特别是主编对专业、人才培养和课程进行深入研究,并植根于成功的教学改革和课程建设的肥田沃土之中,实现对已有教学体系和教学内容创造性的重构,有企业需要的现代新知识和职业素养与技能,有专业和课程需要的地道规范的英语知识,有独到的适合本课程能力培养的模式和载体,有作者将先进的教学法融入其中的教学内容和实践任务的教学设计,有新颖独特的体现本专业职业能力培养的教学栏目设计,有融进使用教材的师生的反馈和时代变化需求对教材的多次修订、重写和不断提高,实现英语应用能力培养和职业英语工作能力养成的有机结合,能真正成为执教教师职业英语能力培养教学改革的推助器,实现专业英语教学内容、教学方法和训练方式的完全转变,还要方便学生自学。我们正是朝着这些方面努力的!

本套教材自出版以来一直受到广大师生和读者的欢迎,得到专家的好评,"代表了目前高职专业英语教材编写的水平,对其他层次专门用途英语教材编写和教学极具启发意义"。这套教材不仅是国内酒店英语精品课程广泛使用的教材,而且为多门酒店英语精品课程的建设助力。编者提出的 DCPEA 理念和"6P"知识载体,所归纳提炼的十种英语服务能力及所设计的教学栏目等被用在一些教师教学改革、课程建设和科研文献中。编者还在《中国外语》等期刊上发表了 DCPEA 课程和教材建设研究文献共 8 篇,教材和文章均受到众多学者的引证和科研运用;DCPEA 教材编写模式也被其他专业英语教材建设所引用。这套教材两次荣幸地获评职业教育国家规划教材,其中的实训还曾获评北京市高等教育精品教材立项项目。借教材再版之机,对广大师生、读者、及学者和专家对本套教材及其研究文献的厚爱表示由衷的感谢!

编 者

2022 年 1 月

前　言

中国酒店业的快速发展有目共睹。到 2020 年中国将成为世界第一旅游大国,这就意味着中国酒店业将持续快速发展。现在在校的酒店管理专业学生毕业后将处于职业环境的黄金时段——酒店业的快速发展,将为具有较高的酒店英语服务技能和管理技能的酒店人才提供前所未有的发展机遇。

高等职业院校酒店管理专业教育培养的是具有一定的职业竞争力的酒店专业人才,要让他们在未来的酒店职业生涯中有能力去发挥,有才华去施展。提高这些学生的酒店英语实用技能,增强他们的职业竞争力,培养受星级酒店欢迎的实用性高技能特色人才,不仅是酒店业快速发展对高水准服务人才和管理人才的迫切要求,更是酒店管理专业课程建设和教学改革的方向和重要任务。

《酒店英语服务实训》是一本根据酒店,特别是五星级酒店对酒店人才的需求特点而编写的实训教材。本书以学习者的酒店英语职业技能发展为中心编写,将英语语言习得与岗位服务功能相结合,将相同岗位不同的英语服务技能构成若干实训项目,以不同的岗位服务功能构成若干酒店英语服务实训模块,通过这些模块的综合实践,提高酒店英语实用职业技能,包括用英语与客人有效沟通的能力、酒店英语礼仪服务得体的应用能力、酒店英语服务的实操能力、用英语销售酒店产品的能力、用英语进行销售策划的能力、用英语处理投诉的能力、用英语解决突发事件的应变能力、用英语进行个性化服务的能力、用英语解决问题的能力、用英语进行创新服务和创新工作的能力。

《酒店英语服务实训(第 3 版)》和《现代酒店服务英语(第 3 版)》为配套教材。本实训教材在编写模式上进行了精心设计,具有一定的创新性。

(1) 以岗位服务为模块,以具体服务为技能,提高学生酒店岗位英语实用服务技能。

(2) 把服务案例编排在技能实训中,在酒店模拟实训(室)和酒店岗位上完成这些实训任务,提高学生酒店英语服务的综合技能。本书也可用作酒店岗位工作中的自我提高教材。

(3) 设计了"Case and Improvement"(案例与提高)栏目。精心选择和编写案例,根据案例设计题目让学生训练和讨论,培养学生创新工作的能力。

(4) 设计了"Hotel Manager's Comments"(酒店经理点评)栏目。在学生进行了上述的"Case and Improvement"的训练和讨论之后,酒店经理人的评讲不仅具有说服力,而且对未来的酒店人将产生深远的职业影响。

本书由胡扬政主编,美籍专家 Glenn L. Hyatt 主审,苑丽娟、王莉莉、刘玥、胡冰冰、胡霞、周欣奕为副主编。胡扬政、王莉莉编写和修订了前台服务（一）、礼宾服务、客房服务（一、二）、餐饮服务共 5 个模块；刘玥编写了酒吧服务、其他服务两个模块，修订了 4 个模块；苑丽娟编写了总机服务、购物服务两个模块；胡冰冰编写了会展服务、前台服务（二）两个模块；胡霞、周欣奕编写了商务中心服务（一、二）和康乐服务三个模块；刘莉参与全书修订，并重写了多个章节。苏玉刚、高亚妹、宋娜修订了三个模块。Glenn L. Hyatt 对全书进行了审校。

　　本书的全部实训项目均配二维码，全书对话刻录成光盘，帮助学习者提高英语听说能力，也可供课堂教学使用。本书主要英文配音：Glenn L. Hyatt、Mariah J. Xu。

　　由于时间仓促，编者水平有限，不足之处在所难免，恳请使用者多提宝贵意见，以便再版时补充更正。

编　者

2017 年 1 月

目　录

Chapter One　Front Office(Ⅰ)
实训模块一　前台服务(一)

Chapter Two   Front Office（Ⅱ）
实训模块二   前台服务（二）

Chapter Three   Concierge
实训模块三   礼 宾 服 务

Chapter Four　Housekeeping(Ⅰ)
实训模块四　客房服务(一)

Chapter Five   Housekeeping(Ⅱ)
实训模块五   客房服务(二)

Chapter Six   Food & Beverage
实训模块六   餐 饮 服 务

Chapter Seven　Bar Service
实训模块七　酒 吧 服 务

Chapter Eight　Telephone
实训模块八　总机服务

Chapter Nine　Business Center（Ⅰ）
实训模块九　商务中心服务(一)

Chapter Ten　Business Center（Ⅱ）
实训模块十　商务中心服务（二）

Chapter Eleven　Health and Recreation
实训模块十一　康 乐 服 务

Chapter Twelve　Convention and Exhibition Services
实训模块十二　会 展 服 务

Chapter Thirteen　Shopping Service
实训模块十三　购 物 服 务

Unit 32　Shopping(Ⅱ)

Chapter Fourteen　Other Services
实训模块十四　其 他 服 务

Unit 33　Lost and Found Service

Unit 34　Safekeeping Service

Unit 35　Introducing Tourism Information

Chapter One　Front Office(Ⅰ)

实训模块一　前台服务(一)

Unit 1
Making Room Reservations
技能实训 1　客房预订服务

Service Procedure 服务流程

◆ Greet the guest.
　向客人问好。

◆ Ask the guest of the reservation information：
　询问客人下列预订信息：

　　The dates of arrival and departure.
　　客人到达和离开酒店的时间。
　　The number of the people.
　　住店的人数。
　　The room type and the number of rooms.
　　客人所要的房型和房间数。

◆ Search for the room available/needed in the computer.
　在计算机上查找所需要的空房。

◆ Get the following information from the guest：
　从客人那里获得下列信息：

　　The name of the guest or name of the group.
　　客人的姓名或团队名称。
　　The guest's telephone number.
　　客人的电话号码。
　　The contact name and his telephone number.
　　如果是代订还要留下代订人的姓名及电话号码。

◆ Confirm the reservation.
　确认预订。

◆ Express your wishes.
　表示祝愿客人。

◆ Form the reservation record.
　形成预订记录。

Skill Points 技能要点

◆ Pay more attention to using polite language. After reservation, be sure to say to the guest,"We look forward to your arrival."

预订中注意使用礼貌服务用语。预订完后别忘了说："我们期盼您的光临。"

◆ Ask the guest about the time of his arrival and departure with the following：

用下列句子询问房间订在什么时间：

What date would that be?

For which/what date?

For when?

How long will you intend to stay?

◆ Ask the guest about his name and telephone number with

"May I have your name and your telephone number?"

用下列句子询问订房人的姓名和电话号码：

"可以记下您的名字和您的电话号码吗？"

◆ Do confirm after getting all of the information about the reservation,for example,

"Mr. White,you've reserved (booked) a single room from July 5 to 7 and your telephone number is 0044-0246-720355."

在获得所有的信息之后一定要 confirm（确认），例如：

"怀特先生，您预订了 7 月 5 日至 7 日的一间单人间，您的电话号码是 0044-0246-720355。"

◆ If you don't understand what the guest says,be sure not to guess or pretend to know at all. Certainly you aren't afraid of this. Ask the guest to say again with,"I beg your pardon.""Pardon me?" or "Sorry,I don't understand. Could you please repeat that?"

没有听懂或没有听清客人说了什么，切忌猜测，更不要假装明白。当然也不用怕。礼貌地请客人再说一遍，如，"对不起，请再说一遍。""请重复一下。"或"对不起，我没有听懂。能否再重复一遍？"

◆ If the rooms are fully booked,or the rooms needed have been reserved,you can recommend the following to the guest in order to solve the problem.

Some other kinds of rooms.

Some other staying date.

Some other hotels.

如果酒店客房已经订满，或者客人所需的房间已经有人预订，可以用下列办法来解决此事。

推荐别的房型。

推荐其他的入住日期。

推荐其他的入住酒店。

Practice 1 Making an FIT Reservation
实训项目 1 散客预订

Task of Service Practice 实训任务

◆ George Brown wants to book a double room with Grand Hyatt Beijing. The room rate per night is 177 dollars.

George Brown 先生想向北京东方君悦大酒店预订一间双人间,房费每天为 177 美元。

◆ The time: from the 20th to the 22nd of April, three days in all.

时间:4 月 20 日至 22 日,一共 3 天。

◆ The telephone number of George Brown is 0044-0246-720598.

George Brown 的电话号码是 0044-0246-720598。

◆ Li Cong handles the reservation.

预订员李聪办理了这个预订手续。

Service Practice 服务实训

Now, let's begin the practice according to *Task of Service Practice*.

请按照上述实训任务开始实训。

Model of Service Practice 实训对照

Li: Li Cong, a reservationist.

Brown: George Brown, a guest.

01 1 Making an FIT Reservation. mp3

Li: Good afternoon, Grand Hyatt Beijing, Room Reservation. How may I help you?

下午好! 北京东方君悦大酒店客房预订部。需要我为您服务吗?

Brown: I'd like to reserve a room from the 20th to the 22nd of April.

我想预订 4 月 20 日到 22 日的一间房。

Li: Please wait a moment. I'll check our available rooms for these days. Thank you for waiting, sir. What type of room would you like?

请稍等,我要查一查那几天有没有空房。先生,让您久等了。您要什么样的房间?

Brown: A double room. What's the room rate per night?

一个双人间。房价多少?

Li: 138 US dollars. Will that be all right?

138 美元,行吗?

Brown: Yes, that will be fine. Thank you.

行,谢谢。

Li: With pleasure! May I have your name and telephone number?

很高兴为您服务。您能留下您的姓名和电话号码吗?

Brown：Sure. My name is George Brown and my telephone number is 0044-0246-720598.

　　　　好，我叫 George Brown，我的电话是 0044-0246-720598。

Li：　Thank you，Mr. Brown. You've booked a double room from the 20th to the 22nd of April，and your telephone number is 0044-0246-720598.

　　　　谢谢您，Brown 先生。您订了 4 月 20 日至 22 日的一间双人间，您的电话号码是 0044-0246-720598。

Brown：Yes，that's right. Thank you.

　　　　是这样，谢谢！

Li：　I'm glad to serve you. We look forward to your arrival.

　　　　很高兴为您服务。我们恭候您的光临。

Practice 2　Making a Group Reservation
实训项目 2　团队预订

Task of Service Practice 实训任务

◆ Li Ming is calling Wang Ying in Room Reservation of Beijing Hotel. He wants to book 16 standard rooms from the 15th to the 21st of May for the visiting scholars，who will attend an important conference in Beijing.

李明正在给北京饭店客房预订部的王晓打电话。他想为访问学者预订 5 月 15 日至 21 日的标准间 16 间，这些访问学者是来北京参加一个重要会议的。

◆ On the 15th of May，there will be only 14 standard rooms available in Beijing Hotel. But some of the junior suites aren't reserved yet. From the 16th to the 22nd of May，there will be exactly 16 standard rooms.

5 月 15 日这一天，北京饭店只有 14 个标准间是空房，不过还有一些普通套间没有订出去。但是 5 月 16 日至 22 日正好有 16 个标准间。

◆ The room rate of a standard room is 180 dollars，a junior suite is 210 dollars. But the rate of junior suite will be 10% deduction for the group reservation during May.

标准间的房价是 180 美元，普通套间是 210 美元。普通套间 5 月团队预订可打九折。

◆ Li Ming's telephone number is 65291256.

李明的电话号码是 65291256。

Service Practice 服务实训

Now，let's begin the practice according to *Task of Service Practice*.

请按照上述实训任务开始实训。

**01 2 Making a Group
Reservation. mp3**

Model of Service Practice 实训对照

Wang：Wang Ying，a reservationist.

Li： Li Ming, a guest.

Wang： Good morning, Beijing Hotel! Can I help you?

上午好，北京饭店。需要我为您服务吗？

Li： I'd like to reserve 16 standard rooms for some visiting scholars.

我想在你们饭店为访问学者订 16 个标准间。

Wang： What date would that be?

预订在什么时间的？

Li： From the 15th to the 21st of May.

5 月 15 日至 21 日。

Wang： Just a moment, please. Let me check the reservation list. I'm very sorry. We only have 14 standard rooms available on the 15th of May. But from the 16th to the 22nd, we have adequate standard rooms for you. Can you change the date of arrival to the 16th?

请等一会儿，我查一查预订单。对不起，5 月 15 日我们只有 14 个标准间，但是从 16 日到 22 日，我们可以为您准备足够的标准间空房，能把到达的时间改在 16 日吗？

Li： Oh, no, we can't, because these visiting scholars will be attending a very important international academic exchange in Beijing.

噢，不，不能，因为这些访问学者是来北京参加一个非常重要的国际学术交流活动的。

Wang： We also have some junior suites available on the 15th. The price of a junior suite is 30 dollars more than that of a standard room, and we have a special group rate for junior suites.

15 日那天我们的普通套间还有一些空房，普通套间的价格只比标准间多 30 美元，而且我们对团队预订普通套间有特价。

Li： How much is a standard room per night? And what is your discount for the junior suites?

标准间每晚价格多少？普通套间怎样打折？

Wang： One hundred and eighty dollars. We'll give you 10 percent off for the reservation of the junior suites.

180 美元。普通套间预订我们给您打九折。

Li： That's great, I'd like to book 14 standard rooms and 2 junior suites altogether. My name is Li Ming and my telephone number is 65291256.

行，我一共订 14 个标准间和两个普通套间。我叫李明，电话号码是 65291256。

Wang： Thank you, Mr. Li. You've booked 14 standard rooms and 2 junior suites from May 15th to the 21st. And your telephone number is 65291256.

谢谢您，李先生！您一共订了 14 个标准间和两个普通套间，时间是 5 月 15 日至 21 日，您的电话号码是 65291256。

Li： That's right. Thank you.

是这样。谢谢。

Wang： You're welcome. My name is Wang Ying. If anything changes, please call me. Goodbye.

不用谢。我叫王英。如果有什么变动，请电话通知我。

Practice 3　Changing a Reservation
实训项目 3　改变预订

Task of Service Practice 实训任务

◆ Mr. Ramsay reserved 20 standard rooms with China World Hotel for the silk trade negotiations for April 7th, 8th, and 9th.

Ramsay 先生用电子邮件在中国大饭店以他的名字在 4 月 7 日、8 日、9 日为丝绸贸易谈判预订了 20 个标准间。

◆ Now he is calling from New York to change the date of the reservation, because the silk trade negotiations have been postponed until the 4th to the 6th of May.

现在他从纽约打电话来改变预订，因为丝绸贸易谈判被延期到 5 月 4 日至 6 日。

◆ The hotel has exactly 20 standard rooms available during the time.

酒店那几天正好有 20 个标准间空房。

◆ Mr. Ramsay books 20 standard rooms and a business suite altogether from the 4th to the 6th of May.

Ramsay 先生共预订了 5 月 4 日至 6 日的 20 个标准间和一个商务套间。

Service Practice 服务实训

Now, let's begin the practice according to *Task of Service Practice*.
请按照上述实训任务开始实训。

01 3 Changing a Reservation. mp3

Model of Service Practice 实训对照

Wang：　Wang Ying, a reservationist.

Ramsay：Marcus Ramsay, a guest.

Wang：　Good morning. China World Hotel, Room Reservation. Can I help you?

　　　　上午好。中国大饭店客房预订部。需要我为您服务吗？

Ramsay：Yes. This is Marcus Ramsay calling from New York. I have to change the date of a reservation.

　　　　需要。我是 Marcus Ramsay, 从纽约给你们打电话, 我得改变预订日期。

Wang：　How and in whose name was the reservation made?

　　　　是以谁的名字, 什么方式预订的?

Ramsay：By E-mail and in my name.

　　　　以我的名字, 电子邮件的方式预订的。

Wang：　Please wait a moment. I'll check it in the computer. Thanks for waiting. You've booked 20 standard rooms for the silk trade negotiations for April 7th, 8th and 9th, is that correct?

请稍等,我查一查计算机。谢谢您,让您久等了。您在 4 月 7 日、8 日、9 日为丝绸贸易谈判预订了 20 个标准间,是这样吗?

Ramsay: Right, but the negotiations have been postponed until the 4th to the 6th of May. Do you think it's possible for us to change the reservation?

是这样,但是谈判推迟到 5 月 4 日至 6 日。你认为我们能够改变预订吗?

Wang: Let me check the reservation list. Fortunately, we have just 20 standard rooms available for the three days.

我查一查预订单。太好了,那 3 天正好有 20 个标准间。

Ramsay: Very well. And we'll book a business suite as well.

我们还要一个商务套间。

Wang: Mr. Ramsay, you need 20 standard rooms and a business suite altogether from the 4th to the 6th of May. Is that right?

Ramsay 先生,5 月 4 日至 6 日您共需要 20 个标准间和一个商务套间,是这样吗?

Ramsay: Yes, it is. Thanks a lot.

是的,太感谢了。

Wang: It's my pleasure. Goodbye.

为您服务很荣幸,再见。

Practice 4　Cancelling a Reservation
实训项目 4　取消预订

Task of Service Practice 实训任务

◆ John Berry wants to cancel a reservation.

John Berry 想取消一项预订。

◆ The date of the reservation is from May 6, for 5 nights altogether.

这项预订的时间是从 5 月 6 日开始共计 5 个晚上。

◆ Zhao Li cancels the reservation for John Berry.

赵莉为 John Berry 取消了这项预订。

Service Practice 服务实训

Now, let's begin the practice according to *Task of Service Practice*.

请按照上述实训任务开始实训。

Model of Service Practice 实训对照

Zhao: Zhao Li, a reservationist.

Berry: John Berry, a guest.

01 4 Cancelling a
Reservation. mp3

Zhao：　Good morning. Room Reservation. May I help you?

　　　　上午好，客房预订部，有什么为您效劳的吗？

Berry：　I'd like to cancel a reservation.

　　　　我要取消一项预订。

Zhao：　In whose name was the reservation made?

　　　　请问，是用谁的名字预订的？

Berry：　John Berry.

　　　　John Berry。

Zhao：　What was the date of the reservation?

　　　　预订日期？

Berry：　From May 6，for 5 nights altogether.

　　　　从 5 月 6 日起共 5 个晚上。

Zhao：　I'll cancel Mr. John Berry's reservation from May 6 for 5 nights altogether. My name is Zhao Li. We look forward to another chance to serve you.

　　　　取消 John Berry 5 月 6 日起共 5 个晚上的预订。我叫赵莉，我们期待能再有机会为您服务。

Hotel Knowledge
新酒店人须知

（1）The function of the Front Office.

前台的功能。

The Front Office (Front Desk / Reception Desk / General Service Counter) is translated into Chinese：前台、总台、总服务台、大堂部。It is mainly responsible for selling the products and services of the hotel，dispatching the operation of the hotel，organizing the guest resource，selling the rooms，and offering a series of services to the guests，such as reserving the rooms，checking in，assigning the rooms，extending the stays，changing the rooms，exchanging the foreign currency，giving the information，and checking out. The service efficiency and quality represent the whole management level of the hotel. The Front Office is called as "Nerve Center" or "Open Window" of a hotel. So，the clerks in the Front Office must have a good command of practical English.

Front Office/Front Desk/Reception Desk/General Service Counter 中文译为前台、总台、总服务台或大堂部，负责销售酒店的产品与服务、调度酒店的经营、组织客源、销售客房、为客人提供订房、办理住宿登记、分房、换房、兑换外币、留言、办理退房手续等一系列的服务。前台的服务效率及服务质量代表着酒店的整体水平，因此，前台被人称为酒店的"神经中枢"（Nerve Center）或"酒店之窗"。因此，前台对职员的英语实用技能的要求也比较高。

（2）Another name for hotel keeping is "the courtesy industry". We advocate old-fashioned and good manners and politeness. Practice these till they become second nature till you are courteous automatically.

酒店行业,又称"礼貌行业"。我们提倡传统的良好仪态和彬彬有礼,要在实践中使这些成为你的第二天性——习惯成自然。

(3) Some useful expressions in the Front Desk:

前台常用词汇:

Reservation	预订部
Information	问询处
Reception	接待处
Cashier's Counter	收银台
Front Office Manager	前厅部经理
Front Office Supervisor	前厅主管
Lobby Assistant Manager	大堂副理
Guest Relations Manager	客务部经理
Reservation Manager	预订部经理
Reservation Supervisor	预订部主管
Reservationist	预订员

Checking In

技能实训 2　入住登记服务

Service Procedure 服务流程

- Greet the guest.
  问候客人。
- Ask the guest whether he or she has a reservation with the hotel.
  询问客人是否有预订。
- Find the reservation in the computer for confirmation.
  在计算机中查找预订记录用于确认。
- Ask the guest to show his identification.
  请客人出示身份证明。
- Ask the guest to fill in the registration list.
  请客人填写入住登记单。
- Ask the guest how to make the payment.
  询问客人怎样付款。
- Form the checking-in record.
  形成入住登记记录。
- Give the room key card to the guest.
  给客人房卡。
- Extend best wishes.
  祝愿客人。

Skill Points 技能要点

- When a guest comes to check in, first ask whether he has a reservation with the hotel. If he is a guest with a reservation, you need to find out his information record. If there is no reservation for this particular guest, you should check the reservation list for the vacancies and then introduce them to the guest.
  客人要办理入住手续，先要询问是否有预订。如果是预订的客人，须找出相关的信息记录;如果是没有预订的客人,须查预订记录单是否有空房,然后向客人介绍。

◆ When you begin to make the registration for the guest,be sure to politely ask the guest to present his valid certificates,such as ID card,passport,or military officer's certification.

当你开始为客人办理入住手续时,要礼貌地请客人出示身份证、护照或军官证等有效的身份证明。

You can ask the guest in this way:"May I see some identification?" or "Could I see your passport?"

可以这样对客人说:"我能看看您的身份证明吗?"或者"我能看一看您的护照吗?"

◆ On the registration card (RC),fill in the guest's name(surname and first name),sex,the date of birth,the nationality,the valid card number,the detailed address,the dates of arrival and departure,and the room type,and ask the guest to sign as well.

在入住登记卡上填写客人的名字(姓和名)、性别、出生日期、国籍、有效证件号码、详细地址、到达日期和离店日期以及房型,还要客人签名。

◆ When you handle the group check in,confirm the group name and the number of rooms, and then ask whether there are any changes in the time schedule and the number of persons.

在做团队入住登记时,不仅要确认团队名称和房间数,还要询问客人的时间安排和人数有无变化。

◆ When asking the guest how to make payment,we can use the following:

询问客人怎样付款,可以这样问:

How will you be paying?

How will you make your payment?

How would you like to settle your bill?

We can also ask the guest with:

还可以这样问:

How would you like to make a payment,by credit card,in cash or with a traveler's check?

请问您怎样付款,用信用卡,现金还是旅行支票?

If the guest pays in cash,he has to hand in some deposit in advance. If the guest pays by credit card,you should ask him to give his credit card to be imprinted.

如果客人用现金付款,须先交押金。如果客人用信用卡付款,须对信用卡查证授权。

◆ Speak to the guest when finishing the registration:

结束入住登记时说:

I hope/ Hope you will enjoy your room/ stay here.

Have an enjoyable stay!

Please enjoy your stay here.

祝您入住愉快!

Practice 1　Checking In a Guest with a Reservation
实训项目 1　为预订的客人办理入住登记

Task of Service Practice 实训任务

◆ The company of John Smith has booked a double room for three nights with Great Wall Hotel for the couple. Now, they are approaching to the Front Desk for check-in. Wang Ping will handle the registration for them.

John Smith 的公司为他们夫妇在长城饭店预订了一间 3 个晚上的双人间，现在他们来到前台。王平将给他们办理入住手续。

◆ Mr. Smith tells Wang Ping that the reservation has been made under John Smith.

Smith 先生告诉王平是以 John Smith 的名字预订的。

◆ Mr. Smith will make the payment by American Express Card.

Smith 先生用美国运通卡付款。

◆ Wang Ping tells the Smiths that their room is on the sixteenth floor. The room number is 1645. Wang Ping also tells them that the bellman will show them to the room.

王平告诉 Smith 夫妇他们的房间在 16 层，房号是 1645。王平还告诉他们服务员会带领他们到房间。

Service Practice 服务实训

Now, let's begin the practice according to *Task of Service Practice*.

请按照上述实训任务开始实训。

02 1 Checking In a Guest with a Reservation. mp3

Model of Service Practice 实训对照

Wang：Wang Ping, a receptionist.

Smith：John Smith, a guest.

Wang：Good morning. Welcome to our Great Wall Hotel. Is there anything I can do for you?

早上好，欢迎来到长城饭店。需要我为您服务吗？

Smith：We'd like to check in, please.

请为我们办理入住登记手续。

Wang：Do you have a reservation?

请问你们有预订吗？

Smith：Yes, our company has booked a double room for us.

有，我们公司为我们预订了一个双人间。

Wang：In whose name was the reservation made?

用谁的名字预订的？

Smith： John Smith.

John Smith。

Wang： Just a moment, please. Let me check the registration list. Thanks for waiting. You have a reservation of a double room for three nights, correct?

请稍等，我查一下预订表。谢谢您，让您久等了。您预订了一个 3 晚上的双人间，对吗？

Smith： That's right.

对。

Wang： May I see your passports?

我可以看看你们的护照吗？

Smith： Sure. Here you are.

可以，给你。

Wang： Thank you. Please fill in this registration form—your nationality, age, occupation, passport number, and your signature.

谢谢。请填写入住登记表——填上您的国籍、年龄、职业、护照号码，还有您的签名。

Smith： OK. Is that all right?

好。这样行吗？

Wang： Yes. Thanks. How would you like to make your payment?

行，谢谢。您用什么方式付款？

Smith： By American Express Card.

用美国运通卡。

Wang： May I take an imprint of the card, please?

请把您的卡让我授权一下，好吗？

Smith： Certainly.

好的。

Wang： Thank you, sir. Your room is 1645 on the sixteenth floor. Here are your key card and your breakfast coupons.

谢谢，先生。您的房间在 16 层 1645 号，这是您的房卡和早餐券。

Smith： Thank you.

谢谢。

Wang： My pleasure. Just a minute, please. A bellman will show you to your room. I hope you will enjoy your stay here.

很高兴为您服务。请稍等。我们的服务员会带你们到房间。祝你们入住愉快。

Practice 2　Checking In a Walk-in Guest

实训项目 2　为无预订的客人办理入住登记

Task of Service Practice 实训任务

◆ Mr. Banks has just come back to Beijing from New York, and he will stay at the hotel for three days. Every time he came to Beijing, he would stay at this hotel.

Banks 先生刚从纽约回到北京,他将要在酒店住 3 天。他每次到北京来都住这个酒店。

◆ He tells Xiao Wang that he has no reservation this time, but he wishes to stay in the suite facing south that he stayed in last time.

他告诉小王这一次他没有跟酒店预订,但是他还想住上一次他住过的那一间朝南的套间。

◆ Xiao Wang tells Mr. Banks that the suite was booked in the morning. He recommends the room facing the little lake and he also tells Mr. Banks that the room rate is the same with the suite facing south.

小王告诉 Banks 先生那个套间上午已被预订,他推荐了面向湖的一个套间,并告诉 Banks 先生房价和朝南的那个套间是一样的。

◆ Mr. Banks pays with US dollars traveler's check.

Banks 先生用美元旅行支票付款。

◆ The suite that Xiao Wang recommends is Room 2457 on the fourth floor.

小王推荐的套间在 4 层,房号是 2457。

◆ Mr. Banks tells Xiao Wang he doesn't need a porter.

Banks 先生告诉小王不需要行李员。

Service Practice 服务实训

Now, let's begin the practice according to *Task of Service Practice*.
请按照上述实训任务开始实训。

02 2 Checking In a Walk-in Guest. mp3

Model of Service Practice 实训对照

Wang:Xiao Wang, a receptionist.

Banks:Mr. Banks, a guest.

Wang: Good afternoon, Mr. Banks. It's nice to have you stay with us again.

下午好。Banks 先生。欢迎您再次入住我们酒店。

Banks: Thank you. It's nice to be back in Beijing, even if I'm only here for three days.

谢谢。回到北京真好,哪怕这次只住 3 天。

Wang: How was your flight from New York, Mr. Banks?

从纽约飞到这里,一路上好吗?

Banks: Fine, thank you. Xiao Wang, I have no reservation with your hotel this time. I'd like the suite facing the south that I stayed in last time.

还好,谢谢。小王,这一次我没有跟你们酒店预订。我想住上次住的那间朝南的套间。

Wang: Please wait a moment. Unfortunately, the suite was booked this morning. But we have a suite available facing the lake. The room rate is just the same as the one you stayed in last time.

请稍等一会儿。真不凑巧,这个套间今天上午被预订了。不过我们还有一个面向湖的套间。价格和您上次住的套间一样。

Banks：OK，I'll take it.

好，我要了。

Wang：How would you like to pay，by credit card?

怎样付款，是用信用卡吗?

Banks：With US dollars traveler's checks，I think.

我想用美元旅行支票。

Wang：Your suite is on the fourth floor，Room 2457. Here's your key card. Do you need a porter，Mr. Banks?

您的套间在 4 层，房号是 2457。Banks 先生，您需要行李员吗?

Banks：It's not necessary. Thank you very much.

不需要。非常感谢。

Wang：It's my pleasure to serve you again. Hope you will enjoy your suite!

很高兴再次为您服务。祝您入住快乐!

Practice 3   Checking In a Group
实训项目3   为团队客人办理入住登记

Task of Service Practice 实训任务

◆ Liu Lu，a tour leader of Huanle Tour Group，is approaching to the Front Desk to check in for the group.

欢乐旅游团领队刘璐到前台办理团队入住登记。

◆ Wang Ping confirms the schedule of breakfast and departure. Breakfast is 7:30 a.m.，departure 8:30 a.m.

王平确认早餐和离店的时间：早餐 7:30，离店早上 8:30。

◆ Liu Lu tells Wang Ping that the schedule has been changed. Breakfast is 6:00 a.m.，departure 7:00 a.m.

刘璐告诉王平，时间安排有改变。早餐时间是 6 点，离店时间是早 7 点。

◆ The Party has been arranged at 8:00 p.m. in the hall on the third floor.

晚会安排在晚 8 点 3 楼大厅。

◆ Wang Ping arranges a morning call at 5:40.

王平安排了一个 5:40 的叫早电话。

Service Practice 服务实训

Now，let's begin the practice according to *Task of Service Practice*.

请按照上述实训任务开始实训。

02 3 Checking In a
Group. mp3

Model of Service Practice 实训对照

Wang：Wang Ping，a receptionist.

Liu：　Liu Lu，a tour leader.

Wang：Good afternoon. Welcome to our hotel. Anything I can do for you?

下午好。欢迎来到我们酒店。有什么为您服务的吗?

Liu：　Good afternoon. I'd like to check in.

下午好。我来办理入住登记手续。

Wang：Are you a tour leader?

请问您是旅行团领队吗?

Liu：　Yes，I'm the tour leader of Huanle Tour Group. My name is Liu Lu. I'd like to check in for our group.

是的,我是欢乐旅游团领队。我叫刘璐。我为我们团办理入住登记。

Wang：I'd like to confirm your schedule here first.

我先要确认一下你们的入住时间安排。

Liu：　I see.

好的。

Wang：Is there any change in the number of your group?

你们团人数上有变化吗?

Liu：　No.

没有。

Wang：You will have a party at 8:00 this evening，right?

晚上 8 点要开一个晚会,是吗?

Liu：　Yes，where will that be?

是的,在哪开晚会?

Wang：The hall on the third floor. Your breakfast tomorrow will be at 7:30 a. m. And your departure time is 8:30 a. m.

在三楼大厅。你们的早餐时间是 7:30,离店时间是早 8:30。

Liu：　No，breakfast needs to be changed to 6 o'clock，and our departure is 7 o'clock.

不,早餐时间改成 6 点,离店 7 点。

Wang：I see. We'll arrange a wake-up call at 5:40. Will that be all right?

我知道了。我们将安排一个 5:40 的叫早电话,行吗?

Liu：　That's fine.

太好了!

Wang：Could you please place your luggage in front of the desk on the left of the lobby at 6:40? The bellman will pick them up. Is there anything else I can do for you?

请你们明天早晨 6:40 把行李放在大堂左边的那张桌子前面好吗? 服务员会来取。还有什么要为您效劳的吗?

Liu：No，that's all.

不，没有了。

Wang：If you have any changes，please contact the Front Desk. Now please fill in the registration card.

如果有什么变化请和前台联系。现在请填一下这张登记表。

Liu：Here you are.

给你。

Wang：Your rooms are on the sixth to ninth floors and there are 7 rooms on each floor. Your room is 2955 on the ninth floor. Would you please sign your name here?

你们的房间安排在6层到9层，每层7个房间。您的房间在9层的2955。请您在这里签名。

Wang：Thank you. Please enjoy your stay here.

谢谢。祝您入住愉快。

Practice 4　Checking In the Handicapped
实训项目4　为残疾客人办理入住登记

Task of Service Practice 实训任务

◆ Alden Adams will register at the Front Desk with his wife Rose Adams.

Alden Adams 和他的妻子 Rose Adams 将要到前台办理入住登记。

◆ His wife is a handicapped woman and is sitting in the wheelchair.

他的妻子是个残疾人，坐在轮椅上。

◆ Room 2308 is arranged for the couple.

给这对夫妇安排的是 2308 房间。

◆ The receptionist Zhang Fang tells Mr. Adams that room 2308 is specially prepared for the handicapped by their hotel. It has a special room，a wide door into the bathroom，with appropriate washing and toilet facilities.

服务员张芳告诉 Adams 先生，2308 房间是他们酒店专门为残疾人准备的房间。这个房间有一个特别的卧室，有一扇很宽的门通往浴室，浴室配备了舒适的专门卫生洁具和洗漱设施。

Service Practice 服务实训

Now，let's begin the practice according to *Task of Service Practice*.

请按照上述实训任务开始实训。

02 4 Checking In the
Handicapped. mp3

Model of Service Practice 实训对照

Zhang：Zhang Fang，a receptionist.

Adams：Alden Adams，a guest.

Zhang：Good afternoon, sir. Welcome to South Grand Hotel.

下午好，先生。欢迎来到南方大酒店。

Adams：Good afternoon. Would you like to check us in, please? I have a reservation in my name Alden Adams. Could you arrange a double room for us? The woman in the wheelchair is my wife.

下午好。请问可以给我们办理入住登记吗？我有预订，是用我的名字 Alden Adams 预订的。能给我们安排一个双人房吗？坐在轮椅上的女士是我的妻子。

Zhang：I see. Could you tell me her name?

我明白了。您能告诉我您妻子的名字吗？

Adams：Rose Adams.

Rose Adams。

Zhang：Thank you, Mr. Adams. Can I see your passports?

谢谢，Adams 先生。我能看一下你们的护照吗？

Adams：Certainly.

当然可以。

Zhang：Thank you. Would you please fill in this registration form?

谢谢。请您填写入住登记表。

Adams：Here you are.

给你。

Zhang：Thank you. This is the key to Room 2308. This is a double room our hotel specially prepared for the handicapped. It has a special bedroom and a wide door in the bathroom. It's equipped with appropriate washing and toilet facilities.

谢谢。这是 2308 房间的钥匙。这个双人间是我们酒店专门为残疾客人准备的。这是一个特殊的房间，浴室有宽大的门，它还配备有舒适的专门卫生洁具和洗漱设施。

Adams：Great! Thank you.

太好了，谢谢你。

Zhang：A bellman will help Mrs. Adams to the room.

服务员会送 Adams 夫人到房间。

Adams：We really appreciate that.

真是太感谢了。

Zhang：You're always welcome. We're glad to serve you at any time. Have a pleasant stay here.

不用谢，我们很高兴随时为您服务。祝你们入住愉快。

Hotel Knowledge
新酒店人须知

（1）The following is the sample of the Registration Card. Please try to fill in the Registration Card.

表 2-1 是入住登记卡的样本。请试着填写入住登记卡。

表 2-1　入住登记卡

Surname 姓	Name 名	Sex 性别
Nationality 国籍	Place of Birth 籍贯	D. O. B. 出生年月日
Type of Visa 签证种类	Validity 有效期　　Yr 年　　Mth 月　　Day 日	
Type of Identification 证件类别	No. 号码	
Permanent Address 永久性住址 Home　　　Office		
Date of Arrival 抵达日期	Date of Departure 离店日期	Room No. 房号
Hosted by 接待单位	Purpose of Stay 停留事由 □Travel 旅游　　□Business 商务　　□Official 官方活动	
Rate 房租	Method of payment 付款方式 □Cash 现金　　□Credit Card 信用卡　□Traveler's Check 旅行支票 □Others 其他	
Remarks 备注		
A safe provided at the Front Desk or in the guest room is available for use free of charge. 饭店前台及房间内的保险箱可免费使用。		
Guest Signature 客人签名	Front Desk Staff 员工签名	

（2）There are some forms at Front Desk：

前台有一些常用表格：

Rooms Revenue Report	客房收入报表
Cancellation List	当日取消订房表
Amendment List	预订更改表
No-show List	未到客人报表
Expected Departure List	次日客人退房表
Difference	入住房数差异表
Discount & Complimentary List	房租折扣及免费表

（3）The rooms will be kept to 6 o'clock in the evening for the reservation without guarantee, and blocked for twenty-four hours for the guarantee reservation in most hotels.

大多数宾馆,饭店将无保证预订房保留到当天下午 6 点钟,有保证预订房延长保留 24 小时。

Unit 3

Extending the Stay and Changing the Room

技能实训3　延宿和换房服务

Service Procedure 服务流程

Extending the Stay

延宿

◆ Greet the guest.

问候客人。

◆ Get the information from the guest：

从客人那里获得下列信息：

The room number.

客人现在所住的房号。

The type and number of rooms.

客人延宿所要的房型和房间数。

The time of extending stay.

客人延宿的时间。

◆ Search for the room available needed in the computer.

在计算机上查找所需要的空房。

◆ Confirm the extending stay.

确认。

◆ Ask the guest how to make the payment.

询问客人怎样付款。

◆ Form the record of extending the stay.

建立延宿记录。

◆ Extend your best wishes.

祝愿客人。

Changing the Room

换房

◆ Greet the guest.

问候客人。

◆ Ask the guest for his room number.

询问客人现在所住的房间号。

◆ Search for the room available needed in the computer.

在计算机上查找所需要的空房。

◆ Form the record of changing the room.

建立换房记录。

◆ Ask the guest to fill in the room changing form.

要求客人填写换房表。

◆ Tell the guest the time of changing room.

告知客人换房的时间。

◆ Extend best wishes.

祝愿客人。

Skill Points 技能要点

◆ When you handle the extending stay, pay more attention to the following.

办理延宿手续要注意下面两点。

> If the guest can not continue to stay in the room that he is staying at now, introduce the new room and the room rate to the guest and the time of changing the room as well.
>
> 如果客人不能继续住在他现在住的房间里,要向客人介绍新的房间、房价及换房的时间。
>
> If the guest pays in cash, politely ask him to hand in some deposit again. If he pays by credit card, politely ask him to give you the card to imprint again.
>
> 如果客人用现金付款,礼貌地请他再交一些押金。如果是用信用卡,礼貌地请他把卡给你再授权一次。

◆ When you handle changing the room, if the rate of the new room is different, you should explain it to the guest clearly.

办理换房手续时,如果新房间的房价不一样,要跟客人讲清楚。

Practice 1 Extending the Stay
实训项目1 延宿

Task of Service Practice 实训任务

◆ Miss Ramirez, secretary of Business Representative Group, is approaching to the Front Desk for extending the stay.

商务代表团的秘书 Ramirez 小姐到前台办理延宿手续。

◆ The receptionist Pan Cheng tells Miss Ramirez that the rooms at which they are staying now have been booked by a tour group. The guests will arrive at the hotel at 3:00 p. m.

服务员潘成告诉 Ramirez 小姐,他们现在住的房间已被一个旅游团预订了,客人们下午 3 点到达酒店。

◆ Pan Cheng recommends a few rooms with sea view on the sixth floor. Pan also tells Miss Ramirez that the rate of these rooms is a little higher.

潘成介绍了 6 楼的几个海景房。潘还告诉 Ramirez 小姐海景房的房价稍高一点。

◆ Miss Ramirez wants to change the rooms at 10 a. m.

Ramirez 小姐想在上午 10 点换房。

◆ Pan Cheng tells Miss Ramirez the guests staying at these rooms will check out at 10 a. m. He thinks they can move into the rooms at 10:40 a. m.

潘成告诉 Ramirez 小姐,住在这几个房间的客人上午 10 点退房,他认为 10:40 他们可以换到新房间。

Service Practice 服务实训

Now,let's begin the practice according to *Task of Service Practice*.

请按照上述实训任务开始实训。

03 1 Extending the Stay. mp3

Model of Service Practice 实训对照

Pan： Pan Cheng,a receptionist.

Ramirez： Miss Ramirez,secretary of Business Representative Group.

Pan： Good morning. What can I do for you?

早上好,有什么可以为您效劳的吗?

Ramirez： Good morning. You can help me a lot. I'm secretary of the Business Representative Group. I'd like to extend our stay for two days to take part in some business activities.

有,您可以帮我的忙。我是商务代表团的秘书,我们团要延宿两天,因为有一些商务活动要参加。

Pan： Certainly,Miss Ramirez. Wait a minute,please. I have to check it in the computer. The eight rooms that you're staying in have been registered by a tour group. The guests will arrive at 3 o'clock this afternoon. Would you mind transferring to rooms on the sixth floor? They are all rooms with a sea view.

当然可以。请等一下,我在计算机上查一查。你们现在住的这 8 间房已被一个旅行团预订了。客人们下午 3 点到达。你们能否换到 6 楼的房间? 它们都是海景房。

Ramirez： OK. I'll take them.

行,就要这些房间。

Pan： By the way,the rate is a little higher.

顺便说一下,房价稍微高一些。

Ramirez: It doesn't matter. Can we change rooms at 10 a. m. ?

没问题。上午 10 点能换房吗？

Pan: The guests in these rooms will check out at 10 o'clock I think you can move into the rooms at 10:40. I'll notify you, and I'll send a few bellboys over to help you with your luggage.

这几个房间的客人上午 10 点退房。我想上午 10:40 你们便可以换房,我会通知你们的,还会派几个服务员帮你们拿行李。

Ramirez: It's very kind of you.

太感谢了。

Pan: You're welcome.

没什么。

Practice 2   Changing Rooms
实训项目 2   换房

Task of Service Practice 实训任务

◆ Miss Mary Smith and her mother are staying in Room 2857, which is a family suite. Miss Smith wants to change into the room facing south. The reasons are they like to stay in the south room. And Miss Smith has found the south rooms facing the park, in which all kinds of flowers are in full bloom. They'll stay here for six days, and she wishes her mother a better stay here.

Mary Smith 小姐和她的母亲住在 2857 房间,这是一个家庭套房。Smith 小姐想把现在住的房间换成朝南的房间。换房的原因是他们本来就喜欢住朝南的房间,Smith 小姐又发现朝南的房间面向花园,园内的花都开了,他们要在这儿住 6 天,她希望她母亲在这儿住得更好一些。

◆ A family suite facing the park has just been checked out. The room rate is the same as the one they are staying in now.

正好有一个朝公园的家庭套房被退宿。房价也正好一样。

◆ Li Yong handles changing the suite for Miss Mary Smith. The room number is 2627. Miss Smith can move into the new suite in half an hour. A bellboy will be sent to her room with the key card of their new suite, and he will help them with the luggage to the new suite. Miss Smith is asked to come to the Front Desk for filling out a room changing form now.

李勇为 Mary Smith 小姐办理了换房,房号是 2627,Smith 小姐半小时后就可搬到新套房。行李员把新套房的钥匙送到房间,并帮她们把行李送到新套房。Smith 小姐现在需要到前台来填写换房登记表。

Service Practice 服务实训

Now, let's begin the practice according to *Task of Service Practice*.

请按照上述实训任务开始实训。

Model of Service Practice 实训对照

03 2 Changing Rooms. mp3

Li： Li Yong, a receptionist.

Smith： Mary Smith, a guest.

Li： Good morning. Front Desk. May I help you?
早上好，前台。需要我为您服务吗？

Smith： Yes, please. I'd like to change our room.
需要，我想换房。

Li： Is there a problem?
请问什么原因您想换房？

Smith： We'd like to stay in a south room. I've noticed the south rooms face the park, where all kinds of flowers are in full bloom. We're here for six days, and I'd like my mother to enjoy her stay more.
我们喜欢住朝南的房间。我发现朝南的房间面向花园，园内的花都开了。我们还要在这儿住 6 天，我希望我母亲在这儿住得更好一些。

Li： I see. May I know your name and room number?
我知道了。您能告诉我您的姓名和房号吗？

Smith： Mary Smith in Room 2857.
Mary Smith，2857 房间。

Li： Miss Smith, you're staying in a family suite, aren't you?
Smith 小姐，你们现在住的是家庭套房，是吗？

Smith： Yes.
是。

Li： Please wait a moment, Miss Smith. I'll have to check in the computer. A family suite facing the park has just been checked out. The room rate is the same.
请稍等，Smith 小姐。我要查一下计算机。正好有一个朝花园的家庭套房退出来。房价也正好一样。

Smith： Fantastic!
太好了！

Li： The room number is 2627. You can move into your new suite in half an hour. I'll send a bellboy with the key card, and he'll help you with your luggage. Would you please come to the Front Desk to fill out a room change form now?
房号是 2627。半小时后您就可以搬到您的新套房。我会派行李员给您送新套房的钥匙，并帮您拿行李。现在您可以到前台来填写换房登记表吗？

Smith： OK. (*One minute later at the Front Desk*) I'm Mary Smith.
好的。（一分钟以后在前台）我是 Mary Smith。

Li： Here's the room change form, Miss Smith.
这是换房登记表，Smith 小姐。

Smith： Here you are. Thank you.

给您登记表。谢谢。

Li： My pleasure. Hope you enjoy yourselves here.

为你们服务我很荣幸。祝你们住得愉快！

Hotel Knowledge
新酒店人须知

(1) The kinds of the guests in hotels：

酒店客人种类：

GITS (group inclusive travelers)	团队客人
FITS (foreign individual travelers)	外国散客
SITS (special interest travelers)	特殊兴趣的客人
corporate business travelers	公司商务客人
walk-in	没有预订直接入住的客人

(2) Some useful expressions for rooms：

客房种类：

standard room	标准间
single room	单人间
double room	双人间
triple room	三人间
junior suite	普通套间
business suite	商务套间
deluxe suite	豪华套间
presidential suite	总统套间（特套间）

Practice Revision 实训回望

◆ Please speak out simply the important elements of the room reservation.

◆ Why need we confirm after we get all of the information about the room reservation?

◆ If the guest is a foreigner，what information need we make sure and record?

◆ What should we pay more attention to when we change the reservation for the guests?

03 C&I Thirteenth or Thirtieth. mp3

Case and Improvement：Thirteenth or Thirtieth
案例与提高：13 号还是 30 号

It was the first day that Wang Yuan practised working at the Front Desk in the Asian Grand Hotel. She received a call for a room reservation from Mexico. The following was the conversation between the Mexican guest and Wang Yuan.

王媛第一天在亚洲大酒店的前台实训，接到一个来自墨西哥的订房电话。下面是王媛和那个客人的对话。

Wang：Good morning，Asian Grand Hotel，Room Reservations. What can I do for you，sir？

上午好，亚洲大酒店客房预订部。我能帮助您吗，先生？

Guest：Good morning. I'm in Mexico. I'd like to book a double room.

上午好。我在墨西哥。我想订一个双人间。

Wang：OK. For when？

好。订在何时？

Guest：The 13th of this month.

本月 13 号。

Wang Yuan didn't hear it very clearly. She wanted to ask the guest，but she didn't for some reason. She thought maybe it was the 30th.

王媛没有听得很清楚，她想问问那个客人，但不知为什么她没有那么做，她以为是 30 号。

Wang：Just a moment，please. Let me check the reservation list. Yes，sir，we have a double room available. May I have your name and your telephone number？

请等一会儿，让我看一看预订单。先生，有一个双人间。您能留下您的姓名和电话号码吗？

Guest：Sure. My name is Hibbard.

可以，我叫 Hibbard。

Wang：Thank you. Anything else？

谢谢，还要别的事吗？

Guest：No. Thanks for your help.

没有。谢谢您的帮助。

Wang：It's my pleasure. We look forward to your arrival.

很高兴为您服务。我们期盼您的光临！

On the 13th, Wang Yuan was just on duty. At 9 o'clock, Mr. Hibbard came to the Asian Grand Hotel with his wife to check in. But there was no room available. It was Wang Yuan who received the Mexican couple. She realized she had made a mistake and brought trouble to the guests. She said sorry to them first and asked them to wait a moment. She got in touch with a few five-star hotels and in the end she booked a double room in a hotel for them. Wang Yuan also called a taxi for the couple and said to them，"I do apologize again for my making trouble for you. I hope I'll have another opportunity to serve you. "

13 号这一天王媛正好当班。9 点钟，Hibbard 和他的妻子来到亚洲大酒店办理入住登记。这时已没有房间了。而接待这对夫妇的正好是王媛。她意识到她犯了错误并给这对夫妇带来了麻烦。她先是道歉，并请求他们等一会儿。她和几家五星级酒店联系，终于在一家酒店为他们订到了一个双人间。王媛还为这对夫妻叫来出租车，对他们说："我为给你们带来的麻烦再次道歉。我希望能另有机会为你们服务！"

Case Topic 案例话题

My opinion about Wang Yuan's service in the case.

我对案例中王媛提供的服务的观点。

Hotel Manager's Comments
酒店经理点评

（1）首先，王媛在服务中得体地使用了礼貌用语。每当我们完成一个服务时，都会对客人说再见，但不同的服务所包含的"再见"的含义是不一样的，在客人预订后我们说："We look forward to your arrival."（我们期盼您的光临。）为客人办理完入住登记后我们说："Hope you'll have a pleasant stay with us."（希望您入住愉快。）无论是主观原因还是客观原因而不能满足客人住店要求时我们说："I hope I'll have another opportunity to serve you."（我希望能另有机会为你们效劳。）它所包含的意思是：尽管您此次不能住店，但还是希望您下次能当"回头客"住店。

（2）王媛在服务中说了"OK"。在酒店用英语进行服务时，应尽量避免使用过于随意的语言，因为它给人以不庄重的感觉。例如，不要说"OK""Yeah"，而要说"Certainly""Very well"等。如果要表示不同意对方的观点，或者要拒绝对方，不要直接说"No"，而用"I'm afraid that..."。

（3）王媛对突发事故处理得很好。

（4）在客房预订中一定要 confirm（确认）。通过确认，一方面可以准确地得到信息；另一方面可以避免事件的发生。住店的客人来自世界各国，他们讲着带有各国口音的英语，本来就难懂，再加上是在电话中，错误理解在所难免（如果王媛做了确认，就可以避免上述错误）。还有数字，如电话号码等，也是很难听懂的，这就要求我们一是提高"听"的能力；二是不断积累"听"的经验，想办法，如电话号码三位数一记。总之，提高英语"听"的能力有助于我们提高服务能力。

（5）客房预订部(Room Reservation Desk)的工作人员必须具备较好的中英文口头和书面的沟通能力。由于经常需要通过电话和海内外的客人交谈，所以较好的中英文（特别是较高的英语服务技能）、悦耳的嗓音和礼貌和蔼的态度对工作很有利。作为客房预订部的工作人员，要对客人做到有问必答，对客房的类型及酒店的设施了如指掌。

Answers to "Practice Revision" 部分参考答案

◆ Please speak out simply the important elements of the room reservation.

The important elements of the room reservation are:

➢ Guest name and his telephone number.

Group name, its code, and the contact telephone number.

Contact name or company name and the contact telephone number.

➢ Dates of arrival and departure.

➢ Numbers of guests, nights and rooms.

➤ Room type and room rate.

➤ Any special requirements of the guests.

➤ Confirmation.

◆ If the guest is a foreigner, what information need we make sure and record?

The information about his passport number, place of issue and date of issue need to be made sure and recorded.

◆ What should we pay more attention to when we change the reservation for the guests?

We should pay more attention to the following:

➤ The name of the guest or company and the telephone number.

➤ Changeable information such as arrival date, room type and room number.

➤ Revising the reservation according to the demand of the guest in the computer and sending out the revised information.

Chapter Two　Front Office(Ⅱ)

实训模块二　前台服务(二)

Unit 4

Dealing with a Complaint and on the Guest's Request

技能实训 4　处理投诉和回应客人要求的服务

Service Procedure 服务流程

◆ Use the polite language of service.
使用礼貌服务语言。

◆ Be patient to listen to what the guest says and take notes.
耐心聆听并作记录。

◆ Say "sorry" or make an apology to the guest.
对客人道歉或表示遗憾。

◆ Tell the guest what will be done at once.
告知客人马上要采取的措施。

◆ Tell the guest the time in which the problem will be solved out.
告诉客人解决问题所需的时间。

◆ Ask the guest to tell his name and room number.
询求客人告知姓名和房号。

◆ Say "Thank you" to the guest.
向客人道谢。

◆ Tell the related clerk to do at once.
通知相关员工马上去做。

◆ Exam the result and make a record.
检查处理结果并作记录存档。

Skill Points 技能要点

◆ On the guest's request, you can say: "I'm sorry to hear that, but I will send someone to...at once."
在回应客人要求时,你可以说:"听到这样的事,我感到遗憾(很抱歉),但是,我马上派人去……"

◆ When a guest makes a complaint against something to you, be sure not to argue with the guest, but you can try your best to make clear what it is. Certainly you can ask some questions of the guest, so the guest can have a chance to explain.

当客人因某事向你投诉时，千万记住别同客人争论，不过，你可以尽自己努力去弄清事实的真相。当然你还可以向客人提问题，这样客人也有机会解释。

◆ Say "sorry" or make an apology to the guest with the following：

对客人道歉或表示遗憾时说：

I'm sorry to hear that...

听到这样的事，我感到遗憾（很抱歉）。

We do apologize for...

我们为……向您道歉。

◆ Show sincereness to the guest with the following：

向客人表示诚恳的句子：

Thank you for bringing the matter to our attention.

感谢您提醒我们注意。

I assure you that it won't happen again.

您尽可以放心，不会再发生这种事情了。

Practice 1　Meeting the Guest's Request
实训项目 1　满足客人要求

Task of Service Practice 实训任务

◆ Mr. Smith in Room 1645 calls Wang Ping at the Front Desk because there are no towels and toilet paper in the bathroom.

1645 号房的 Smith 先生打电话给前台的王平，因为卫生间里没有浴巾和厕纸。

◆ Mr. Smith asks Wang Ping whether he has an extra pillow and a hair-dryer.

Smith 先生问王平能否多要一个枕头和一个吹风机。

◆ Wang Ping sends a housemaid to meet his request at once.

王平马上派了一个服务员去满足了他的要求。

Service Practice 服务实训

Now, let's begin the practice according to *Task of Service Practice*.

请按照上述实训任务开始实训。

Model of Service Practice 实训对照

04 1 Meeting the
Guest's Request. mp3

Wang：Wang Ping，a receptionist.

Smith：John Smith，a guest.

Wang：Good evening，Front Office. Is there anything I can do for you?

晚上好，这里是前台。有什么可以为您效劳的吗?

Smith：This is Mr. Smith in Room 1645. There are no towels and toilet paper in the bathroom.

我是 1645 号房的 Smith 先生。卫生间里没有浴巾和厕纸。

Wang：I'm very sorry. We might have overlooked some details. Thank you for bringing the matter to our attention. I'll send a housemaid immediately.

非常抱歉，我们可能忽略了一些细小的地方。感谢您提醒我们注意。我马上派一个服务员过去。

Smith：Thank you. Can I have an extra pillow? And I need a hair-dryer.

谢谢，我能多要一个枕头吗? 我还需要一个吹风机。

Wang：Certainly. The housemaid will bring them to you.

当然，我会叫服务员把枕头和吹风机一起给您送去。

Smith：Thank you very much.

非常感谢。

Wang：We do apologize for the inconvenience.

我们为给您带来的不便深表歉意。

Practice 2 Dealing with a Complaint
实训项目2 处理投诉

Task of Service Practice 实训任务

◆ Mr. Smith in Room 1156 calls Wang Li at the Front Desk because the toilet is out of order，and there is something wrong with the air-conditioner as well.

1156 号房间的 Smith 先生打电话给前台的王莉，因为抽水马桶不能用，空调也坏了。

◆ Mr. Smith tells Wang Li，"The toilet is clogged. When I flushed it，it overflowed! The room is very cold."

Smith 先生告诉王莉:"抽水马桶堵住了，我一冲水，水就冒出来。房间里非常冷。"

◆ Wang Li tells Mr. Smith that the repairman will come to his room within five minutes to repair the water closet and the air-conditioner.

王莉告诉 Smith 先生维修人员 5 分钟内到达他的房间修理空调和马桶。

◆ A complimentary flowers will be sent to Mr. Smith in fifteen minutes.

15 分钟后 Smith 先生将收到一个免费的花篮。

Service Practice 服务实训

Now，let's begin the practice according to *Task of Service Practice*.
请按照上述实训任务开始实训。

Model of Service Practice 实训对照

04 2 Dealing with a
Complaint. mp3

Wang：Wang Li，a receptionist.

Smith：Mr. Smith，a guest.

Wang：Good evening，Front Office. Can I help you?

晚上好，这里是前台，我可以帮您吗?

Smith：This is Mr. Smith in Room 1156. The toilet is out of order，and there's something wrong with the air-conditioner as well.

我是 1156 号房间的 Smith 先生，抽水马桶不能用了，空调也坏了。

Wang：May I know what's wrong?

请问有什么问题吗?

Smith：The toilet is clogged. When I flushed it，it overflowed! The room is very cold.

抽水马桶堵住了，我一冲水，水就冒出来。房间里非常冷。

Wang：First，we do apologize for the inconvenience. My name is Wang Li. Our repairman will come to your room within five minutes.

首先，我们为给您带来的不便深表歉意。我叫王莉。我们的维修人员 5 分钟内到达您的房间。

Smith：That's fine.

好吧。

(Fifteen minutes later)

(15 分钟以后)

Wang：Hello，this is Wang Li speaking. Is everything all right?

您好，我是王莉。一切都好了吗?

Smith：Everything is OK. Thank you.

都好了，谢谢你。

Wang：You're welcome. We have sent you complimentary flowers to express our regrets for all the trouble. A chambermaid is waiting outside your door with them. Please open your door.

不用谢，我们给您带来了那么多麻烦，为了表示歉意，我们送您一个免费的花篮。拿着花篮的服务员正等在您的门口，请您开门。

Smith：Thank you very much indeed. I'll go open the door.

非常感谢，我去开门了。

Hotel Knowledge
新酒店人须知

（1）Keep the following in mind：

始终记住：

An argument with the guest is the most undesirable thing that can happen to a staff member and a hotel.

对于酒店员工和酒店来说，最不可取的就是和客人争吵。

（2）A dissatisfied guest means a loss of potential future business for the hotel, whereas a pleased guest leaves the hotel with a warm memory of the hospitality he has enjoyed and an inclination to repeat his visit to our hotel.

一位扫兴而归的客人，意味着酒店会失去将来可能得到的一笔生意；而一位满意的客人则带着自己在酒店所受到的热情周到的服务的美好回忆离开，并且会愿意再次光顾我们的酒店。

Unit 5

Foreign Currency Exchange

技能实训 5　外币兑换服务

Service Procedure 服务流程

◆ Greet the guest.

问候客人。

◆ Introduce today's exchange rate to the guest.

给客人介绍当天的汇率。

◆ Ask the guest how much he wants to change and receive the money from the guest.

询问客人要兑换多少钱，并接收客人递过来的外币。

◆ See the passport of the guest.

查看客人的护照。

◆ Fill in the exchange memo.

填写外汇兑换水单。

◆ Tell the guest about the money amount of changing.

告知客人所兑换的金额。

◆ Give the money to the guest and ask him to count.

把兑换的钱给客人，并要求客人清点。

◆ Give the receipt to the guest, and ask him to keep it well.

把收据给客人，并要求他妥善保管。

Skill Points 技能要点

◆ Since the exchange rate is changing every day, firstly you should explain today's exchange rate very clearly to the guest.

由于汇率每天都在变，所以首先你需要向客人清楚地介绍当天的汇率。

◆ Seeing the passport of the guest, you need to get the information as to the name, nationality and the passport number.

查看客人护照时，你需要关注客人的姓名、国籍和护照号码。

◆ When filling in the exchange memo, ask the guest to fill in his passport number, the total sum, room number or permanent address and sign his name.

填写外汇兑换水单时，要求客人填写护照号码、兑换金额、房间号或永久性地址并签名。

◆ Ask the guest to keep the memo well, and remind the guest, "You need to show it at the customs when you go back to your country."

告知客人要妥善保存外汇兑换水单，并提醒客人："回国时在海关您要出示这张水单。"

◆ If you can not exchange for the guest, you should explain the reason and give him some suggestion.

如果不能给客人兑换，你要给客人解释原因并提出建议。

Practice 1　Changing Euros to RMB
实训项目 1　欧元兑换人民币

Task of Service Practice 实训任务

◆ Mr. Carter wants to change 200 euros into RMB for some souvenirs.

Carter 先生想换 200 欧元的人民币买纪念品。

◆ Today's exchange rate：Every 100 euros in cash comes to 1 005 RMB.

今天的汇率：100 欧元兑换人民币 1 005 元。

◆ Li Ming tells Mr. Carter that they change foreign currencies according to today's exchange rate, 200 euros, an equivalent of 2 010 RMB. After exchanging, Li Ming urges Mr. Carter to keep this memo well because he is required to show it at the customs when he goes back to his country.

李明告诉 Carter 先生，按照今天的外汇汇率，200 欧元可以兑换人民币 2 010 元。兑换完毕，李明特意叮嘱 Carter 先生妥善保存外汇兑换水单，因为他回国时在海关需要出示它。

◆ Mr. Carter wonders how he can change his RMB left back into euros when he goes back to his country.

Carter 先生还想知道，他回国时怎样将剩下的人民币换回欧元。

◆ Li Ming tells Mr. Carter that he can change it back into euros at the Bank of China or the Airport Exchange Office, and there he will be required to show the memo, too.

李明告诉 Carter 先生，可以在中国银行或机场外币兑换处兑换回欧元，兑换时他还得出示这张水单。

Service Practice 服务实训

Now, let's begin the practice according to *Task of Service Practice*.

请按照上述实训任务开始实训。

Model of Service Practice 实训对照

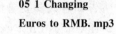

05 1 Changing Euros to RMB. mp3

Li： Li Ming，a cashier.

Carter： Mr. Carter，a guest.

Li： Good afternoon. Is there anything I can do for you?

下午好，有什么可以为您服务的吗？

Carter： I'd like to change some euros into Chinese RMB for souvenirs.

我想把一些欧元换成人民币去买纪念品。

Li： At today's rate of exchange，100 euros comes to 1 005 RMB①. How much would you like to change，sir?

根据今天的兑换率，100 欧元可兑换人民币 1 005 元。先生，您要换多少欧元？

Carter： Two hundred euros. Here you are.

200 欧元。把欧元给你。

Li： Two hundred euros. The exchange is 2 010 RMB. May I see your passport，sir?

200 欧元。兑换人民币 2 010 元。先生，我能看一下您的护照吗？

Carter： Sure. Here you are.

当然可以。给你。

Li： Please，fill in the exchange memo. Be careful to fill in your passport number，the total，your room number or permanent address，and sign your name here as well.

请您填写外汇兑换水单，仔细填写您的护照号、兑换金额、房间号或永久性地址，并在这里签名。

Carter： Here you are. Is that all right?

给你，你看行吗？

Li： That's all right. Thanks. What denominations would you like?

行，谢谢。您要什么面值的货币？

Carter： Any kind will be OK.

都行。

Li： Here is 2 010 yuan. Please count it. Here's your memo. Please hold on to it. You're required to show it at the customs when you go back to your country.

这是 2 010 元，请清点一下。这是您的兑换水单，请妥善保存，您回国时，在海关需要出示它。

Carter： No problem. By the way，how can I change my remaining RMB back into euros when I go back to my country?

没问题。顺便问一下，我回国时怎样将剩下的人民币换回欧元？

Li： You can change it back into euros at the Bank of China or the Airport Exchange

① 书写时要写成 RMB 1 005。

Office,and you'll be required to show the memo there,too.

您可以在中国银行或机场外币兑换处兑换回欧元,兑换时您还得出示这张兑换

水单。

Carter：Thanks for your help.

谢谢你的帮助。

Li：You're welcome. Glad to have served you.

不客气。很高兴为您服务。

Practice 2　Going to the Bank of China for Changing
实训项目2　到中国银行兑换

Task of Service Practice 实训任务

◆ A guest wants to change some KRW and US dollars into RMB in the hotel. But only US
dollars can be changed in the hotel. KRW can be changed in the Bank of China instead.
一位客人想在酒店将一些韩元和美元换成人民币。但是酒店只兑换美元,韩元可以在中
国银行兑换。

◆ The exchange rate of US dollars to RMB is 1:7.25.
美元兑换人民币汇率为 1:7.25。

◆ The guest wants to change 3 500 US dollars into RMB.
这位客人想将 3 500 美元兑换成人民币。

◆ If the large amounts can be changed in a hotel,the cash supply may run out and the other
guests will not be served in foreign currency exchange in the hotel. Zhou Yuan says to
the guest,"You'd better go to the Bank of China for changing. "
如果酒店进行大额兑换,就可能造成资金短缺,那么酒店就不能为其他的客人提供外币兑
换服务了。周媛建议客人:"您最好到中国银行去兑换。"

◆ Go out of the hotel,turn left and the Bank of China will be seen.
出酒店后向左转,就看见中国银行了。

Service Practice 服务实训

Now,let's begin the practice according to *Task of Service Practice*.
请按照上述实训任务开始实训。

05 2 Going to the
Bank of China for
Changing. mp3

Model of Service Practice 实训对照

Zhou：Zhou Yuan,a cashier.
Guest：a guest.

Zhou：Good morning,sir. Can I help you?

早上好,先生。需要我为您服务吗?

Guest: Good morning, I'd like to change some KRW and US dollars into RMB.

早上好,我想将一些韩元和美元换成人民币。

Zhou: I'm afraid that you'll have to change KRW at the Bank of China. We can't change KRW. But you can change US dollars here. The exchange rate of US dollars to RMB is 1:7.25. How much would you like to change, sir?

恐怕您得到中国银行去兑换韩元,因为我们酒店不能兑换韩元。您可以在我们这儿兑换美元,美元兑换人民币的汇率为 1:7.25,先生您想兑换多少?

Guest: I have to change 3 500 US dollars①.

我要换 3 500 美元。

Zhou: I'm very sorry, sir, but we can't.

非常抱歉,先生。我们不能兑换。

Guest: Why not?

为什么不能?

Zhou: If we change large amounts, our cash supply may run out and we won't be able to serve our other guests. You'll have to go to the Bank of China.

如果我们进行大额兑换,就可能造成资金短缺,那么我们就不能为其他的客人提供服务了。您最好到中国银行去兑换。

Guest: How can I get to the Bank of China?

我怎样才能到中国银行?

Zhou: It's very convenient. Please go out of our hotel, turn left, and you will see it.

很方便,出我们酒店后向左转,您就看见中国银行了。

Guest: Thanks a lot. Goodbye.

非常感谢。再见。

Zhou: Goodbye.

再见。

Hotel Knowledge
新酒店人须知

(1) Some useful expressions about foreign currency exchange:

外汇兑换相关词汇:

currency	货币
foreign currency	外币
exchange	交换,交易
today's exchange rate	今天的兑换率

---

① 书写时要写成 US$ 3 500。

exchange memo	外汇兑换水单
denomination	货币的面额/面值
receipt	收据
one-way change	单向兑换
full change	全向兑换
cash a check	兑现支票
account	账号户头
foreign exchange bank	外汇兑换银行
foreign exchange counter	外币兑换柜台
non-convertible currency	不可兑换的货币

（2）Several international credit cards：

几种国际上通用的信用卡：

American Express（AE/AX）	美国运通卡
Master Card（MC）	万事达信用卡
Visa（VS）	维萨卡
EN Route（ER）	在途卡
Eurocard（EC）	欧洲卡
International Great Wall	长城卡
International Dinner's Club	国际大来俱乐部卡
Federal Card	联邦卡

Unit 6
Checking Out

技能实训6　结账退宿服务

Service Procedure 服务流程

◆ Greet the guest.

问候客人。

◆ Ask about the name and the room number.

询问客人的名字和房号。

◆ Ask the guest to give you the room key card.

要求客人交回房卡。

◆ Draw up the bill.

结账。

◆ Tell the guest the total and give the bill to the guest for checking.

告知客人消费总额，并把账单给客人核查。

◆ Explain the items if necessary.

必要时解释账目。

◆ Ask the guest how to pay and handle making the payment.

询问客人怎样付款并办理付款手续。

◆ Bid farewell to the guest.

与客人道别。

Skill Points 技能要点

◆ Checking out in cash, ask the guest to give you the receipt of deposit.

用现金结账的时候，要客人把交押金的收据给你。

◆ Checking out by credit card, firstly you should make sure whether the credit card can be accepted or not in the hotel. Secondly you must pay special attention to the valid date and credit limit.

用信用卡结账的时候，首先要确定酒店是否能接收这种信用卡。还要特别留意信用卡的有效日期和信用额度。

◆ Checking out with Traveler's Check, first examine whether the check is good; pay more attention to asking the guest to sign his name in correct place. If the guest signs his name in wrong place, the hotel can not cash the check.

用旅行支票结账的时候，首先要检查支票是否完好，要求客人在正确的位置签名。如果客人签名签错地方，酒店将无法兑现这张支票。

Practice 1   Checking Out by Credit Card
实训项目1   信用卡结账

Task of Service Practice 实训任务

◆ Mr. Peters in Room 2796 is going to the Front Desk to check out.

住在 2796 号房间的 Peters 先生到前台办理结账退宿手续。

◆ Mr. Peters' bill is 1 465 US dollars.

Peters 先生账单上的消费金额为 1 465 美元。

◆ The hotel accepts American Express, Master Card, Visa and Federal Card.

酒店接收美国运通卡、万事达卡、维萨卡、联邦卡。

◆ Mr. Peters pays by American Express.

Peters 先生用美国运通卡付款。

◆ Wang Hong tells Mr. Peters that he has to pay a 5% merchant commission if he uses a credit card.

王虹告诉 Peters 先生如果他使用信用卡买单，他还要付 5% 的贸易商委托费。

Service Practice 服务实训

Now, let's begin the practice according to *Task of Service Practice*.

请按照上述实训任务开始实训。

Model of Service Practice 实训对照

06 1 Checking Out by Credit Card. mp3

Wang：Wang Hong, a cashier.

Peters：George Peters, a guest.

Wang：Good morning, sir. Can I help you?

早上好，先生。有什么需要我帮忙的吗？

Peters：Yes, I'm checking out. Could I have my bill?

有，我要结账退宿。能把账单给我吗？

Wang：Certainly. May I have your name and your room number, please?

当然可以。能告诉您的姓名和房间号吗？

Peters：George Peters, Room 2796. Here's the room key card.
George Peters, 2796 号房间。给你房卡。

Wang：Thank you, Mr. Peters. Just a moment, please. Thanks for waiting so long. Mr. Peters, here's your bill. The total is 1 465 US dollars.
谢谢。Peters 先生，请稍等。谢谢您，让您久等了。给您账单，一共是 1 465 美元。

Peters：That figure seems right.
这些数字是对的。

Wang：How will you be paying, sir?
先生，您用什么方式付款？

Peters：By credit card. What credit cards do you honor?
信用卡。你们收什么信用卡？

Wang：There's a 5% merchant commission you must pay if you use a credit card, We accept American Express, Master Card, Visa and Federal Card.
如果您用信用卡买单要付 5% 的贸易商委托费。我们接收美国运通卡、万事达卡、维萨卡、联邦卡。

Peters：American Express. Here you are.
美国运通卡，给你。

Wang：Thank you, sir.
谢谢您，先生。

Wang：If you could just sign here, please. Thanks. Here's your card and your receipt.
先生，请您在这里签字。谢谢，这是您的卡和收据。

Peters：Thank you.
谢谢。

Wang：We hope you'll be staying with us again. Have a good trip!
欢迎您下次光临我们酒店。祝您旅途顺利！

Practice 2 Checking Out in Cash
实训项目2 现金结账

Task of Service Practice 实训任务

◆ Mr. Peter Temple in Room 1256 wants to check out.
住在 1256 房间的 Peter Temple 先生想办理退宿手续。

◆ He paid a deposit of 3 000 yuan when he checked in.
他在办理入住登记时已预付押金人民币 3 000 元。

◆ The total of the bill is 2 829 yuan.
账单总额是 2 829 元。

◆ Xiao Ling handles checking out for Mr. Peter Temple.
肖玲为 Peter Temple 先生办理结账退宿。

Service Practice 服务实训

Now, let's begin the practice according to *Task of Service Practice*.
请按照上述实训任务开始实训。

Model of Service Practice 实训对照

06 2 Checking Out
in Cash. mp3

Xiao： Xiao Ling, a cashier.

Temple： Peter Temple, a guest.

Xiao： Good morning, sir. Can I help you?

早上好,先生。需要我帮忙吗?

Temple： Good morning. I'd like to check out.

早上好。我要办理退宿。

Xiao： Would you please tell me your name and room number?

能告诉我您的名字和房间号吗?

Temple： Peter Temple in Room 1256.

Peter Temple, 1256 号房间。

Xiao： May I have the key card, please?

请把房卡给我,好吗?

Temple： Here you are.

给你。

Xiao： Thank you. Please wait a moment, Mr. Temple. I'll draw up your bill for you. Here is your bill, 2 829 yuan in all. Please check it.

谢谢。请等一会儿,我为您结单。这是您的账单,共计 2 829 元,请核对。

Temple： That's right.

没错。

Xiao： You paid a deposit of 3 000 yuan. May I have your receipt, please?

您已预交 3 000 元。能把收据给我吗?

Temple： OK. Here you are.

好的,给你。

Xiao： Thank you. Here is the invoice and your change. Please check it over.

谢谢,这是您的发票和退还您的钱,请清点一下。

Temple： It's quite all right. Thank you.

完全正确,谢谢你。

Xiao： You're welcome. We hope you have enjoyed your stay in the hotel. We hope we will have another opportunity to serve you.

不客气,希望您对我们的服务满意。我们希望能再有机会为您服务。

Practice 3　Checking Out by Traveler's Check
实训项目3　旅行支票结账

Task of Service Practice 实训任务

◆ Xiao Ling is handling checking out for Mr. Berry.

　肖玲正在为Berry先生办理结账退宿。

◆ Xiao Ling asks Mr. Berry to give her his room key card.

　肖玲要求Berry先生把他的房卡给她。

◆ The bill totals 14 480 yuan. It includes two room services and six suppers in the Chinese Restaurant.

　账单总计14 480元人民币,包括两次客房送餐,6次中餐厅晚餐。

◆ Mr. Berry pays with traveler's card. Today's US dollars for traveler's check is 709 yuan against 100 US dollars.

　Berry先生用旅行支票结账。当天旅行支票的美金兑换率为100美元兑换709元人民币。

◆ The traveler's check is 2 000 US dollars, an equivalent of 14 180 yuan. Mr. Berry pays the rest, 300 yuan in cash.

　您的旅行支票2 000美元兑换成14 180元人民币。用人民币现金支付剩余部分为300元。

Service Practice 服务实训

Now, let's begin the practice according to *Task of Service Practice*.

请按照上述实训任务开始实训。

Model of Service Practice 实训对照

06 3 Checking Out by Traveler's Check. mp3

Xiao： Xiao Ling, a cashier.

Berry： Mr. Berry, a guest.

Xiao： Good morning, sir. How can I help you?

　　　早上好,先生。需要我为您服务吗?

Berry： Good morning. I'd like to settle my bill.

　　　早上好。我想结账。

Xiao： Certainly, sir. Could you give me your room key card?

　　　好的,请给我您的房卡好吗?

Berry： OK. Here you are.

　　　好的,给你。

Xiao： Please wait a moment, Mr. Berry. I'll draw up your bill. Your bill totals 14 480 yuan. Would you like to check it?

先生请稍等,我帮您结算账单。您的账单总计 14 480 元,请您查看一下。

Berry： Are food and beverage included?

餐饮都计算在内了吗?

Xiao： Yes,we charged you for two room service meals and two suppers in the Chinese Restaurant. Is that right?

计算在内了,两次客房送餐,两次在中餐厅晚餐,对吗?

Berry： That's right.

对。

Xiao： How would you like to pay?

您怎样付款?

Berry： I'll pay with a Traveler's check.

旅行支票。

Xiao： Traveler's check is welcome.

欢迎您用旅行支票付账。

Berry： May I know today's US dollars exchange rate?

请告诉我今天旅行支票的美元兑换率好吗?

Xiao： 709 yuan against 100 US dollars. Your passport,please.

100 美元兑换 709 元。请出示您的护照。

Berry： Here you are.

给你。

Xiao： Please sign your name here again on the traveler's check and sign the memo.

请在支票上再签一下,并在兑换水单上签名。

Berry： OK. Is that all right?

好的。行吗?

Xiao： That's right. Your traveler's check is 2 000 US dollars,an equivalent of 14 180 RMB. How would you like to pay the rest,300 yuan?

行。您的旅行支票是 2 000 美元,兑换 14 180 元。您怎样支付剩余部分的 300 元?

Berry： RMB in cash. Here you are.

用人民币现金支付。给你。

Xiao： Here is your invoice. And here is the exchange memo.

给您发票和兑换水单。

Berry： Thank you.

谢谢。

Xiao： You're welcome. Hope you enjoy your trip.

不用谢。祝您旅途愉快!

Hotel Knowledge
新酒店人须知

（1）Some useful expressions：

常用词汇：

merchant commission	贸易商委托费
extra charge	附加费用
credit limit	信用卡限额
deposit	押金
IOU（I Owe You）	欠单
service charge	服务费
receipt	收据
invoice	发票
rental	租金
check	支票
cash withdrawal	提取现金
transfer	转账
cashier	收银员
ATM machine	自动提款机

（2）Some abbreviations in the bills：

账单上的一些缩写词：

Room＝Room Charge	房费
T＝Telephone Call Charge	电话费
L. DIST＝Long Distance Call	长途电话费
RESTR＝Restaurant	餐饮费
L＝Laundry	洗衣费
MISC＝Miscellaneous	杂费
TR. CH＝Transfer Charge	转出
TR. CR＝Transfer Credit	转入
PD. OUT＝Paid Out	代付
PAID＝Paid	付现
C. I. A.（Cash In Advance）	预付现金
P. I. A.（Paid In Advance）	已预付
B. N. P.（Bill Not Paid）	未结账

Practice Revision 实训回望

◆ As we know，getting into an argument with the guest is the most undesirable thing to a staff member and a hotel. In order to avoid the argument and deal with a complaint，what should you do?

◆ Could you speak out some English sentences of apology?

◆ The guests check out mainly in three ways，what are they? What's the difference between them in checking-in and checking-out?

◆ What will be done when checking-out?

Case and Improvement：Sorry for Overcharging You
案例与提高:抱歉向您多收了钱

Xiao： Xiao Ling，a cashier.

Johnson： Samuel Johnson，a guest.

06 C&I Sorry for Overcharging You. mp3

Xiao： Good morning，sir. How can I help you?
早上好，先生。需要我为您服务吗?

Johnson： Good morning. I'd like to change some currency and check out.
早上好。我想兑换外币，还要结账。

Xiao： Which one would you like to handle first?
您想先办哪一件?

Johnson： Foreign currency exchange. I have some Chinese RMB left，and I want to change the money left back into US dollars. I'm going back to America this afternoon.
先兑换外币。我还有一些没用完的人民币，我想换回美元，因为下午我就要回美国了。

Xiao： I'm afraid that we only offer one-way change. We can't handle full change. There is a foreign exchange bank on the second floor of our hotel. You can go there after checking out.
恐怕我们只能提供单向兑换，我们不能办理全向兑换。我们酒店的二楼有一家外汇银行，您结账之后可以前去兑换。

Johnson： OK. Thank you. Please draw up the bill for me.
好的，谢谢。请帮我结算账单。

Xiao： May I have your name and your room number?
请您告诉我您的姓名和房号。

Johnson： Samuel Johnson in Room 2653.
Samuel Johnson，房间号 2653。

Xiao： Your bill totals 9 700 yuan. How would you like to pay?

您的账单总计 9 700 元。请问您怎样付款？

Johnson： By credit card. Do you accept Visa?

用信用卡。你们接受维萨卡吗？

Xiao： Certainly.

当然接受。

Johnson： Here you are.

给你。

Xiao： Here is your card and your receipt. Goodbye.

这是您的卡。再见。

(Twenty minutes later, Mr. Johnson is walking back to Xiao Ling.)

（20 分钟后，Johnson 先生回到肖玲这里。）

Xiao： Have you changed the money?

您兑换了钱吗？

Johnson： Yes, I have.

换了。

Xiao： Is there anything else I can do for you?

还有什么需要我帮忙吗？

Johnson： Yes. I think there's something wrong with the bill. You've overcharged.

有。我认为账单有错，你多收了钱。

Xiao： So you've been overcharged. Please wait a moment, Mr. Johnson. I'll check it. It's all right.

也就是说账单有错，我们多收了您的钱。请稍等，Johnson 先生。我查一下。没错啊。

Johnson： What do they mean?

这个是什么意思？

Xiao： L means laundry, while RESTR stands for restaurant.

L 是洗衣费，RESTR 是餐饮费。

Johnson： The restaurant is 1 857 yuan, but I just had two room services and four suppers in the Chinese Restaurant. It can't be so much.

餐饮费 1 857 元，但我只有两次客房送餐，四次中餐厅的晚餐。

Xiao： You had no lunch in the Western Restaurant, right?

您没有西餐厅的午餐，是吗？

Johnson： No, I have never been to the Western Restaurant. I have just been to the Chinese Restaurant.

没有，我从没去过西餐厅，我只去过中餐厅。

Xiao： Don't worry. Please wait a moment. I see, Mr. Johnson, but I have to confirm it. It's Samuel Johnson in Room 2623 who had the three lunches in the Western Restaurant, but we have charged your account by mistake, because your names are the same. We're terribly sorry for overcharging you. I must apologize for the inconvenience.

别着急。请等一会儿。我已明白是怎么一回事了,Johnson 先生,但我还得确认一下。是 2623 房间的 Samuel Johnson 先生在西餐厅用过三次西餐,但我们误记在您的账上,因为你们同名同姓。非常抱歉向您多收了钱。给您带来了不便,向您道歉。

Johnson：Everyone makes mistakes.

每个人都可能会犯错误。

Xiao：We'll correct your bill by deducting 800 yuan from the total. I'll return the money you've overpaid. Which currency would you like to get, Chinese RMB or US dollars?

我们将把账单更正过来,从总额中减去 800 元人民币,我把您多付的钱退还给您。您要哪一种货币,人民币还是美元?

Johnson：US dollars.

美元。

Xiao：Today's rate of RMB against US dollars is 700∶100. Here's the 114 dollars you overpaid.

今天人民币兑美元是 700∶100。这是您多付的 114 美元。

Johnson：Thank you.

谢谢。

Xiao：Have a good trip.

祝您旅途愉快!

Case Topic 案例话题

Talk about Xiao Ling's service.

就肖玲的服务发表你的看法。

> **Hotel Manager's Comments**
> **酒店经理点评**

前台收银是酒店非常重要的岗位之一。Cashier(前台收银员)的工作是:负责将客人在各营业点的实际消费记入客人账单,在客人退房时收取费用,外币兑换,旅行支票兑换,与财务部门协调有关客人信用卡及账单等问题,并在工作结束时进行账目结算。而直接服务于客人的是这样三项:结账退房、外币兑换和旅行支票兑换。值得注意的是:

(1) 前台收银员必须能用英语有效地与外国客人交流和沟通,并满足客人的要求,解决客人提出的问题。

(2) 前台收银员要为酒店树立良好的形象。

我们知道,前台收银员最主要的职责是客人退房时结账,收银员是客人最后接触到的前台人员。第一印象和最后的印象都非常重要,从某种角度而言,最后的印象比第一印象更重要。因为客人将把这种印象带回家,并且记忆深刻。这将影响到客人今后与朋友或同事谈起酒店服务或设施时所持的态度。所以,客人来结账时要很热情地打招呼,提供快捷的服务并且向客人诚挚地道别,这些都是很重要的。在结账时,收银员应该询问客人近来的消费,因为可能有漏账的情况。所有客人的消费都应该及时记入账单。除了客房的租金,还可能有电话费、洗衣费、在餐厅用餐及客房送餐的费用等。

案例中,肖玲在礼貌服务方面和服务流程方面做得都不到位,这也是同学们实践中经常犯的错误。

(3) 认真对待客人对账单的投诉。

接到客人对账单的投诉,需确认投诉的要点,可以重复客人的话以确认。例如,肖玲说:"So you've been overcharged. Please wait a moment, Mr. Johnson. I'll check it. "(也就是说账单有错,我们多收了您的钱。请稍等,Johnson 先生,我查一下。)

肖玲有两件事做得很好,值得大家学习。

第一,查错并向客人致歉。出了错道歉这是天经地义的。肖玲说:"We're terribly sorry for overcharging you. "(非常抱歉向您多收了钱。)还可以说:"Please accept my apologies for our mistakes. "(让我为我们所犯的错误向您道歉,请您接受。)

第二,改错。有错改错,客人不仅原谅你,而且你的改错态度也会改变他对你的印象,如案例中的 Johnson:"Everyone makes mistakes. "(每个人都可能会犯错误。)客人记住的是你的改错过程和结果,而不是"错"的这件事。

(4) 不能兑换外币时,要向客人解释清楚。酒店能兑换外币,但酒店兑换外币又有很多限制,如只能单向兑换,不能像外汇银行那样全向兑换,具有时间限制和额度限制等。这时,你要耐心地向客人解释,必要时还要向客人提出兑换的建议。

(5) 收银员在礼貌待客的同时还必须讲究工作效率。多数客人在上午 9～10 点钟结账,有的还要赶飞机或火车,所以希望收银员能以最快的速度(一般在 3 分钟之内)为他们结完账。如果出了差错,就会给酒店造成很大的损失,而且这种损失日后无法弥补。因此,平时要多加训练,练好基本功,这样真正工作起来才能做到三个字——静、快、好。

Answers to "Practice Revision" 部分参考答案

◆ As we know, getting into an argument with the guest is the most undesirable thing to a staff member and a hotel. In order to avoid the argument and deal with a complaint, what should you do?

We should always be polite and helpful, listen to what the guest says attentively and take down what he has said. We will never interrupt him unless necessary. We will say sorry to him or make an apology to him. We need to try our best to look at the guest's problem in his way, and take actions quickly to remove the complaint. Certainly we also need to tell the guest what measures will be taken and what time they will be carried out.

◆ The guests check out mainly in three ways, what are they? What's the difference between them in checking-in and checking-out?

They're cash, credit card and traveler's check.

➢ If the guest makes the payment in cash, he will be asked to hand in some deposit in advance in checking-in and give the receipt of the deposit in checking-out.

➢ If the guest makes the payment by credit card, he will be asked to give his card to be imprinted(be pre-authorized) in checking-in. When dealing with checking-out, we need to pay special attention to the number, valid date and limit of the credit card of the guest. After he gives his card to print to finish the payment, we need to ask him to sign his name.

➢ Checking-out with the traveler's check, we need to examine whether the check is good, and then ask the guest to sign his name in the correct place. If the guest signs his name in wrong place, the hotel can't cash the check.

Chapter Three　Concierge

实训模块三　礼宾服务

Accompanying the Guest

技能实训 7　陪送客人

Service Procedure 服务流程

◆ Greet the guest.
问候客人。
◆ Help the guest with the luggage out of the taxi.
帮客人从出租车里提出行李。
◆ Confirm the pieces of the luggage.
确认行李件数。
◆ Put the luggage on the luggage cart.
将行李放上行李车。
◆ Accompany the guest to the Front Desk for checking in.
陪送客人到前台登记。
◆ Wait for the guest while he is checking in.
客人登记时在旁等候。
◆ Accompany the guest to the room.
陪送客人到房间。
◆ Open the room and introduce the room facilities simply.
开房,简单地介绍房间设施。
◆ Extend your wishes to the guest.
表达祝愿。

Skill Points 技能要点

◆ Before helping the guest with his luggage,confirm the pieces of the luggage.
在帮客人送行李前,要确认行李件数。
◆ Accompanying the guest,the clerk of the hotel must go after the guest of the hotel.
陪送客人时,酒店职员必须走在酒店客人的后面。
◆ Accompanying a guest into the elevator,say to the guest,"You go first,please."When

going out of the elevator, say to the guest, "After you, sir."
陪送客人进电梯,要说:"先生,您请进。"出电梯时对客人说:"先生,您先请。"

◆ Accompanying the guest to his room, you can introduce the facilities and services of the hotel to him.
陪送客人到房间的途中,你可以介绍酒店的设施和服务。

Practice 1　Accompanying the Guest to the Front Office
实训项目1　陪送客人到前台

Task of Service Practice 实训任务

◆ A guest has arrived at Holiday Inn. She has just taken three pieces of his luggage out of the taxi and two pieces are still in it.
一个客人到达假日酒店。她从出租车里拿出了三件行李,还有两件在里面。

◆ Zhao Jun helps the guest to take the two pieces of luggage out of the taxi. Then he brings a luggage cart and shows the guest to the Front Desk for checking in.
赵军帮客人从出租车里取出了那两件行李。然后他推出一辆行李车,送客人到前台办理入住登记。

◆ Zhao Jun also tells the guest that he will accompany her to the room when she finishes checking in.
赵军还告诉客人,她办理完入住登记手续后就送她到房间。

Service Practice 服务实训

Now, let's begin the practice according to *Task of Service Practice*.
请按照上述实训任务开始实训。

Model of Service Practice 实训对照

07 1 Accompanying the Guest to the Front Office. mp3

Zhao：Zhao Jun, a bellman.
Guest：a guest.

Zhao：I trust you had a good trip. Welcome to Holiday Inn.
旅途愉快! 欢迎您光临假日酒店。
Guest：Thank you.
谢谢。
Zhao：May I help you with your luggage?
我来帮您提行李吧?
Guest：Yes, please.
谢谢。

Zhao：How many pieces of luggage do you have?

您有多少件行李？

Guest：Five pieces.

5件。

Zhao：But there are just three pieces here.

但是这里只有3件。

Guest：Oh, two pieces of luggage are still in the taxi.

哦，还有两件在出租车里。

Zhao：I'll carry them for you.

我来帮您拿吧。

Guest：Thank you.

谢谢。

Zhao：Just a moment, please. I'll bring a luggage cart. But first I'll show you to the Front Desk. This way, please.

请等一下，我去推一辆行李车来。现在我带您到前台，请这边走。

Guest：Thank you.

谢谢。

Zhao：I'll show you to your room when you finish checking in.

您办完入住登记后，我送您到您的房间去。

Guest：OK.

好的。

Practice 2　Accompanying the Guest to the Room
实训项目2　陪送客人去房间

Task of Service Practice 实训任务

◆ The guest finishes checking in, and then Zhao Jun shows the guest to Room 3878 on the eighth floor.

客人完成登记以后，赵军送客人到8层的3878房间。

◆ The elevators on the right are the express ones to the tenth floor and above. The elevators on the left go to the tenth floor only. They stop at every floor. Zhao Jun shows the guest to take the elevator on the left.

右边是10层以上的直达电梯。左边的电梯只到10层。电梯每一层都停。赵军引领客人乘左边的电梯。

◆ Zhao Jun introduces to the guest that the elevator on the left goes to the Health Center and the restaurant as well. The restaurant is on the second floor. The Health Center is on the third floor. Zhao Jun recommends the guest to play table tennis, billiards and bowling there.

赵军向客人介绍:左边的这部电梯还通向餐厅和康乐中心,餐厅在2层,康乐中心在3层。赵军向客人建议可在那里打乒乓球、台球和保龄球。

◆ Zhao Jun opens the air conditioner for the guest.
   赵军为客人打开空调。
◆ Zhao Jun answers that the price list for the mini bar is under the hotel service guide.
   赵军回答客人迷你吧的价目表在服务简介的下面。

Service Practice 服务实训

Now, let's begin the practice according to *Task of Service Practice*.
请按照上述实训任务开始实训。

Model of Service Practice 实训对照

07 2 Accompanying the Guest to the Room. mp3

Zhao： Zhao Jun, a bellman.
Guest： a guest.

Zhao： Finished, ma'am?
         已办完登记了吗?
Guest： Finished.
         办完了。
Zhao： Your room number, please?
         请问您的房间号码是多少?
Guest： 3878.
         3878。
Zhao： I'll show you to your room.
         我送您去您的房间。
Guest： OK. Thank you.
         好的。谢谢。
Zhao： This way, please. The elevators on the right are the express ones to the tenth floor and above. The elevators on the left go to the tenth floor only. They stop at every floor. Your room is on the eighth floor. We'll take the elevator on the left. You go first, please.
         请这边走。右边是10层以上的直达电梯。左边的电梯只到10层。电梯每一层都停。您的房间在8层,我们乘左边的电梯。您请进。
Guest： OK.
         好的。
Zhao： By the way, the elevators go to the Health Center and restaurant as well. The restaurant is on the second floor. The Health Center is on the third floor. You can play table tennis, billiards and bowling there.
         顺便说一下,这部电梯也通向餐厅和康乐中心。餐厅在2层。康乐中心在3层。您可以在那儿打乒乓球、台球和保龄球。

Zhao： Here we are. After you, please. This is your room. May I have your key card?

我们到了，您先走。这是您的房间。我能用一下您的房卡吗？

Guest： Here you are.

给你。

Zhao： After you, ma'am. May I put your suitcases here?

您先请。我能把行李放在这里吗？

Guest： Sure, just put them anywhere.

可以，放在哪里都行。

Zhao： Shall I turn on the air conditioner?

需要打开空调吗？

Guest： Yes, thank you.

打开吧，谢谢。

Guest： Where's the price list for the mini bar?

迷你吧的价目表在哪儿？

Zhao： It's under the hotel service guide. Is there anything else I can do for you?

在服务简介下面。还有什么需要我为您服务的吗？

Guest： No. Thank you.

没有了，谢谢。

Zhao： You're welcome. I hope you have a pleasant stay here.

不用客气。祝您入住愉快！

Hotel Knowledge
新酒店人须知

（1）Try your best to give your guests your best in service and in kindness in the practice in the hotel.

酒店实训中尽自己努力让客人得到最佳的服务和最实际的好处。

（2）Some soft drinks in the mini bar in the room：

迷你吧里的软饮料种类：

Coca-cola	可口可乐
Pepsi	百事可乐
Sprite	雪碧
Mineral Water	矿泉水
7-Up	七喜
Evian	依云矿泉水
Fresh Milk	鲜奶
Yogurt	酸奶
Distilled Water	蒸馏水
Lipton Tea	立顿（茶）
American Ginseng Tea	美国参茶（花旗参茶）

Unit 8

Introducing the Facilities and Services

技能实训8　介绍设施和服务

Skill Points 技能要点

◆ It is a very important job for a clerk of the Concierge Department to introduce the facilities in the room, the services and the service equipment of the hotel. After accompanying the guest into his room, you can introduce them to him on your own initiative. If he asks about some service facility, you ought to explain clearly or show him how to use it.

介绍房间设施及酒店的服务和服务设施是礼宾部员工的一项重要的工作。当陪送客人进入房间之后,可以主动地介绍房间设施、酒店的服务和酒店的设备。如果客人问起某个服务设施,要跟客人解释清楚或教他怎样使用。

◆ When receiving a group, you are always needed to introduce and explain clearly the services of the hotel and service arrangements to the guests in order to serve the group guests in order.

接待团队客人时,要向客人介绍或说明酒店服务和服务安排,以确保对团队服务工作的有序开展。

◆ Pay attention to using the polite language.

注意使用礼宾语言。

Practice 1　Introducing the Facilities and Services
实训项目1　介绍设施和服务

Task of Service Practice 实训任务

◆ Zhang Xiao opens the room and draws back the curtain. Miss Wells is very glad because her room just faces a little mountain and a little river.

张晓打开房门,拉开窗帘。Wells 小姐非常高兴,因为房间正好面临小山和小河。

◆ Zhang Xiao tells Miss Wells that she can make tea and coffee by using the electric kettle on the desk.

张晓告知 Wells 小姐用桌上的电水壶烧水泡茶或冲咖啡。

◆ Zhang Xiao introduces that the hair salon is on the left side of the south gate and it opens from 9：00 a. m. to 11：00 p. m.

张晓介绍美发沙龙在南大门的左边，营业时间是上午 9 点到晚上 11 点。

◆ The Chinese Restaurant in the hotel is good at Beijing food and the guest can try Beijing roast duck here. Today is Mid-autumn Festival，one of the Chinese traditional festivals. The guest can try all kind of moon cakes.

酒店的中餐厅擅长北京菜，客人在这里可以品尝北京烤鸭。今天是中秋节，是中国的传统节日。客人还可以品尝到各种月饼。

◆ Today is the birthday of Miss Wells. She wants to spend a Chinese birthday with her parents at Chinese Restaurant in the hotel.

今天是 Wells 小姐的生日，她想在酒店的中餐厅里和她的父母一起过一个中国式的生日。

◆ The Chinese Restaurant will present Miss Wells a bowl of longevity noodles with a poached egg. In Chinese people's eyes，noodles symbolize longevity，and poached eggs will bring good luck.

中餐厅将赠送给她一碗带荷包蛋的长寿面。在中国人的眼里，面条代表长寿，荷包蛋能带来好运。

◆ Miss Wells gives the tip to Zhang Xiao，but he doesn't accept it.

Wells 小姐给张晓小费，但是他没有接受。

Service Practice 服务实训

Now，let's begin the practice according to *Task of Service Practice*.

请按照上述实训任务开始实训。

Model of Service Practice 实训对照

08 1 Introducing
the Facilities and
Services. mp3

Zhang：Zhang Xiao，a bellman.

Wells：Miss Wells，a guest.

Zhang：Here's your room，Miss Wells. After you，please.

这是您的房间，Wells 小姐，您先请。

Wells：Thank you.

谢谢。

Zhang：Shall I draw back the curtain for you?

我为您拉开窗帘，好吗？

Wells：OK. Thank you. Oh，wonderful! My room just faces the little mountain. The flowers are in bloom.

好的。谢谢你。啊，太美了！我的房间正好面临小山，花都开了。

Zhang： I'm very glad you like it.

您喜欢我非常高兴。

Wells： How can I make tea or coffee?

我怎样泡茶或者冲咖啡？

Zhang： You can make your own tea and coffee by using the electric kettle on the desk.

您可以用桌上的电水壶烧水泡茶或冲咖啡。

Wells： Is there a hair salon in your hotel?

你们酒店有美发沙龙吗？

Zhang： Yes, it's on the left side of the south gate. It's open from 9：00 a. m. to 11：00 p. m.

有，在南大门的左边。营业时间是上午 9 点到晚上 11 点。

Wells： Can you tell me a bit about your hotel's Chinese Restaurant?

能介绍一下你们酒店的中餐厅吗？

Zhang： Certainly. We are good at Beijing food. You can try Beijing roast duck here. By the way, today is the Mid-autumn Festival, one of the Chinese traditional festivals. You can try all kinds of moon cakes.

当然可以。我们擅长北京菜，您在我们这可以品尝到北京烤鸭。顺便说一下，今天是中秋节，是中国的一个传统节日。您可以品尝到各种月饼。

Wells： Thank you very much. Today is my birthday. I want to spend a Chinese birthday with my parents at the Chinese Restaurant in the hotel.

非常感谢。今天是我的生日，我想在酒店的中餐厅里和我父母一起过一个中国式的生日。

Zhang： Wonderful! The Chinese Restaurant will present you a bowl of longevity noodles with a poached egg.

太好了！中餐厅会赠送给您带荷包蛋的长寿面。

Wells： Why?

为什么？

Zhang： In the Chinese people's eyes, noodles symbolize longevity, and the poached eggs will bring good luck to you.

在中国人的眼里，面条代表长寿，荷包蛋能给你带来好运。

Wells： It's very nice of you. Where is your service brochure? I want to get more information about the facilities and services of your hotel.

真是太好了。你们的服务小册子在哪儿？我还想知道你们酒店的设施和服务方面更多的信息。

Zhang： It's in the first drawer of the dresser. Is there anything else I can do for you?

在梳妆台的第一个抽屉里。还有什么可以为您服务的吗？

Wells： No, nothing. Here's something for you.

没有。这里有给您的一件东西。

Zhang： It's very kind of you, but I'm afraid we don't accept tips. Thank you all the same. If there is anything I can do for you, please call me. I'm always at your service. Happy birthday!

您真是太好了,不过我们是不收小费的。还是一样地感谢您。如果有什么我能效劳的,请给我打电话,我随时乐意为您服务。祝您生日快乐!

Practice 2　Introducing the Services to the Group
实训项目 2　向团队客人介绍服务安排

Task of Service Practice 实训任务

Zhou Jin introduces the service arrangements to the guests of the group.

周瑾向团队客人介绍服务安排。

◆ How to take the room key card and the breakfast meal vouchers?

怎样拿自己的房卡和早餐券?

The room-keys cards and breakfast meal vouchers are in the envelops on the desk. Every envelop is written the name of a guest. The rooms are arranged in alphabetical order of the family names.

房卡和早餐券在桌上的信封里,每个信封都写着客人的名字,房间是按照客人姓的字母顺序排列的。

◆ How to make calls?

怎样打电话?

Room-to-room calls：dial directly the room number you want.

酒店内线电话：直拨您要的房间。

Outside calls：dial 0 first.

外线电话：先拨 0。

◆ There is a service brochure of the hotel on the desk in the room.

房间的桌子上有一本酒店服务小册子。

◆ Some service arrangements：

服务安排：

The guests will have lunch at the Chinese Restaurant on the second floor in forty minutes.

客人 40 分钟后到二层中餐厅就餐。

There will be a party in the hall on the third floor at 7：00 this evening.

晚上 7 点钟在三层的大厅里有一个晚会。

The luggage will be delivered to the rooms according to the luggage labels within fifteen minutes.

15 分钟内将根据行李上的标签将行李送到房间。

The breakfast of the next day will be at 6 o'clock. The departure time is 7 o'clock.

第二天的早餐时间为 6 点。离店时间是第二天的早上 7 点。

Service Practice 服务实训

Now, let's begin the practice according to *Task of Service Practice*.
请按照上述实训任务开始实训。

08 2 Introducing the Services to the Group. mp3

Model of Service Practice 实训对照

Zhou：Zhou Jin, a concierge.

Good afternoon, ladies and gentlemen. Welcome to our hotel!
下午好,女士们、先生们。欢迎大家来到我们酒店。

Your room key cards and breakfast meal vouchers are in the envelopes on the desk. They are arranged in alphabetical by family name. Please take the one with your name.

你们的房卡和早餐券在桌上的信封里,是按照姓的字母顺序排列的。请拿上写有您的名字的信封。

We will deliver your luggage to your room according to the luggage label within fifteen minutes. If you find something wrong, please call me. My name is Zhou Jin. I'm in charge of services to your group in our hotel. My telephone number is 66465231.

15 分钟内我们将根据行李上的标签将行李送到您的房间。如果有差错,请打电话告诉我。我叫周瑾,负责贵团在本酒店的服务,我的电话是 66465231。

If you want to make a room-to-room call from your room, please dial the room number that you want directly. Outside calls may be made from your room by dialing "0" first and then the number. We have a guide to hotel service on the desk in your room. If you have some special requiment or difficulties, please tell me.

从房间打酒店内线电话,请直拨您要的房间号码;外线电话要先拨"0",再拨您要的号码。在您房间的桌子上有一本我们酒店的服务指南。如果您对酒店的服务有特殊要求,或有需要我们协助解决的问题,请您告诉我。

Feel free to have a rest in your room or have a walk in the little garden, and go have lunch at the Chinese restaurant on the second floor in forty minutes. You will have a party in the hall on the third floor at 7 o'clock. Starting at 8:30 you are welcome to enjoy the Recreation Center on the first floor.

请大家在房间稍事休息,或在小花园里散散步,40 分钟后到 2 层中餐厅就餐。晚上 7 点钟在 3 层的大厅里有一个晚会,8:30 大家可以在一层的娱乐中心参加自己喜欢的活动。

Your breakfast tomorrow will be at 6 o'clock. Your departure time is 7 o'clock. Hope you have a pleasant time here.

明天的早餐时间为 6 点,离店时间是明早 7 点。祝大家在这里度过美好的时光!

Hotel Knowledge
新酒店人须知

(1) How to translate them? Pay attention to the meaning of the word "express".

在下列句子中"express"这个词如何翻译?

① Li Yuan can express herself in English to the guest.

李媛能够用英语向客人表达自己的意思。

② The guest left for Shanghai on the express.

客人通过高速公路去上海了。

③ The cashier printed the American Express Card for the guest.

收银员为客人刷美国运通卡。

④ They took the express train to Shanghai.

他们乘快车去上海。

⑤ They have taken the express elevator to the fifth floor.

他们乘直达电梯到 5 层。

⑥ Miss Smith expressed a letter to the hotel.

Smith 小姐给酒店快递了一封信。

⑦ He expressed his regret to the guest.

他向客人表示遗憾。

⑧ We express the juice from grapes for the guests every day.

我们每天为客人压榨葡萄汁。

⑨ He sent an express telegram to his friend.

他向他的朋友发了一份加急电报。

(2) Some useful expressions:

常用术语:

Foreign Exchange	外币兑换
Cafe	咖啡厅
Business Center	商务中心
Shopping Center	购物中心
Travel Counter	旅游代办处
Parking	停车场
Health Club	健身俱乐部
Recreation Center	娱乐中心
Beauty Parlor	美容室
Hair Salon	美发厅
Barber's Shop	理发室
Toilet	盥洗室
Cloakroom	寄存处

Unit 9

Other Concierge Services

技能实训 9　其他礼宾服务

Main Services 主要服务

◆ Airport picking up service.
接机服务。

◆ Arranging a bus to send the guests.
安排车接送客人。

◆ Calling a taxi for the guest.
为客人叫出租车。

◆ Helping the guest with the luggage.
帮客人拿行李。

◆ Arranging the tour of the city.
安排城市观光。

Skill Points 技能要点

◆ When receiving guests at the airport, take the picking-up board with you and hold high while you are waiting. If there is any change, delay or cancellation of the flight, or no show of guests, contact the Chief Concierge as soon as possible and wait for further instructions. When the guests arrive, greet them politely with a friendly smile. Then help them with the luggage to the hotel car or limousine waiting outside in the airport parking lot. On the way back to the hotel, introduce our city and some beautiful tourist attractions in our city.
机场迎宾时,高举接机牌等候客人。如果有变化——航班延误、航班取消或客人没来,要及时与礼宾部领班联系,等候下一步指令。客人到达之后,面带微笑,礼貌地问候,然后帮助客人把行李搬到停在停车场的酒店的轿车或豪华客车上。在回酒店的路途中要向客人介绍我们的城市和城市的旅游景点。

◆ When calling a taxi for a guest, introduce the price to him or give him some budget advice if the guest asks.
在为客人叫出租车时,如果客人询问,向客人介绍出租车价格,或者提出怎样坐车省钱的建议。

◆ It's a very important job for a clerk in Concierge to handle the luggage of the guests of the hotel. You are needed to help the guests with their luggage, deliver the luggage to the room or collect the luggage from the guest. No matter what you do, pay more attention to the following: the number of luggage, damaged or undamaged, and the luggage tags as well(Particularly for the group guests).

对礼宾部员工来说处理行李是一件很重要的工作。为客人拿行李,送或分发客人行李到房间,从客人那里收取行李,无论你做哪一项,都要留意下面三点:行李的件数、行李是否被损坏、行李的标签(特别是团队客人)。

Practice 1　Receiving a Guest at the Airport
实训项目 1　机场接客人

Task of Service Practice 实训任务

◆ Wang Yang from the Beijing Hotel receives Mrs. Rose Brown from New York at the airport.
北京饭店的王阳到机场接来自纽约的 Rose Brown 夫人。

◆ Mrs. Rose Brown has five pieces of luggage.
Rose Brown 夫人随身带有五件行李。

◆ The car of the hotel is in the airport parking lot.
酒店接客人的车已停在机场的停车场。

◆ It is the first time that Mrs. Rose Brown comes to Beijing. She is looking forward to visiting the Forbidden City and the Great Wall. And she wants to see the Summer Palace as well.
Rose Brown 夫人是第一次来北京,她一直想看看紫禁城和长城,还有颐和园。

◆ Wang Yang tells Mrs. Rose Brown that it's very convenient to go to the Forbidden City from the hotel because so many buses can go there. She can visit it as soon as they arrive at the hotel. Wang Yang suggests renting a car to visit the Summer Palace and the Great Wall.
王阳告诉 Rose Brown 夫人,从酒店去紫禁城很方便,有很多车到那儿,他们一到酒店她就可以去紫禁城。王阳建议租车到颐和园和长城。

◆ They arrive at the Beijing Hotel. The bellman Xiao Li has been waiting there and he'll escort Mrs. Rose Brown to her room assigned.
他们到达北京饭店,行李员小李已等候在那儿,他将送 Rose Brown 夫人去她的房间。

Service Practice 服务实训

Now, let's begin the practice according to *Task of Service Practice*.
请按照上述实训任务开始实训。

Model of Service Practice 实训对照

Brown：Rose Brown，a guest from New York.

Wang：Wang Yang，an airport representative.

Brown：Excuse me. Are you a clerk from the Beijing Hotel?

打扰了，你是北京饭店的职员吗?

Wang：Yes，I'm Wang Yang from the Beijing Hotel. Are you …

是，我是北京饭店的王阳，您是……

09 1 Receiving a Guest at the Airport. mp3

Brown：I am Rose Brown from New York.

我是来自纽约的 Rose Brown。

Wang：Mrs. Brown，I hope you had a good trip. I'm here to meet you. Welcome to Beijing.

Brown 夫人，一路顺利。我是来接您的。欢迎您来到北京。

Brown：Thank you. Glad to meet you.

谢谢。见到你真高兴。

Wang：Glad to meet you，too. Let me help you with your luggage cart.

见到您我也很高兴。我来推行李车。

Brown：Thank you.

谢谢你。

Wang：How many pieces of luggage do you have?

您一共有多少件行李?

Brown：Five.

五件。

Wang：This way，please. We have a car in the airport parking lot to take you to our hotel.

请这边走。接您到酒店的车已停在机场的停车场。

Brown：OK.

好的。

Wang：This is our car. Let's go please. Is this your first visit to Beijing?

这就是我们的车。咱们走吧。这是您第一次来北京吗?

Brown：Yes，it is. I'm looking forward to visiting the Forbidden City and the Great Wall. I want to see the Summer Palace as well.

是的。我一直想看看紫禁城和长城，还有颐和园。

Wang：You can go to visit the Forbidden City as soon as you arrive at our hotel. It's very convenient to go there from our hotel. Many buses go there.

您一到我们酒店就可以去参观紫禁城。到那儿很方便，有很多车到那儿。

Brown：What about the Summer Palace and the Great Wall?

怎样到颐和园和长城?

Wang：You can rent a car. This is our hotel. The bellman，Xiao Li，is waiting there，and he'll escort you to your assigned room.

可以租车到这两个地方。这就是我们酒店。行李员小李正等在那儿，他将送您到
您的房间。

Brown： I really appreciate your kindness.

不胜感激。

Wang： You're welcome, madam. This way, please.

不用谢，夫人。请您这边走。

Brown： Goodbye.

再见。

Wang： Goodbye. Hope you have a very pleasant time in Beijing.

再见。祝您在北京度过美好的时光！

Practice 2　Calling a Taxi for the Guest
实训项目 2　为客人叫出租车

Task of Service Practice 实训任务

◆ Mrs. Rose Brown needs to call a taxi, because she plans to visit the Summer Palace in the morning and the Great Wall in the afternoon. She wants to get some advice on how to rent a taxi from Zhou Tao…

Rose Brown 夫人想叫一辆出租车，她计划上午去颐和园，下午去长城。她想从周涛那里
获得租车的建议。

◆ Zhou Tao tells Mrs. Brown that it is good for her to take the return tour by taxi.

周涛告诉 Brown 夫人包车来回合适。

◆ The taxi arrives at the hotel in 15 minutes.

出租车 15 分钟后到达酒店。

Service Practice 服务实训

Now, let's begin the practice according to *Task of Service Practice*.

请按照上述实训任务开始实训。

Model of Service Practice 实训对照

09 2 Calling a Taxi
for the Guest. mp3

Zhou： Zhou Tao, a doorman.

Brown： Rose Brown, a guest from New York.

Zhou： Good morning. I'm the doorman here. How can I help you?

早上好。我是这儿的门童。需要我的帮助吗？

Brown： Could you call a taxi for me?

你能帮我叫一辆出租车吗?

Zhou： Certainly. Where are you going?

当然可以。您要去哪里?

Brown： I want to visit the Summer Palace in the morning and the Great Wall in the afternoon. It's the first time I've been to Beijing. Could you please give me some advice?

我们计划上午去颐和园,下午去长城。这是我第一次到北京来,请你给我提一些建议。

Zhou： It's good for you to book a round trip by taxi.

包车来回划算。

Brown： OK. I'll take the round trip by taxi.

好,我就包车来回。

Zhou： Please wait a moment. I'll get in touch with a taxi dispatcher. The taxi is expected to come in 15 minutes. Oh, the taxi is coming.

请稍等,我和出租车调度联系一下。出租车15分钟就到。噢,车来了。

Brown： Thank you very much.

太感谢你了。

Zhou： You're welcome. Have a good trip.

没什么,祝您旅途愉快。

Practice 3　Helping the Guest with the Luggage
实训项目3　为客人搬运和保管行李

Task of Service Practice 实训任务

◆ Hugo Carter in Room 2656 has to check out and go to see an old friend of his in twenty-five minutes. He has no time to deal with his luggage. So he calls the Concierge for help.

2656 房间的 Hugo Carter 得在 25 分钟内办理退宿手续并赶去看他的一个老朋友。他没有时间来处理他的行李,于是他打电话给礼宾部寻求帮助。

◆ Li Ming receives the call and sends a bellman to fetch the luggage.

李明接了这个电话,并派了一个行李员去取行李。

◆ Li Ming asks Mr. Carter to be sure to put his name tag on the cases. Li Ming also tells Mr. Carter they will take good care of his luggage until he comes back for it.

李明要求 Carter 先生务必在行李上贴上名签。李明还告诉 Carter 他们将妥善保管好他的行李,直到他来取。

◆ Mr. Carter will come back to collect his luggage at the Concierge Desk at 2:00 p. m.

Carter 先生将在下午两点到礼宾部取行李。

Service Practice 服务实训

Now, let's begin the practice according to *Task of Service Practice*.

请按照上述实训任务开始实训。

Model of Service Practice 实训对照

Li：Li Ming, a concierge.

Carter：Hugo Carter, a guest.

09 3 Helping the Guest with the Luggage. mp3

Li：Good morning. Concierge. How can I help you?

上午好,礼宾部。需要我为您服务吗?

Carter：Good morning. I have to check out and go to see an old friend of mine in twenty-five minutes. I'm calling you because I have no time and I don't know how to deal with my luggage.

上午好,我得在 25 分钟内办理退宿手续并赶去看我的一个老朋友。我打电话给你,是因为我没有时间也不知道怎样处理我的行李。

Li：Don't worry, sir. May I have your name and your room number?

别着急,先生。请告诉我您的姓名和房间号。

Carter：Hugo Carter, Room 2656.

Hugo Carter, 2656 房间。

Li：Mr. Carter, I'll send a bellman to Room 2656 to fetch your luggage at once. Please be sure to put name tags on the cases. When will you come back to our hotel for the luggage?

Carter 先生,我马上派一个行李员到 2656 房间去取您的行李。请您务必把您的名签贴在行李上。您什么时候回酒店取行李?

Carter：At 2:00 p. m.

下午两点。

Li：My name is Li Ming. We'll take good care of your luggage until you come back to our hotel for it.

我们会妥善保管您的行李,直到您回来取。

Carter：Thank you very much indeed. And where shall I collect my luggage at that time?

真是太感谢了。到时候我在哪里取行李?

Li：At the Concierge Desk.

礼宾部。

Carter：That's very kind of you. See you.

您真是太好了,再见。

Li：See you then.

再见。

Hotel Knowledge

新酒店人须知

(1) In order to assure high quality guest service, the staff must follow the 6 points.

为了确保优质服务,酒店员工必须遵循以下 6 点。

① Every time you see a guest, smile and offer an appropriate hospitality comment.

每次见到客人,面带微笑,进行友好而得体的寒暄。

② Speak to the guest in a friendly, enthusiastic and courteous tone and manner.

与客人交谈友好、热情、彬彬有礼。

③ Serve the people with polite language.

使用礼貌语言为客人服务。

④ Answer the guest's questions and requests quickly and efficiently, or take personal responsibility to get the answer.

迅速有效地回答客人的问题或对客人的要求做出反应,答复不了的问题应自己寻求答案。

⑤ Anticipate the guest's needs and resolve guest's problems.

预测客人的需求并解决客人的难题。

⑥ Follow up wherever and whenever necessary and possible.

随时随地,只要有必要、有可能,就应当追踪落实解决情况。

（2）Some useful expressions in the concierge:

礼宾部常用术语:

parking attendant	停车场服务员
doorman	门童
head porter	行李领班
airport rep.	机场代表
group baggage record	团队行李登记
airport pick-up service	机场接送服务
flight number	航班号
travel agency	旅行社
luggage tag	行李箱
rooming list	分房单
luggage	行李
luggage cart	行李车
luggage belt	行李带
automobile	小汽车
shuttle bus	穿梭巴士

Practice Revision 实训回望

◆ What will you say to the guest when accompanying him into and out of the elevator?

◆ We have known that it's a very important job for a clerk in the Concierge to handle the luggage of the guest of the hotel. What should you pay more attention to when handling the luggage of the guest when you practice in the Concierge?

◆ What must the staff follow in order to assure high quality of service in the hotel?

◆ Please talk about the work of receiving a guest at the airport.

Case and Improvement: Birthday Cake and Marigold, Birthday Cards and Flowers
案例与提高：生日蛋糕和万寿菊，生日贺卡和鲜花

When Mr. Banks finished his last work, it was midnight. He was tired, but he was very glad, because everything was ready. Beijing International Trade Exhibition would open at 9:00 tomorrow morning. He took off his coat in order to sleep. At that time it suddenly occurred to him that today was his mother's birthday and the grand birthday party for his mother would begin in four hours. But he had been keeping busy with preparing for the exhibition so that he forgot to prepare the presents for his mother.

当 Banks 先生结束他最后一项工作时，已经是午夜 12 点了。他很累，但很高兴，一切准备就绪，明天上午 9 点北京国际贸易展览会就要开幕了。他脱掉外套准备睡觉。这时他猛然想起，今天是他母亲的生日，为母亲举行的生日聚会 4 个小时后就要开始了。他一直忙于筹备展览，以至忘了给母亲准备礼物。

The mother was eighty years old this year. The three brothers planned to hold a grand birthday party for his mother a month ago. As Mr. Banks had to hold the exhibition in China, he was only responsible to prepare the big birthday cake and marigold for the party. But now he was in China and his wife was on business in France. He called a few express companies, but they couldn't express these gifts for him in such a short of time. He put on his coat and went to the Concierge for help.

母亲今年 80 岁，三个兄弟一个月前就计划为母亲举行一个大型聚会。由于 Banks 先生要在中国开展览会，他只负责为聚会准备大蛋糕和万寿菊。但是现在他在中国，妻子在法国出差。他给几家快递公司打电话，他们都无法在这么短的时间内为他运送礼物。他穿上外套到礼宾部寻求帮助。

Li Ming was on duty. He found out Mr. Banks walking to him, looking worried and said to him, "Good night, Mr. Banks. You haven't gone to sleep so late. Is there anything I can do for you?" "I need your help, indeed." Mr. Banks told him the reason.

李明正在值班。他发现 Banks 先生面容焦虑正向他走来，于是说："晚上好，Banks 先生。这么晚您还没有休息，有什么需要我帮忙?""我的确需要你的帮助。"Banks 先生向李明讲明了原委。

"Don't worry, Mr. Banks. Maybe our manager can help you. Oh, he has just gone home. Wait a moment, please. Let me think. I know we have some cooperation with a hotel in New York. Let me have a try." Li Ming called the Concierge Department of the hotel. It was the Concierge Manager Mr. White himself that received the call. He told Li Ming that they could offer the help. Li Ming said to Mr. Banks, "Our cooperation hotel in New York can help you. The Concierge Manager promised to buy the presents and sent them to your mother with his two clerks. Please write down the demands for the presents, for example, where to buy the cake, the shape and color of the cake. And then I will send an e-mail to

Mr. White. "

"别着急，Banks 先生，可能我们的经理可以帮您。哦，他刚回到家。请您等一会儿，让我想一想。Banks 先生，我知道我们跟纽约的一家酒店有一些合作，我来试一试。"李明给这家酒店的礼宾部打电话，礼宾部经理 White 先生亲自接了电话。他当即告诉李明他们能够提供帮助。李明对 Banks 先生说："礼宾部经理承诺自己和两名员工去购买礼物并将礼物送到您的母亲手中。请您写下您对所要购买的礼物的要求，例如，在哪儿购买蛋糕，蛋糕的外形和颜色。然后我给 White 先生发一个邮件。"

At the birthday party, Mr. White said to the lady, "Happy birthday, Mrs. Banks! We are pleased to be asked by your son Mr. Banks to send the birthday cake and the marigold. And here are two cards and two bunches of flowers in the names of our hotel staff and the staff of the Chinese hotel which your son is staying at. We wish you a long life. "

生日宴会上，White 先生对老夫人说："生日快乐，Banks 夫人！承蒙令郎 Banks 先生之托，我们为您送来生日蛋糕和万寿菊。这是我们酒店职员和令郎现在所住的一家中国酒店的职员送给您的鲜花和生日贺卡，我们祝您长寿！"

The old lady was so glad and couldn't help calling the sleeping son Mr. Banks, asking him to express her appreciation to the Chinese hotel.

老妇人太高兴了，情不自禁地给睡梦中的儿子 Banks 先生打电话，要求他转达她对中国酒店由衷的感激之情。

Case Topic 案例话题

The enlightenment I gain from what Li Ming did.
我从李明所做的工作中得到的启发。

Hotel Manager's Comments
酒店经理点评

实训模块三的案例是根据真实的服务事例改写成的案例故事，旨在提高同学们对服务、个性化服务以及服务质量等概念的感性和理性的认识。

我们来看一看案例中李明提供的个性化服务的特点。

案例故事中有这么一段：

He found out Mr. Banks walking to him, looking worried and said to him, "Good night, Mr. Banks. You haven't gone to sleep so late. Is there anything I can do for you?" "I need your help, indeed. " Mr. Banks told him the reason.

首先是：Mr. Banks walking to him, looking worried; haven't gone to sleep so late, 李明的结论是客人需要帮助，于是"Is there anything I can do for you?"

李明服务的第一个特点是能预测客人的需求。李明服务的第二个特点是解决了客人的难题。

我们知道，不是李明自己去买礼物、送礼物，而是 the Concierge Manager Mr. White 帮他解决了客人 Banks 先生的难题。我们来看这一段：

Wait a moment, please. Let me think. I know we have some cooperation with a hotel in New York. 说明李明有这方面的信息资源积累。"Let me have a try. "李明敢于尝试,他找到了帮客人解决问题的 the Concierge Manager Mr. White,生日蛋糕和万寿菊、生日贺卡和鲜花都送到了老妇人手中。

实训中应怎样提高服务能力呢?

一方面要严格按酒店常规服务流程和服务要求为客人服务;另一方面要提高观察力和洞察力,以预测客人的需求。平时注意积累自己和他人的服务经验,遇到难题时可得到启迪和借鉴;平时注意收集服务信息,需要时信手拈来;还要有智慧、有勇气。这样我们就能像李明那样既能预测客人的需求,还能解决客人的难题。在实训中,同学们也能让客人得到最佳的服务和最实际的好处。

Answers to "Practice Revision" 部分参考答案

◆ We have known that it's a very important job for a clerk in the Concierge to handle the luggage of the guest of the hotel. What should you pay more attention to when handling the luggage of the guest when you practice in the Concierge?

Handling the luggage of the guest contains three parts: helping the guest with his luggage, delivering the luggage to the guest rooms and collect the luggage from the guest. No matter what you do, make sure of the number of the luggage, damaged or undamaged, and the luggage tags as well.

Chapter Four　Housekeeping（Ⅰ）

实训模块四　客房服务（一）

Unit 10

Cleaning the Room

技能实训 10 打扫房间

Service Procedure 服务流程

◆ Knock at the door gently three times.

轻轻地敲门三次。

◆ Say, "Housekeeping. "

通报:"客房服务。"

◆ Ask the guest whether to come into the room.

问客人能否进房间。

◆ Greet the guest.

问候客人。

◆ Ask the guest whether to clean the room now.

问客人现在能否打扫房间。

◆ Clean the room.

打扫房间。

　Open the window;

　开窗;

　Dispose of the rubbish;

　倒垃圾;

　Make the bed;

　铺床;

　Clean the bathroom;

　清洁卫生间;

　Replenish the supplies;

　补充客房物品;

　Vacuum the floor;

　吸尘;

Self-check.

检查。

◆ Express your wishes to the guest.

表达祝愿。

Skill Points 技能要点

◆ Before entering a guest room, knock at the door three times slightly, and then announce: "Housekeeping. May I come in?"

在进客人房间前,轻敲门三下,然后通报:"客房服务,我能进来吗?"

◆ Entering the room, greet the guest in a warm and natural voice, "Good morning. May I clean the room now?"

进入房间后,热情而自然地问候客人:"上午好。我现在可以打扫房间吗?"

◆ If the guest doesn't want the room to be cleaned now, ask what time is convenient and come back to the room for cleaning at the convenient time.

如果客人不想马上打扫房间,要询问何时方便,然后在客人认为方便的时间再回房间打扫。

Practice 1　Cleaning the Room Now
实训项目 1　现在打扫房间

Task of Service Practice 实训任务

◆ Wang Ying is going to clean the room for Mr. White now.

王英现在要打扫 White 先生的房间。

◆ Mr. White agrees her to do the room now, but he asks Wang Ying to clean the bathroom first.

White 先生同意她现在打扫房间,不过需先打扫卫生间。

◆ When Wang Ying finishes cleaning the room, Mr. White asks her to give him three coat hangers and another blanket.

王英打扫完房间,White 先生要求王英给他三个衣架并再添一条毯子。

◆ Wang Ying tells Mr. White another housemaid will bring them to his room immediately.

王英告诉 White 先生另外一个服务员会马上把这些东西送到他的房间。

Service Practice 服务实训

Now, let's begin the practice according to *Task of Service Practice*.

请按照上述实训任务开始实训。

Model of Service Practice 实训对照

Wang：Wang Ying，a housemaid.
White：Mr. White，a guest.

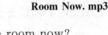

10 1 Cleaning the Room Now. mp3

Wang：Housekeeping. May I come in?
客房部工作人员。我能进来吗？

White：Come in，please.
请进。

Wang：Good morning，Mr. White. Sorry to disturb you. May I do the room now?
早上好，White 先生。对不起，打扰了。我现在可以打扫房间吗？

White：OK. Can you clean the bathroom first?
好的，你能先打扫浴室吗？

Wang：Certainly. I have finished cleaning the room. Anything else I can do for you，sir?
当然可以。我已打扫完房间。先生，还有什么需要我做的吗？

White：I have washed some clothes. I need three coat hangers and I'd like you to give me another blanket.
我洗了一些衣服，还需要三个衣架。我想再要一条毯子。

Wang：Another housemaid will bring them to your room immediately.
另外一个服务员会马上把这些东西送到您的房间。

White：Thank you.
谢谢。

Wang：You're welcome. I hope you have a good day.
不用谢。祝您快乐！

Practice 2 What Time Can I Clean the Room
实训项目2 什么时间可以打扫房间

Task of Service Practice 实训任务

◆ Mr. White doesn't agree Wang Ying to do the room now because several old friends of his will come here in fifteen minutes.
White 先生不同意王英现在打扫房间，因为他的几个老朋友 15 分钟后就要到这儿来。

◆ Wang Ying asks Mr. White when she can come back to clean the room. It is hard for Mr. White to tell the time of cleaning，for they haven't seen each other for twenty years.
王英问她何时可以回来打扫房间。White 先生却很难告知王英回来打扫房间的时间，因为他们老朋友之间已经 20 年没见面了。

◆ Wang Ying gives him two pieces of advice. One is when the friends come，press this PND sign outside your door. When the cleaning can be done, place this MUR outside your door. The other is to call the Floor Service Desk. So she can come back for service immediately.

王英给了两条建议。一条是：朋友来了之后，就把"请勿打扰"牌挂在门外；当可以打扫房间时，请把"请打扫房间"牌挂在门外。另一条是：打电话到楼层服务台。这样她就可以马上过来服务。

Service Practice 服务实训

Now, let's begin the practice according to *Task of Service Practice*.
请按照上述实训任务开始实训。

Model of Service Practice 实训对照

10 2 What Time Can I Clean the Room. mp3

Wang：Wang Ying, a housemaid.

White：Mr. White, a guest.

Wang：Housekeeping. May I come in?

客房服务员。我可以进来吗？

White：Come in, please.

请进。

Wang：Good morning, Mr. White. May I do your room now?

早上好，White 先生。我现在可以打扫房间吗？

White：No, not now. A few old friends of mine are coming in fifteen minutes.

不，现在不行。我的几个老朋友 15 分钟后就要到这里。

Wang：When would you like me to clean your room, Mr. White?

我何时可以回来打扫房间，White 先生？

White：It's hard to say. We haven't seen each other for twenty years.

很难说，因为我们之间已经 20 年没见面了。

Wang：When your friends come, please place this PND sign outside your door. When you want me to come back to do the room, please place this MUR sign outside your door. You can also call the Floor Service Desk. I'll be back at once.

您的朋友来了之后，请把"请勿打扰"牌挂在门外；当您需要我打扫房间时，请把"请打扫房间"牌挂在门外。当然您还可以打电话到楼层服务台，我马上过来为您服务。

White：OK. Thank you.

好的，谢谢你。

Wang：It's my pleasure. I hope you enjoy yourselves.

不用谢。祝您玩得愉快！

Hotel Knowledge

新酒店人须知

(1) The room attendant can know the name of the guest by the following：

客房服务员可以通过以下途径了解客人的姓名：

luggage tags	行李标签
arrival list	来客单
registration	入住登记
restaurant reservation	餐厅预订
convention or meeting name tags	会议用姓名标牌
asking the guest	询问客人

(2) Useful expressions：

常用词汇：

pillow	枕头	quilt	被子
blanket	毯子	extra blanket	备用毯
sheet	床单	bed cover/bed spread	床罩
mattress	床垫	curtain	窗帘
carpet	地毯	coffee table	咖啡桌
electric pot	电水壶	thermos	热水瓶
extra bed	加床	table lamp/reading lamp	台灯/阅读灯
king-size beds	大床/双人床	ashtray	烟灰缸
envelope	信封	sewing	针线包
laundry bag	洗衣袋	laundry list	洗衣单
coat hanger	衣架	shoe shine cloth	擦鞋布
shoe horn/shoe lifter	鞋拔子	shoe basket	鞋筐
clothes brush	衣刷	rubbish bin	垃圾桶
postcard	明信片		

Unit 11

Turn-down Service and Extending a Bed Service

技能实训 11　晚床服务和加床服务

Service Procedure 服务流程

Turn-down Service
晚床服务

◆ Knock at the door gently three times.
轻轻地敲门三次。

◆ Announce "Housekeeping".
通报"客房服务"。

◆ Greet the guest.
问候客人。

◆ Ask the guest if he wants turn-door service now.
问客人现在能否做晚床。

◆ Turn down the bed.
做晚床。

◆ Drop the curtain together.
放下窗帘。

◆ Clean the bathroom and bring in the fresh towels.
清洁浴室,放上干净的毛巾。

◆ Have a look around to be sure everything is done.
回望一下,以确保该做的事都做了。

◆ Express the wishes to the guest.
表达祝愿。

Extending a Bed Service
加床服务

◆ Ask the guest to go to handle the formality of extending a bed at the Front Office.
要求客人到前台办理加床手续。

◆ With the permission of the Front Office, put an extra bed for the guest.
前台允许之后,给客人加床。

Skill Points 技能要点

Turn-down Service

晚床服务

◆ Before entering a guest room, knock at the door three times slightly, and then announce "Housekeeping" with a pleasant smile.

在进客人房间前，轻敲门三下，然后微笑着通报"客房服务"。

◆ Entering the room, greet the guest in a warm voice: "Good evening, Mr. or Mrs. …May I turn down your bed?"

进入房间后，热情地问候客人："晚上好。"然后说："我现在可以为您做晚床吗？"

◆ If the guest doesn't want the bed to be turned down now, ask what time is convenient, and come back to the room to do it at the convenient time.

如果客人不想现在做晚床，要询问何时方便，然后在客人认为方便的时间再回房间完成此项服务。

Extending a Bed Service

加床服务

◆ In the Housekeeping, some guests always ask the house attendants to put an extra bed for them. But the house attendants have no right to put extra beds for the guests directly. At that time, you should ask the guest to call the Front Office for permission or ask him to handle the formality of extending the bed. Only with the permission, you can put an extra bed for the guest.

客房服务中，总有些客人会向客房部工作人员提出加床要求，但是客房部工作人员没有权利直接给客人加床。这时，要求客人打电话到前台以获得许可，或者要求客人直接到前台办理加床手续。只有在获得前台许可之后你才能给客人加床。

Practice Turning Down the Bed and Asking an Extra Bed
实训项目 做晚床与要求加床

Task of Service Practice 实训任务

◆ Wang Li introduces to Mr. Brown what turning down means.

王莉向 Brown 先生介绍了做晚床。

◆ Mr. Brown asks Wang Li to come back for turning down the bed at 10:15. But now, he wants Wang Li to clean the bathroom for him, for he has just had a bath and the bathroom is in disarray. His former classmates will come here at once.

Brown 先生要求王莉在 10:15 回来做晚床。但是现在他希望王莉把浴室打扫一下，因为他刚刚洗过澡，浴室很乱。他的老同学马上就要到这里来。

◆ Wang Li says that she will be able to finish cleaning the bathroom within five minutes.

王莉说她能在 5 分钟之内打扫完浴室。

◆ Mr. Brown asks Wang Li to put an extra bed because one of his former classmates will stay here with him for a night.

Brown 先生要求王莉给他加床,因为他的一个老同学将在这里和他住一夜。

◆ With the permission of the Front Office, Wang Li will bring in the extended bed when she comes back for turning down the bed.

经前台的允许,王莉将在回来做晚床时给他带来加床。

Service Practice 服务实训

Now, let's begin the practice according to *Task of Service Practice*.

请按照上述实训任务开始实训。

Model of Service Practice 实训对照

11 1 Turning Down the Bed and Asking an Extra Bed. mp3

Wang：　Wang Li, a housemaid.

Brown：　Mr. Brown, a guest.

Wang：　Good evening. Housekeeping. May I come in?

晚上好。客房服务,我可以进来吗?

Brown：　Come in, please.

请进。

Wang：　Good evening, sir. May I provide turn-down service now?

晚上好,先生。我现在可以做晚床吗?

Brown：　What do you mean by that?

做晚床是什么意思?

Wang：　For the turn-down service, I'll take away the bed cover, take a quilt corner by the telephone side and fold it into a triangle. I'll place the pillow properly. Then I'll draw the curtains and turn on some lights. Finally I'll tidy up the bathroom, bring in fresh towels and just-boiled water as well.

做晚床就是将床罩拿走,将靠电话那一边的被子角掀起,折成三角形,放好枕头。接着我会放好窗帘,打开一些灯。最后收拾好浴室,放上一些干净的毛巾并准备好热水。

Brown：　Oh, I see. Please come back to turn down the bed at 10：15. Could you clean the bathroom now? I just had a bath and the bathroom is in disarray. My former classmates will be here shortly.

噢,我明白了,请在 10：15 过来做晚床。你能帮我打扫一下浴室吗? 我刚刚洗过澡,浴室很乱。我的老同学马上就要来了。

Wang：　I will be able to finish cleaning the bathroom in five minutes.

5 分钟我就可以打扫完浴室。

Brown： Could I have an extra bed? One of my former classmates will stay here with me for a night.

能给我加床吗? 我的老同学将在这里和我过一夜。

Wang： Of course. But please call the Front Desk first. With the permission of the Front Office，I'll get you one when I come back to turn down your bed.

当然可以。请先给前台打电话,经过前台的允许,我回来做晚床时给您带来加床。

Brown： OK，I'll call them then.

好的,我给他们打电话。

Wang： The bathroom is all right.

浴室打扫完了。

Brown： Thank you very much.

非常感谢。

Wang： You're welcome. I hope you have a very pleasant evening.

不用谢。祝您度过一个美好的夜晚。

Hotel Knowledge
新酒店人须知

Useful expressions：
常用词汇：

tissues	面巾纸	towels	毛巾
face towel	面巾	bath towel	浴巾
shower cap	浴帽	soap	肥皂
shampoo	洗发水	conditioner	护发素
toothpaste	牙膏	toothbrush	牙刷
comb	梳子	a hour drier	吹风筒
shaving kit	剃须包	razor	剃须刀
shaving cream	剃须膏	toilet paper	卫生纸
foot mat	脚垫	bathtub	浴缸
slipper	拖鞋	wash basin	面盆
cotton buds	棉签	shower curtain	浴帘
bathroom	浴室	toilet cover	马桶盖

Unit 12
Laundry Service

技能实训 12　洗衣服务

Skill Points 技能要点

◆ Same day service：collect the clothes by 11：00 a. m. and deliver them to the guests' room by 9：00 p. m. in the same day；collect the clothes before 3：00 p. m. and deliver them to the guests' room by noon the next day.

当日服务：上午 11 点前收洗的衣服，晚 9 点前送回客人房间；下午 3 点前收洗的衣服，第二天中午前送回客房。

◆ Express service：collect the clothes by 2：00 p. m. and deliver them within four hours at a 50％ extra charge.

快洗服务：下午 2 点前收洗的衣服在 4 小时内送回客房，增收 50％的费用。

◆ When collecting the laundry，ask the guest to make a note in the laundry list whether the clothes need ironing，washing or dry-cleaning and what time he wants to get them back.

收取客人要洗的衣服时，要求客人在洗衣单上注明衣服是熨烫，水洗还是干洗，还要注明何时需要取回衣服。

◆ When collecting the laundry list，pay attention to the room number，the name of the guest，and the special demands of the guest as well.

收取洗衣单时，要注意客人的房号、姓名及特殊要求。

◆ When there is no such service or necessary equipment，say "I'm sorry. " And then give the reason politely. For example："I'm sorry. We can only do simple mending. "

如果没有某种服务或设备，先对客人说"抱歉"，然后礼貌地解释。例如，"很抱歉，我们只能做简单的织补。"

Practice 1　Introducing Laundry Service
实训项目 1　介绍洗衣服务

Task of Service Practice 实训任务

◆ Mr. Williams asks Chen Yuan if there is laundry service in the hotel.

Williams 先生询问陈嫒酒店是否有洗衣服务。

◆ Chen Yuan answers "yes" and introduces to Mr. Williams that if a guest has any clothes to be cleaned, he should put them into the laundry bag behind the bathroom door and make a note in the laundry list whether the clothes need ironing, washing or dry-cleaning and what time the guest wants them back.

陈嫒回答"有",还向 Williams 先生介绍,如果客人有要洗的衣服,请放在浴室门后的洗衣袋里,在洗衣单上要注明衣服需要熨烫,水洗还是干洗,还要注明何时需要取衣服。

◆ There is a hole in the sweater of Williams. He wants to deal with it.

Williams 的毛衣上有一个洞,他需要织补。

◆ The hotel can deal with it, but this kind of special demand should be written clearly in the laundry list.

酒店能够织补,但是这种特殊的服务需要在洗衣单上填写清楚。

◆ Mr. Williams wants his leather coat to be cleaned, but the hotel has no special equipment.

Williams 先生还想洗他的皮外套,但是酒店没有这种特殊的设备。

Service Practice 服务实训

Now, let's begin the practice according to *Task of Service Practice*.

请按照上述实训任务开始实训。

Model of Service Practice 实训对照

12 1 Introducing
Laundry Service. mp3

Chen: Chen Yuan, a room maid.

Williams: Mr. Williams, a guest.

Chen: Good morning. Housekeeping. How can I help you?

早上好,客房部,需要我们的服务吗?

Williams: Do you have laundry service?

你们有洗衣服务吗?

Chen: Yes, we have. If you have any laundry, please leave it in the laundry bag behind the bathroom door. Please note on the laundry list whether you need your clothes ironed, washed, or dry-cleaned and what time you want to get them back.

有。如果您有要洗的衣服,请放在浴室门后的洗衣袋里。请在洗衣单上注明您的衣服是需要熨烫,水洗还是干洗,还要注明何时需要取衣服。

Williams: There's a hole in my sweater. I wonder if you can deal with it.

我的毛衣上有个洞,我想知道你们能否织补。

Chen: Certainly, we can. Please note that on the laundry list, too.

当然有办法处理,也请您在洗衣单上注明。

Williams：My leather coat needs cleaning.

我的皮外套需要清洗。

Chen：I'm sorry，but we don't have the special equipment to clean leather.

很抱歉，我们没有清洗皮料所需要的特制设备。

Williams：Thank you for the information.

谢谢你提供信息。

Practice 2　Quick Service
实训项目2　快洗服务

Task of Service Practice 实训任务

◆ John Smith in Room 8656 asks Chen Yuan to send someone up for his laundry.

8656 房间的 John Smith 要求陈媛派人来取他要洗的衣服。

◆ John Smith also asks whether he can get his clothes back in two hours.

John Smith 还询问能否在两个小时之内送回他的衣服。

◆ Chen Yuan answers "yes" because the hotel has two-hour quick service. But the hotel will charge 50% more for the quick service.

陈媛回答可以，因为酒店有两小时的特急服务。不过酒店对特急服务要加收 50% 的费用。

◆ Mr. Smith agrees with it.

Smith 先生同意加收服务费。

◆ Chen Yuan tells Mr. Smith that a room attendant will come to his room to pick up his laundry in five minutes.

陈媛告知 Smith 先生客房服务员 5 分钟后到他的房间取走他要洗的衣服。

Service Practice 服务实训

Now，let's begin the practice according to *Task of Service Practice*.

请按照上述实训任务开始实训。

Model of Service Practice 实训对照

Chen：Chen Yuan，a room attendant.

Smith：John Smith，a guest.

12　2　Quick Service. mp3

Chen：Good morning. Housekeeping. How can I help you?

早上好。客房部。需要我为您服务吗？

Smith：Good morning. This is John Smith in Room 8656. Could you send someone up for my laundry?

早上好,我是 8656 房间的 John Smith,能派个人来取我要洗的衣服吗?

Chen：Certainly.

当然可以。

Smith：Can you deliver it back to my room in two hours?

能在两小时之后送回到我的房间吗?

Chen：Yes,we can. We have a two-hour quick service.

可以,我们有两小时的特急服务。

Smith：What's the difference in price?

价格上有什么不同?

Chen：We charge 50% more for the quick service.

特急服务加收 50%的费用。

Smith：That's fine. Let's do it this way.

很好,就这样了。

Chen：Mr. Smith,a room attendant will come to your Room 8656 to pick up your laundry in five minutes.

Smith 先生,客房服务员 5 分钟后到您的 8656 房间取走您要洗的衣服。

Smith：Thanks a lot.

非常感谢。

Chen：It's my pleasure.

很高兴为您服务。

Hotel Knowledge
新酒店人须知

(1) The staff of the Laundry Department：

洗衣部员工：

Laundry Supervisor	洗衣主管
valet	熨衣工
laundryman	洗衣工

(2) Some useful expressions in laundry service：

洗衣服务术语：

dressing/ironing	熨烫
dry cleaning	干洗
hand wash	手洗
do not wash	不能水洗
laundry list	洗衣单
rate list	价目
pressing only	单烫

washing	水洗
machine wash	机洗
quick service	快洗服务
laundry bag	洗衣袋
extra charge	附加费
date sent	送洗日期
slacks/pants	西裤
dress	连衣裙
overcoat/long coat	大衣
scarf	围巾
suit	西装
skirt	短裙
sweater	毛衣/羊毛衫
jacket	短上衣,夹克
waist coat	背心,马甲

Chapter Five   Housekeeping(Ⅱ)

实训模块五   客房服务(二)

Unit 13
Room Service

技能实训 13　客房送餐服务

Service Procedure 服务流程

◆ Greet the guest.
问候客人。

◆ Get the information from the guest：
从客人那里获得下列信息：
　　What he wants.
　　他想要什么。
　　Special demands for cooking.
　　对烹饪的特殊要求。
　　The guest's name and his room number.
　　客人的名字和房间号。

◆ Confirm.
确认。

◆ Tell the guest the order will be ready soon.
告知客人点餐很快就能准备好。

◆ Deliver the food to the guest room.
送餐到客人房间。

◆ Speak out the order and give the bill to the guest.
报点餐，把账单给客人。

◆ Ask the guest to sign the name and room number.
要求客人签署姓名和房间号。

◆ Express your wishes.
祝愿。

Skill Points 技能要点

◆ The guest can get the room service by telephone or by door knob menu.
客人可以通过电话或者填写门把菜单来获得客房送餐服务。

◆ Ask the guest about the demands for cooking when the guest orders by telephone. You can ask:"How would you like your…"

电话订餐时,要询问客人对点餐的要求。可以这样问:"我们怎么做您点的……"

◆ If there is minimum charge or service charge,you have to explain it clearly in advance.

如果有最低消费或服务费,应事先说明。

Practice 1   Booking the Room Service by Telephone
实训项目 1   客房电话送餐预订

Task of Service Practice 实训任务

◆ The hotel offers three types of breakfast:American,Continental and Chinese.

酒店提供三种早餐:美式、欧式和中式早餐。

◆ After knowing that the Continental breakfast has orange juice,toast with butter,coffee or tea,Mr. Black in Room 1926 books a Continental breakfast,straight coffee and very black,and a soft boiled egg.

在知道欧式早餐有橙汁、黄油吐司、咖啡或茶之后,1926 房间的 John Black 先生订了一份欧式早餐、纯咖啡,还有一个煮得很嫩的鸡蛋。

◆ The hotel adds a 10% service charge for the room service.

客房用餐酒店要加收 10% 的服务费。

◆ The order will be sent to the room in 15 minutes.

餐点 15 分钟内送到。

Service Practice 服务实训

Now,let's begin the practice according to *Task of Service Practice*.

请按照上述实训任务开始实训。

Model of Service Practice 实训对照

13 1 Booking the
Room Service by
Telephone. mp3

Liu: Liu Ying,a room service waitress.
Black:John Black.

Liu: Good morning,Room Service. May I help you?
         这里是送餐中心,有什么吩咐?

Black:I'd like to order breakfast from room service.
         我要预订早餐。

Liu: We offer three types of breakfast:American,Continental and Chinese. Which one would you prefer?
         我们提供美式、欧式和中式早餐,您要订哪一种?

Black:What does a Continental breakfast have?

欧式早餐有什么?

Liu: Orange juice, toast with butter, and coffee or tea.

橙汁、黄油吐司、咖啡或茶。

Black: That's fine.

我就要这个。

Liu: Coffee or tea?

您要咖啡还是茶?

Black: Coffee. You can forget the sugar and the cream.

咖啡。不要放糖和奶油。

Liu: I see, no sugar, no cream, black coffee. Is that all, sir?

我知道了,不要糖,不要奶油,纯咖啡。先生,是这样吗?

Black: And I'd like a boiled egg as well.

我还要一个煮鸡蛋。

Liu: How would you like your egg?

煮鸡蛋怎样做?

Black: Soft boiled.

煮得嫩一点。

Liu: May I have your name and room number, please?

请问您的名字和房间号?

Black: John Black in Room 1926.

1926 房间的 John Black。

Liu: Let me confirm your order: Mr. John Black in Room 1926 has booked a Continental breakfast and a soft boiled egg. Is that right?

我确认一下:1926 房间的 John Black 先生订了一份欧式早餐,还有一个煮鸡蛋。

Black: Exactly. Is there an extra charge for room service?

是这样。客房送餐要另加费用吗?

Liu: We add a 10% service charge.

我们要另加 10% 的服务费。

Black: OK. Please send them as soon as possible.

知道了,请尽快送餐。

Liu: Your order will arrive in 15 minutes. See you.

您的餐点 15 分钟送到,再见。

Practice 2　Sending the Ordered Breakfast to the Guest's Room
实训项目2　客房送早餐

Task of Service Practice 实训任务

◆ Put the ordered breakfast on the table over there.

所点的早餐放在那边的桌子上。

◆ Here is the Continental breakfast：orange juice，toast with butter，black coffee，and a boiled egg.

这是一份欧式早餐：橙汁、黄油吐司、纯咖啡，还有一个煮鸡蛋。

◆ How to pay? Add the cost to the room bill. The guest needs to sign the name and room number on the bill.

怎样付账？把费用加在房间的账单上。在账单上签上客人的姓名和房间号。

Service Practice 服务实训

Now，let's begin the practice according to *Task of Service Practice*.
请按照上述实训任务开始实训。

Model of Service Practice 实训对照

13 2 Sending the Ordered Breakfast to the Guest's Room. mp3

Liu： Liu Ying，a room service waitress.

Black： John Black，a guest.

Liu： (*Knocking at the door*) It's room service. May I come in?
(敲门)客房送餐，我能进来吗？

Black： Come in，please.
请进。

Liu： Thank you，Mr. Black. Where would you like me to put them?
我把您的餐点放在哪儿？

Black： Please put them on the table over there.
请放在那张桌子上。

Liu： All right. Here is your Continental breakfast：orange juice，toast with butter，black coffee. And a boiled egg. Is it correct?
这是一份欧式早餐：橙汁、黄油吐司、纯咖啡，还有一个煮鸡蛋，对吗？

Black： Yes，it is. Thanks a lot.
是这样，谢谢。

Liu： Mr. Black，here is your bill. Please check it.
Black 先生，这是您的账单，请核对。

Black： It's OK. How can I pay the bill?
没问题。我怎样付款？

Liu： We'll charge it to your room. Please sign your name and room number here on the bill. Thank you for using room service. Enjoy yourself. Goodbye.
我们会把费用加在您房间的账单上。请在账单上签上您的姓名和房间号。谢谢您使用送餐服务。请慢用，再见。

Black： Goodbye.
再见。

Hotel Knowledge
新酒店人须知

(1) Some useful expressions in room service：
常用送餐服务术语：

Room Service Center	客房送餐中心
Room Service Supervisor	客房送餐主管
breakfast tray	早餐托盘
room service menu	客房送餐菜单
door knob menu	挂在门把上的送餐菜单

(2) Some Chinese food as breakfast：
几种中式早餐食品：

noodles with soup	汤面
beef noodles	牛肉面
stretched noodles	拉面
noodles with soybean paste	炸酱面
Sichuan style noodles with peppery sauce	担担面
deep-fried dough sticks	油条
dumpling	饺子
meat pie	馅饼
meat bun	包子
millet gruel	小米粥
sweet dumpling	汤圆
rice noodles	米粉
soybean milk	豆浆
streamed bun	馒头
wonton/dumpling	馄饨

Maintenance Service

实训项目 14　维修服务

Service Procedure 服务流程

For the housekeeper

客房服务员

◆ Greet the guest.

问候客人。

◆ Patiently and carefully listen to what the guest says.

耐心且仔细听客人述说并记录。

◆ Say "sorry" or "apologize" to the guest.

向客人道歉。

◆ Get the room number from the guest.

问明客人房号。

◆ Tell the guest what will be done at once.

告知客人马上要采取的措施。

◆ Inform the repairman to repair at once.

马上通知维修人员修理。

◆ Check what has been made by the repairman.

检查维修结果。

For the repairman

维修人员

◆ Knock at the door, saying:"Maintenance. May I come in?"

敲门通报:"维修人员,可以进来吗?"

◆ Say "sorry" to the guest and ask the guest about the problem in details.

向客人道歉并仔细询问问题所在。

◆ Check and repair.

检修。

◆ Tell the guest that everything is all right.

告诉客人检修完毕。

◆ Extend the wishes to the guest.
祝愿。

Skill Points 技能要点

For the housekeeper
客房服务员

When the guest finishes the complaint, say sorry to him and tell him that the repairman will come to the room to fix/repair at once/as soon as possible/in five minutes.
当客人投诉完毕,道歉并告诉客人检修人员会立刻(尽快,5分钟内)到房间检修。

For the repairman
维修人员

After checking, if you think the problem can't be solved in a short period of time, you have to inform the Housekeeping Department(or the Front Desk) to take other measures.
检查完毕,如果你认为问题不能在短时间内解决,要通知客房部(或前台)采取其他措施。

Practice 1 Complaining About the Bathroom Problem
实训项目 1 卫生间设备问题投诉

Task of Service Practice 实训任务

◆ It's 11 o'clock, but the guest can't use the bathroom, so he calls Chen Ying in the House-keeping to complain.
已经 11 点了,但是客人不能使用卫生间,于是他打电话向客房部的陈颖投诉。

◆ There's something wrong with the toilet, shower head and washbasin faucet.
马桶坏了,淋浴头及水盆上的水龙头都坏了。

◆ The repairman will come to the room of the guest in five minutes.
维修人员 5 分钟内到达客人房间修理。

◆ The room number is 3587.
房间号 3587。

◆ The color TV doesn't give a clear picture.
房间电视图像不清楚。

Service Practice 服务实训

Now, let's begin the practice according to *Task of Service Practice*.
请按照上述实训任务开始实训。

Model of Service Practice 实训对照

Chen： Chen Ying, a housekeeper.

Guest： a guest.

Chen： Good evening. Housekeeping. May I help you?

晚上好,客房部。有什么需要我做的吗?

Guest： Yes. It's 11 o'clock, but I still can't use the bathroom.

有,现在已经 11 点了,但是我还不能使用卫生间。

14 1 Complaining
About the Bathroom
Problem. mp3

Chen： What's the trouble, sir?

有什么问题吗,先生?

Guest： There's something wrong with the toilet, shower head and washbasin faucet.

马桶坏了,淋浴头及水盆上的水龙头都坏了。

Chen： I'm sorry to hear that. I'll tell the Maintenance Department to repair them right away. Would you please tell me your room number?

听说这些,非常抱歉,我马上通知维修部前来修理。能告诉我您的房间号吗?

Guest： 3587.

3587 房间。

Chen： Room 3587. Any other problems?

3587 房间。还有别的问题吗?

Guest： The TV doesn't give a clear picture.

房间的电视图像不清楚。

Chen： Thank you for bringing the problems to our attention. And I apologize to you for the inconvenience as well. The repairman will come to your room in five minutes.

感谢您提出问题让我们注意,同时我也为给您带来的不便向您道歉。维修人员 5 分钟内到达您的房间修理。

Guest： OK. I see.

我知道了。

Practice 2   Repairing the Bathroom Facilities
实训项目2   修理卫生间设备

Task of Service Practice 实训任务

◆ The shower head is clogged. The toilet can't flush. The guest can't turn off the faucet above the washbasin.

花洒堵住了,马桶不能冲水,水池上的水龙头拧不动。

◆ Everything in the bathroom is OK in fifteen minutes and the repairman Xiao Jun tells the guest that he can use the bathroom now.

15 分钟内卫生间修好了,维修员肖君告诉客人现在卫生间可以用了。

◆ An electrician from the Maintenance Department will come to the room to repair the TV at 9:30 the next morning.

明天上午 9:30,维修部的电工来客人房间修理电视机。

Service Practice 服务实训

Now, let's begin the practice according to *Task of Service Practice*.

请按照上述实训任务开始实训。

Model of Service Practice 实训对照

14 2 Repairing the Bathroom Facilities . mp3

Xiao: Xiao Jun, a repairman.

Guest: A guest.

Xiao: (*Knocking at the door*) Housekeeping. May I come in?

(敲门)客房部。我可以进来吗?

Guest: Come in, please.

请进。

Xiao: Good evening, sir. I've come to repair the facilities in the bathroom. Can you please tell me what the trouble is in detail?

晚上好,先生。我是来维修卫生间的设施的,请您详细地告诉我什么坏了,好吗?

Guest: The shower head is clogged. The toilet can't flush. I can't turn off the wash basin faucet.

花洒堵住了,马桶不能冲水了,我拧不开水池上的水龙头。

Xiao: Thank you.

谢谢您告诉我这一切。

Guest: How long will I have to wait?

我需要等多长时间?

Xiao: About fifteen minutes.

大约 15 分钟。

Xiao: Everything is all right, sir. You can use the bathroom now, sir. By the way, an electrician from the Maintenance Department will come to your room to repair the TV at 9:30 tomorrow morning.

修好了,先生。您现在可以用卫生间了。顺便告诉您一声,明天上午 9:30,我们维修部的电工来您房间修理电视机。

Guest: OK. Thank you very much.

好。谢谢你。

Xiao： Not at all. Good night.

没什么。晚安。

Hotel Knowledge
新酒店人须知

（1）Generally speaking, there is no potable water in Chinese hotels. So we can warn the foreign guests to drink boiled water or bottled water.

一般来说，中国酒店没有直饮水。因此我们可以提醒外宾喝煮开的水或瓶装水。

（2）Some abbreviations：

常用缩写：

D. N. A(Do Not Arrive)　　　　客人未到

F. I. T(Free Individual Tourist)　散客

ARR(Arrival)　　　　　　　　抵店

C/I(Check-In)　　　　　　　　入住

C/O(Check-Out)　　　　　　　退房

O. N. O(One Night Only)　　　只住一晚

Other Housekeeping Services

技能实训 15   客房其他服务

Services Procedure 服务流程

◆ Use the electric eacilities.
  使用电器设备服务。
◆ Use the safety deposit box.
  使用保险箱服务。

Skill Points 技能要点

How to use the electric facilities in the room
怎样使用房内电器

◆ In a lot of five-star hotels, the room facilities are introduced by the floor attendant. For some guests, how to use the electric facilities may be a problem. It will take them some time to understand how to use them. So if the students practice in these hotels, when you introduce the room facilities to the guest, you can pay more attention to explaining how to use the electric facilities.

  在许多五星级酒店,房间设备是由楼层服务员来介绍的。对于某些客人而言,怎样使用电器设备会是一个问题,他们需花上一定的时间来弄清楚怎样使用这些房间的电器设备。所以同学们在这些酒店实训,当介绍房间设施时,可以将重点放在如何使用电器设备上。

◆ If the guest doesn't know how to use the electric facilities in the room, show him how to use it carefully or give some explanations.

  如果客人不会使用房间电器设备,给客人演示或解释。

How to use the safety deposit box in the room
怎样使用房间内保险箱

◆ Ask the guest to open the safe and set the new code when "Open" is showed; put the documents and valuables inside and the safe will be locked when closed.

  告知客人打开保险箱,见到"Open"字样时设定新密码;然后放入文件和贵重物品,关上门,保险箱就锁上了。

◆ Warn the guest to remember the new code in order to open it smoothly.
告诫客人记住自己设置的密码以便自己顺利地打开它。

Practice 1 Showing How to Use Electric Appliances
实训项目 1 教客人如何使用电器设备（设施）

Task of Service Practice 实训任务

◆ Show the guest how to make an outside call.
告知客人怎样打外线电话。

◆ Show the guest how to use the air conditioner.
告知客人怎样使用空调。

◆ Press the button on the up-right corner in order to turn on the TV.
按右上角的按钮，就可以打开电视。

◆ The electric shaver of the guest is operated by 110 volts.
客人的电动剃须刀要用 110 伏电源。

◆ The hotel has prepared transformers to loan to the guests. Li Lin will fetch one for him.
酒店为客人准备了变压器，李林为客人拿来一个。

Service Practice 服务实训

Now, let's begin the practice according to *Task of Service Practice*.
请按照上述实训任务开始实训。

15 1 Showing How
to Use Electric
Appliances. mp3

Model of Service Practice 实训对照

Li： Li Lin, a housekeeper.
White： Mr. White, a guest.

Li： Welcome to our hotel, Mr. White. I'm the room attendant. My
name is Li Lin. Is there anything I can do for you?
欢迎您光临我们酒店，White 先生。我是客房服务员李琳，有什
么需要我做的吗？

White： Yes. Would you please show me how to use some of these devices?
请告诉我怎样使用房间的一些电器设备，好吗？

Li： Certainly.
当然可以。

White： How can I make an outside call?
怎样打外线电话？

Li： Please dial "9" first, and then dial the telephone number you want.

请先拨"9"，然后再拨你要的电话号码。

White： How about the air-conditioner?

怎样使用空调？

Li： This is the temperature control of the air-conditioner. You can turn it to adjust the temperature as you like.

这是空调的温度控制开关，您可以随意旋转来调节温度。

White： I like watching TV in the evening.

晚上我喜欢看电视。

Li： Just press the button on the upper-right corner in order to turn on the TV. There are 50 channels.

按右上角的按钮，就可以打开电视，有 50 多个频道。

White： My electric shaver operates at 110 volts.

我的电动剃须刀需要用 110 伏电源。

Li： The electrical current in your room is 220 volts. But we have prepared transformers to loan for the guests. I'll bring you one at once.

您房间的额定电压是 220 伏，不过我们为客人准备了变压器，我马上去给您拿一个。

White： I'd appreciate that.

谢谢。

Li： You're welcome. I'm always at your service.

不用客气，我愿意随时为您服务。

Practice 2　Showing How to Use the Room Safe
实训项目 2　教客人怎样使用保险箱

Task of Service Practice 实训任务

◆ The guest wants to keep some documents and valuables in the safe in the room, but she doesn't know how to use it, so she calls Housekeeping.

客人想把一些文件和贵重物品存放在房间的保险箱里，但她不知道怎样使用它，于是打电话到客房部询问。

◆ Li Lin tells the guest in the call: Open the safe, when "Open" is displayed, set the code by inputting a six-digit password. Then the documents and valuables can be put inside and the safe will be locked when closed. At that time "Lock" will be displayed. Remember the password you have input; otherwise it will cause much trouble.

李琳在电话里告诉客人：打开保险箱，当显示"Open"字样时，输入六位阿拉伯数字来设定密码。然后放入文件和贵重物品，关上门，保险箱就锁上了。这时会出现"Lock"字样。记住自己所设置的密码，否则就麻烦了。

◆ Li Lin tells the guest to put in the six-digit password to open it.

   李琳告诉客人输入那个六位数的密码,保险箱就开了。

◆ If the wrong number is put in, the safe will never be opened. So be sure to remember the password.

   如果输入的数字不正确,保险箱绝对打不开,所以一定要记住所设定的密码。

Service Practice 服务实训

Now, let's begin the practice according to *Task of Service Practice*.
请按照上述实训任务开始实训。

Model of Service Practice 实训对照

15 2 Showing How to Use the Room Safe. mp3

Li：Li Lin, a housekeeper.

Guest：a guest.

Li：Good morning, Housekeeping. How can I help you?

   早上好,客房部,需要我为您服务吗?

Guest：I want to keep some documents and valuables in the safe in my room, but I don't know how to use it.

   我想把一些文件和贵重物品存放在我房间的保险箱里,但我不知道怎样使用它。

Li：Please open the safe. When "Open" is displayed, you must set the code by inputting a six-digit password. Then you put the documents and valuables inside and the safe will be locked when closed. At that time "Lock" will be displayed. You must not forget the password you set; otherwise it will cause a lot of trouble.

   请打开保险箱。当显示"Open"字样时,您得输入六位阿拉伯数字来设定密码。然后放入文件和贵重物品,关上门,保险箱就锁上了。这时会出现"Lock"字样。您千万别忘记您所设置的密码,否则就麻烦了。

Guest：How can I open it?

   我怎么打开它?

Li：Just put in the six-digit password and the safe will open.

   只要输入那六位数的密码,保险箱就开了。

Guest：If I put in the wrong number...

   如果我输入的数字不正确……

Li：It will show "Error" and will not open. So you have to remember the password that you set.

   它会显示"Error",保险箱绝对打不开,所以您得记住您所设定的密码。

Guest：OK. Thanks a lot.

   好的,谢谢你。

Hotel Knowledge
新酒店人须知

(1) Hotel keeping is known as the "hospitality industry" or "courtesy industry" or "service industry". Our aim is to create a "home away from home" for all our guests.

酒店业是一个被称为"殷勤待客"的服务行业,又称"礼貌行业"。我们的宗旨在于为所有宾客创造一种"宾至如归"的气氛。

(2) Some useful expressions in Housekeeping:

客房部常用术语:

housekeeping manager	客房部经理
floor supervisor	客房部主管
floor captain	楼层领班
room attendant	客房服务员
cloak man/woman	衣帽间服务人员
PA cleaner	公共区域清洁员

Practice Revision 实训回望

◆ How can the room attendant know the name of the guest?

◆ Please talk about the procedure of room service.

◆ The aim of the hotel is to create a home away from the home for all the travelling guests who need rest, food and drink. How to create a home in the hotel? What will you try?

◆ The guest in Room 2356 asks Zhao Li practicing in the Housekeeping to put an extra bed for him. What should Zhao Li do?

Case and Improvement: How to Create a Home Away from Home
案例与提高:怎样营造"家外之家"

Ji Yuan and her classmates have practised in Asia Grant Hotel for three months. They made great progress in serving the guests, and the housekeeping manager praised them for it at the meeting.

纪媛和她的同学在亚洲大酒店实训已近三个月,他们在为客人服务方面有很大进步,为此客房部经理在会上表扬了他们。

Ji Yuan was thinking what the housekeeping manager said to the students at the meeting. "The aim of the hotel is to create a home away from home for all the traveling guests who need—rest, food and drink. How to create a home in the hotel? Firstly, we should regard our guests as our family members and try our best to meet the demands that the guests have put to us. Secondly we should be good at finding out or predicting the demands that the guests don't put to us and satisfy them. If we can provide our guests with the most sincere service to make their stay here convenient, comfortable and enjoyable, they'll have the feeling of staying at their home. I know it's very hard for you to do so, but you can have a try and have a practice. I believe you will do very well. "Ji Yuan was determined to create a home away from home for the guests in her service.

纪媛思考着客房部经理在会上对同学们说的话:"酒店经营的目的是为在外旅行需要休息、需要餐饮的客人创造一个'家外之家'。怎样在酒店创造一个'家外之家'? 首先我们要把客人当成家庭成员来看待,尽我们的能力满足客人所提出的要求。其次,我们要善于发现和预见客人没有向我们提出的要求,并满足他们。如果我们能够给客人提供最真诚的服务,使他们住店方便舒适、舒心,他们就会有家的感觉。我知道对你们来说,这样做很难,但只要你们能够试一试,能够实践,我相信你们会做得很好的。"纪媛决定在她的服务中为客人创造一个"家外之家"。

Seven guests, who would attend an important international conference, stayed in the rooms that she was in charge of. These guests were very busy.

七名客人住进了她负责的房间,他们是来参加一个重要的国际会议的。这些客人非常繁忙。

From the registration list, she found that the next day would be Miss White's birthday. She made a beautiful birthday card and bought some flowers for her and sent them to Miss. White in the morning.

从登记单上她发现第二天是 White 小姐的生日,她制作了漂亮的生日贺卡,买来了鲜花,上午送给 White 小姐。

> **Ji:** Happy Birthday, Miss White. Here is a bunch of flowers and a birthday card from our hotel staff.
> 生日快乐,White 小姐! 这是我们酒店职员给您送的鲜花和生日贺卡。
>
> **White:** How beautiful! I don't know how to express my appreciation.
> 真美! 我不知怎样感谢你们才好。
>
> **Ji:** It's really our great pleasure.
> 为您服务是我们的荣幸。

15 C&I How to Create a Home Away from Home. mp3

Mr. Cashbox in Room 2586 had a cold and coughed seriously, but he had no medicine for his cough. He felt a little cold at night. After knowing of these, Ji Yuan brought an extra woolen blanket for him at once and bought the medicine for his cough from the drugstore in her spare time.

住在 2586 房间的 Cashbox 先生患了感冒,咳嗽得很厉害,但他没有治咳嗽的药,晚上感觉有些冷。知道这些之后,纪媛马上为他加了一条毛毯,还利用休息时间给他买了治咳嗽的药。

Dr. Wang, secretary of the conference, was drinking Chinese medicine and he also had a habit of drinking a glass of hot milk at 11 for sleeping. Ji Yuan prepared Chinese medicine and hot milk for Dr. Wang for four days.

会议秘书王博士正在吃中药,他还有一个习惯,11点钟时喝一杯热牛奶睡觉。纪媛一连四天为王博士准备中药和热牛奶。

When leaving the hotel,they said to Ji Yuan:"You have an eye for details. Your service is the first."

离开酒店时,他们对纪媛说:"你心细如丝,你的服务是一流的。"

The housekeeping manager received a letter of thanks,saying:"Your services are meticulous. You create a warm 'home' in the hotel for us."

客房部经理收到一封感谢信,信中说:"你们的服务细致入微,你们在酒店中为我们营造了一个温馨的'家'。"

Case Topic 案例话题

(1) How to create a home away from home in the hotel?
怎样在酒店营造一个"家外之家"?
(2) Please talk about your experience of serving a guest.
请谈一下你的对客服务经验。

Hotel Manager's Comments
酒店经理点评

同学们已研读了以上案例,并就案例话题展开了热烈的讨论。同学们的讨论涉及服务、服务质量、个性化服务,还有如何营造"家外之家",大家现在对这些问题有了一些感性认识,许多同学还在探索实践中,这很好。现在我们回到理论上来,我想问同学们几个问题。

第一个问题:什么是酒店的商品?

酒店以有形的设施和空间及无形的时间和劳动向客人提供的各种服务可谓酒店的商品。前者包括酒店的客房餐厅等各种服务设施;后者包括酒店向客人提供的各种劳务服务,以及通过这些服务使客人获得的物质、精神满足和享受,以及节省的时间的价值。

第二个问题:酒店商品的主要特性是什么?

(1) 酒店商品的不可捉摸性。酒店的服务是无形的,因而对服务质量的衡量并无具体的尺度。顾客对商品的满意程度主要来自于感受,所以带有较强的个人主观性和特殊性。这种主观性和特殊性又往往成为对酒店商品肯定与否定的主要依据。

(2) 酒店商品的可变性。酒店是按照一定的秩序向客人提供服务的,但客人的需求因个人的习惯、爱好、情绪及当时的特殊需要不同而不同,不能固定在一个模式上,因而判断服务质量只能以满足客人需要为标准。

(3) 酒店商品的品质。服务质量决定着酒店的社会形象,影响着酒店的客人。酒店的客人在选择酒店时,多从酒店的社会形象和信誉方面进行考虑和比较,特别注重酒店的软件——服务。客人是否前来酒店消费往往取决于客人对酒店的信任和酒店在客人心目中的地位。换句话说:"酒店员工的优质服务会赢得客人。"而酒店员工任何一点小的失误都会给酒店带来负面影响,使酒店的经营受到损失。

第三个问题：客房的盈利可以占到酒店总盈利的多大比例？

如果我们像案例中的纪媛那样为客人提供优质服务，为客人营造一个"家外之家"，能够使客房的盈利占酒店总盈利的 1/2 甚至 3/5。

同学们在为客人服务中要有三个意识。第一，要有服务意识，即按照酒店的服务规范为客人服务，这是对我们酒店人的最基本的要求。第二是客人意识。这就要求我们向案例中的纪媛那样，善于观察，在工作中做有心人，发现和预测客人的需求。第三是服务质量意识。我们要认识到服务质量决定着酒店的信誉和生存。

作为新的酒店人，一定要注意积累服务经验，不断提高创新服务的能力。用自己热情周到的服务，为客人营造"家外之家"，为酒店赢得信誉，赢得再次光顾的客人，同时也能提高自己的职业竞争能力。

Answers to "Practice Revision" 部分参考答案

◆ How can the room attendant know the name of the guest?

The room attendant can know the name of the hotel by the following: Luggage tag, arrival list，room registration，restaurant registration，convention name tag or asking the name.

◆ The guest in Room 2356 asks Zhao Li practicing in the Housekeeping to put an extra bed for him. What should Zhao Li do?

Firstly，Zhao Li needs to explain to the guest the reason why she cannot put an extra bed for him directly. Secondly，tell the guest to call the Front Office for permission or go to the Front Office to handle the formality of extending the bed. Thirdly，with the permission of the Front Office，Zhao Li puts the bed for the guest.

Chapter Six   Food & Beverage

实训模块六　餐饮服务

Unit 16

Table Reservation

技能实训 16　用餐预订服务

Service Procedure 服务流程

◆ Greet the guests.

问候客人。

◆ Ask the guest about the information of the table reservation：

从客人那里获得下列用餐预订信息：

The number of the persons.

就餐人数。

A table in the lobby or a private room is needed by the guest.

客人需要订餐厅大堂的餐台还是包间。

The demands for the table or the private room.

客人对餐台或包间的要求。

The time of arrival.

到达的时间。

Under whose name the reservation is made.

以谁的名字订餐。

The contact telephone number or the room number.

联系电话号码或房间号。

◆ Confirm.

确认。

◆ Express your expectation to the guests.

表达对客人的期盼。

Skill Points 技能要点

◆ When the guest asks you to reserve a table for him, pay attention to asking him whether he wants a table in the lobby or a private room.

当客人要求你为他订餐时，要注意询问他是要订餐台还是要订包间。

◆ When handling the reservation of a banquet, you should get the following information.
宴会预订，还要获取下列信息。

For whose company.

为哪一家公司预订。

The expected number of the persons or the number of the table needed.

预计用餐的人数或所需的餐台数。

The time of the banquet.

宴会时间。

The banquet menu.

宴会菜单。

The budget for the banquet.

宴会预算。

How to arrange the table or seats, and how to decorate the banquet hall.

怎样安排餐台和座位，怎样装饰宴会大厅。

Some special requests.

某些特殊的要求。

How to pay.

付款方式。

Ask the guest to hand in some deposit to secure the reservation in advance.

要求客人预先交押金以确保预订。

◆ If the restaurant has extra charge, such as the cover charge or minimum charge, you should make it clear in advance to the person who makes the reservation of a private or a banquet.
如果餐厅有像茶位费这样的额外收费，或有最低消费限制，要事先跟包间或宴会预订人解释清楚。

Practice 1　Booking a Table
实训项目 1　餐台预订

Task of Service Practice 实训任务

◆ Mr. Abraham Jones in Room 2687 wants to book a table in the hall for four at 11:20 this morning, but the tables have been fully booked for that time. So Chen Xiao suggests that Mr. Jones make the reservation at another time.
2687 房间的 Abraham Jones 先生想预订今天上午 11:20 大厅里的四人餐台，但那个时间的餐台已经订满了，于是陈晓建议 Jones 先生把预订改在其他时间。

◆ Mr. Jones has to book a table at 11:20 tomorrow morning. He hopes that Chen Xiao can arrange the table by the south window for him.
Jones 先生只得预订明天 11:20 的餐台，他希望陈晓能为他安排靠南边窗台的餐台。

◆ Chen Xiao handles the reservation of a table according to the request of Mr. Jones.

陈晓按照 Jones 先生的要求办理了用餐预订。

Service Practice 服务实训

Now，let's begin the practice according to *Task of Service Practice*.

请按照上述实训任务开始实训。

Model of Service Practice 实训对照

16 1 Booking a Table. mp3

Chen：Chen Xiao，a reservation clerk.

Jones：Abraham Jones，a guest.

Chen：Good morning，Chinese Restaurant. How can I help you?

早上好，中餐厅。有什么需要帮助的吗？

Jones：I'd like to make a reservation in your restaurant.

我想在贵餐厅订餐。

Chen：For how many people，and when will you be coming?

订几个人的餐？什么时候来？

Jones：Four people，and today.

四个人，今天。

Chen：Would you like a table in the dining hall or a private room?

您是订大厅里的餐台还是要一个包间？

Jones：A table in the hall.

大厅里的餐台。

Chen：What time would you like your table?

什么时间就餐？

Jones：At 11：20.

11：20。

Chen：I'm afraid the tables have been fully booked for that time. Would you like to make the reservation at another time?

恐怕那个时间的餐台已经订满了。您是否可以换个其他的时间？

Jones：At 11：20 tomorrow morning.

明天上午 11：20。

Chen：May I have your name and your room number?

能告诉我您的名字和房间号吗？

Jones：My name is Abraham Jones and my room number is 2687. If possible，try to arrange a table by the south window.

我叫 Abraham Jones，我的房间号是 2687。如果可能的话，最好订靠南边窗户的桌子。

Chen: No problem. Mr. Jones, you've booked a table by the south window for four people at 11:20 tomorrow morning. Your room number is 2687. Is that right?

没问题。Jones 先生,您预订了明天上午 11:20 靠南边窗户的四人台位。您的房间号 2687,是这样吗?

Jones: Exactly. Thanks for your help.

是这样。谢谢你的帮助。

Chen: You're welcome. We look forward to your arrival tomorrow. Thank you for calling.

不用谢。我们恭候您明天光临。谢谢您的来电。

Practice 2　Booking a Private Room
实训项目 2　包房预订

Task of Service Practice 实训任务

◆ Mr. George Jones in Room 2357 would like to reserve a south private room in Jiangnan Restaurant for fourteen people for next Saturday, May 3.

2357 房间的 George Jones 先生想在江南餐厅预订 5 月 3 日下周六可容纳 14 人的一个南边的包间。

◆ There are three south private rooms in the restaurant, but each of them can be seated for eleven people at most. The restaurant has a private room facing the east, which can be seated for fourteen people. This private room is called Red Rose. It is decorated elegantly.

酒店有三个南包间,但每一间最多只能坐 11 位。酒店还有一个包间向东,里面能坐 14 位。这个包间叫红玫瑰,装饰典雅华丽。

◆ Mr. George Jones has booked the private room Red Rose for fourteen people for next Saturday, May 3. The time of their arrival is 5:40. The price of the western cuisine is 320 yuan per person excluding drinks. Their drinks are Champaign and Great Wall. The cell phone number of Mr. Jones is 132×××8526, and his room number is 2357. The private room that Mr. Jones has booked can be kept till 7:30 p. m. , since that will be the peak season.

George Jones 先生预订了 5 月 3 日下周六 14 人餐位的红玫瑰包间,他们到达的时间是 5:40。每人西餐消费 320 元,不包括酒水。酒水为香槟和长城。Jones 先生的手机号是 132×××8526,房间号 2357。Jones 先生预订的包房只能保留到晚上 7:30,因为那段时间是高峰期。

Service Practice 服务实训

Now, let's begin the practice according to *Task of Service Practice*.

请按照上述实训任务开始实训。

Model of Service Practice 实训对照

Chen：Chen Xiao，a reservation clerk.

Jones：George Jones，a guest.

16 2 Booking a Private Room. mp3

Chen：Good afternoon. Jiangnan Restaurant. Can I help you?

　　　下午好，江南餐厅。需要我为您服务吗？

Jones：Yes，could I make a reservation for next Saturday，May 3?

　　　我能在贵餐厅预订 5 月 3 日，也就是下周三的用餐吗？

Chen：Certainly. What time would you like to book your table?

　　　当然可以。您要订在什么时间？

Jones：What time do you open and close?

　　　请告诉我你们餐馆的营业时间。

Chen：At 5:30 a. m. ，and we close at midnight.

　　　早晨 5:30 开始营业，午夜停止营业。

Jones：I'd like a private south room in the evening. We'll arrive at your restaurant at 5:40.

　　　我要晚上一个朝南的包间。我们 5:40 到餐厅。

Chen：For how many people?

　　　您几位？

Jones：Let me see，eleven people. We need a bigger table. Three others may come at 7:00.

　　　让我想想，11 位。我们需要一个大一点的桌子，可能 7 点钟还会来 3 位。

Chen：We have three private south rooms，but each of them can seat eleven at most. We have a private room facing the east，which can seat fourteen people. This private room is called the Red Rose. It's decorated elegantly.

　　　我们有 3 个朝南的包间，但每一间最多能坐 11 位。我们还有一个包间向东，里面能坐 14 位。这个包间叫红玫瑰，装饰典雅华丽。

Jones：OK. I'll take it.

　　　好，我就要这个包间。

Chen：And what is it going to be，Chinese food or Western food?

　　　您打算订中餐还是西餐？

Jones：Western food.

　　　西餐。

Chen：How much food per person would you like? By the way，the minimum charge for a private room in the evening is 200 yuan per person.

　　　每个人消费多少？顺便说一下，晚上包间每位最低消费是 200 元。

Jones：Well，320 yuan per person.

　　　每位 320 元。

Chen：320 yuan. And what drinks are you going to have，Budweiser or Champaign?

　　　320 元。你们要什么酒水？百威啤酒还是香槟？

Jones：Champaign. And we want to try some Chinese wine.

香槟。我们还想试试中国葡萄酒。

Chen：Which one would you like, Dynasty or Great Wall?

您要哪一种,王朝还是长城?

Jones：Great Wall.

长城。

Chen：In whose name should the reservation be?

以谁的名字预订?

Jones：Please reserve it under my name, George Jones.

请用我的名字 George Jones 预订。

Chen：Thank you. What about your telephone number and your room number?

谢谢,您的电话号码和房间号?

Jones：My cell phone number is 132××××8526, and my room number is 2357.

手机号 132××××8526,房间号 2357。

Chen：Thank you, Mr. Jones. You've booked the private room Red Rose for fourteen people for next Saturday, May 3. The time of your arrival is 5:40. The price of the western cuisine is 320 yuan per person excluding drinks. Your drinks are Champaign and Great Wall. Your cell phone number is 132××××8526, and your room number is 2357. By the way, we can only keep your private room till 7:30 p.m., since that will be the peak time.

谢谢您,Jones 先生。您预订了5月3日下周六 14 人餐位的红玫瑰包间,到达的时间是 5:40。每人西餐消费 320 元,不包括酒水。酒水为香槟和长城。您的手机号是 132××××8526,房间号 2357。顺便说一下,您预订的包房只能保留到晚上 7:30,因为那段时间是高峰期。

Jones：That's right. Thank you.

好的,谢谢你。

Chen：We look forward to having you visit us.

我们期盼你们前来就餐。

Practice 3　Reserving the Banquets
实训项目3　宴会预订

Task of Service Practice 实训任务

◆ George Brown would like to book two banquets for May 6 in the restaurant of the hotel, for their company, New York International Trade Company will have a conference in the Meeting Center in the hotel and they plan to have lunch and supper in the restaurant in the hotel.

George Brown 先生要在酒店的餐厅预订 5 月 6 日两个宴会,因为他们的公司纽约国际贸易公司将在酒店的会议中心召开会议,计划在酒店的餐厅用午餐和晚餐。

◆ The time of the banquets will be 11:30 a. m. and 6:00 p. m.

宴会的时间为上午 11:30,下午 6:00。

◆ The Lunch Banquet for 400 people will be served the Buffet Western Food and everyone can spend 220 yuan.

400 人的午宴是自助式西餐,人均消费 220 元。

◆ 15 VIPs will come in the evening. The Dinner Banquet will be the Chinese Food, and everyone can spend 280 yuan excluding drinks. A bottle of Maotai and two bottles of Dynasty will be prepared for every table firstly. 41 tables are needed. George Brown asks Wang Qian to set up a big table which can be seated for 16 in the front of the hall. It will be for the VIP. And it is required to decorate with some flowers.

晚上要来 15 位贵宾。晚宴用中餐,每人消费为 280 元人民币,不含酒水;先为每张餐台准备一瓶茅台,两瓶王朝。晚宴需要 41 张餐台。George Brown 先生要求王倩在餐厅前面摆放一张能坐 16 人的大餐台。这张餐台是专为贵宾准备的,需要用鲜花来装饰。

◆ The meeting planners hope that the participants can try some Chinese famous cuisines. But George Brown is not familiar with the Chinese cuisines. He just heard that there are four major cuisines in China. He asks Wang Qian to introduce them simply.

会议组织者希望与会者能品尝一些中国的名菜,但是 George Brown 先生对中国菜并不熟悉,他只是听说中国菜主要有四大菜系,他要求王倩就此向他简单地介绍一下。

◆ The four major Chinese cuisines are: Shandong Cuisine, Guangdong Cuisine, Sichuan Cuisine and Huaiyang Cuisine. Generally speaking, Shandong Cuisine is heavy, Guangdong Cuisine is light, Sichuan Cuisine is spicy and hot. But Huaiyang food is well known for its cutting technique and original.

这四种主要的中国菜系是:山东菜、广东菜、四川菜和淮扬菜。一般来说,山东菜味重香浓,广东菜清淡,四川菜麻辣。而淮扬菜则以其刀工和原味而著名。

◆ Wang Qian tells Mr. Brown that they serve Beijing Cuisine, Cantonese (Guangdong) Cuisine, Shandong Cuisine, Sichuan Cuisine, Jiangsu Cuisine and Zhejiang Cuisine in the restaurant and they are good at cooking the famous foods of them.

王倩告诉 Brown 先生他们有北京菜、广东菜、山东菜、四川菜、江苏菜和浙江菜,并擅长做这些菜系中的名菜。

◆ George Brown and Wang Qian choose ten dishes from the six cuisines on the menu for the Dinner Banquet.

George Brown 和王倩在菜单上从这六种菜系里为晚宴挑选了十道菜。

Roast Beijing Duck	北京烤鸭
Meat Balls Braised with Brown Sauce	红烧狮子头
Roasted Suckling Pig	烤乳猪
White Sweet and Sour Trotter	白云猪手
Braised Abalone with Shells	扒原壳鲍鱼

Fried Sea Cucumber with Spring Onion	葱烧海参
Sichuan Style Bean Curd	麻婆豆腐
Shredded Pork with Spicy Garlic Sauce	鱼香肉丝
Fried Mandarin Fish in Squirrel Shape	松鼠鳜鱼
Fried Shrimp Meat with Longjing Tea	龙井虾仁

◆ George Brown hand in the deposit of 20 000 yuan.

George Brown 交了押金 20 000 元。

◆ George Brown's cell phone number is 139×××5567.

George Brown 的手机号码是 139×××5567。

Service Practice 服务实训

Now, let's begin the practice according to *Task of Service Practice*.

请按照上述实训任务开始实训。

Model of Service Practice 实训对照

Wang：Wang Qian, a reservation clerk.

Brown：George Brown, a guest.

16 3 Reserving the Banquets. mp3

Wang：Good morning, sir. Welcome to our restaurant. How can I help you?

上午好,先生。欢迎来到我们餐厅。需要我为您服务吗?

Brown：Good morning. I'd like to book two banquets in your restaurant for our company.

上午好。我想在贵餐厅为我们公司预订两个宴会。

Wang：When would you like to book?

您订在什么时候?

Brown：May 6. Our New York International Trade Company will have a conference in the Meeting Center in your hotel, so we plan to have lunch and supper in your restaurant.

5 月 6 日。我们纽约国际贸易公司将在贵酒店的会议中心召开会议,所以计划在贵餐厅用中餐和晚餐。

Wang：When would you like your tables?

什么时间用餐?

Brown：At 11:30 a. m. for lunch and at 6:00 p. m. for supper.

上午 11:30 中餐,下午 6:00 晚餐。

Wang：For how many people?

多少人?

Brown：400 people. And 15 VIPs will come in the evening.

400 人,还有 15 位贵宾晚上到。

Wang：And what is it going to be, Chinese food or Western food?

您打算订中餐还是西餐?

Brown：The lunch banquet is a western food buffet，while the dinner banquet is Chinese food.

午餐是自助式西餐，晚宴为中餐。

Wang：How many tables would you like? And how would you like us to set up the banquets?

您需要多少张餐台？请问我们怎样布置宴会厅？

Brown：Please arrange 41 tables for the dinner banquet. Please set up a large table in the front of the hall which can seat 16. This table will be for our VIPs，and We'd like it decorated with some flowers.

晚宴需要 41 张餐台。请在餐厅前面摆放一张能坐 16 人的大餐台。这张餐台是专为贵宾准备的，需要用鲜花来装饰。

Wang：How much would you like to spend per head?

每位消费多少？

Brown：220 yuan for the lunch banquet，and 280 yuan for the dinner banquet excluding drinks.

午宴每位消费 220 元，晚宴每位消费 280 元，不包括酒水。

Wang：And what drinks are you going to have?

用什么酒水？

Brown：Please prepare a bottle of Maotai and two bottles of Dynasty for each table to start with.

晚宴上请先为每张餐台准备一瓶茅台，两瓶王朝。

Wang：Do you have any special requirements for the banquet menu?

您对宴会菜单有什么特别要求？

Brown：Chinese cuisine is universally recognized as one of the great cuisines of the world. We hope our participants can try some famous Chinese cuisine. But I'm not familiar with Chinese cuisine. I heard that there are four major cuisines in China. Could you introduce the basics to me?

中国的烹调是大家公认的世界上最具特色的风味之一，我们希望与会代表能品尝一些中国的名菜，但我对中国菜不是非常熟悉。我听说，中国菜主要有四大菜系，你能简单地介绍一下吗？

Wang：Certainly. The four major Chinese cuisines are：Shandong cuisine，Guangdong cuisine，Sichuan cuisine and Huaiyang cuisine. Generally speaking，Shandong cuisine is heavy，Guangdong cuisine is light，but Sichuan cuisine is spicy and hot.

可以。这四种主要的中国菜系是：山东菜、广东菜、四川菜和淮扬菜。一般来说，山东菜味重香浓，广东菜清淡可口，四川菜麻辣浓香。

Brown：How about Huaiyang cuisine?

淮扬菜怎样？

Wang：Huaiyang food is well known for its cutting technique and original flavour.

淮扬菜则以其刀工和原味而闻名。

119

Brown：Please show me your menu. What cuisines can you serve?

请把菜单给我看看。你们有什么菜？

Wang：Here you are. We serve Beijing cuisine, Cantonese (Guangdong) cuisine, Shandong cuisine, Sichuan cuisine, Jiangsu cuisine and Zhejiang cuisine. We are good at cooking some of the famous foods from each of them.

给您菜单。我们有北京菜、广东菜、山东菜、四川菜、江苏菜还有浙江菜。我们擅长做这些菜系里的一些名菜。

Brown：Let's choose ten dishes altogether for our dinner banquet from your menu: roast Beijing duck, meat balls braised with brown sauce, roasted suckling pig, white sweet and sour trotter, braised abalone with shells, fried sea cucumber with spring onion, Sichuan style bean curd, shredded pork with spicy garlic sauce, fried Mandarin fish in squirrel shape, fried shrimp meat with longjing tea.

我们一起看看菜单，从中为我们的晚宴挑选 10 道菜：北京烤鸭、红烧狮子头、烤乳猪、白云猪手、扒原壳鲍鱼、葱烧海参、麻婆豆腐、鱼香肉丝、松鼠鳜鱼、龙井虾仁。

Wang：How would you like to pay for the banquets?

请问宴会怎样付款？

Brown：We'll pay by credit card.

信用卡。

Wang：How about the deposit?

怎样交押金？

Brown：Here you are, 20 000.

给你，20 000 元。

Wang：Thank you. This is the receipt for your deposit. Please hold onto it. May I have your name and your cell phone number?

谢谢您。这是您交押金的收据，请您保管好。能告诉我您的姓名和手机号码吗？

Brown：My name is George Brown and my cell phone number is 139××××5567.

我叫 George Brown，我的电话号码是 139××××5567。

Wang：Thank you, Mr. Brown. You have booked two banquets for May 6, for the New York International Trade Company. The times are 11:30 a. m. and 6:00 p. m. The lunch banquet for 400 people will be a western food buffet, at around 220 RMB per head. The dinner banquet for 415 people will be Chinese food, at 280 yuan per head, excluding drinks. A bottle of "Maotai" and two bottles of "Dynasty" will be put on every dinner banquet table to start. 41 tables will be arranged for the dinner banquet. A large table which can seat 16 will be set up in the front of the hall. This table is for your VIPs. It is to be decorated with some flowers. These are the names of the dishes chosen. Your name is George Brown and your cell phone number is 139××××5567. Is there anything else I can do for you?

谢谢您，Brown 先生。您为纽约国际贸易公司预订了 5 月 6 日的两个宴会。用餐时间是上午 11:30，下午 6:00。400 人的午宴采用自助式西餐，人均消费大约 220 元。

415 人晚宴用中餐，每人消费 280 元，不含酒水。每张晚宴餐台上先准备一瓶"茅台"和两瓶"王朝"。晚宴安排 41 张餐台。在餐厅前面摆放一张大餐台，能坐 16 人。这张餐台是专为贵宾准备的，需要用鲜花来装饰。这是宴会菜单。是这样吗？您的电话号码是 139×××5567。还有什么需要我做的吗？

Brown：No. Thank you.

没有了。谢谢你。

Wang：My name is Wang Qian. If you need anything, please call me. We look forward to your arrival.

我叫王倩，有事请打电话给我。我们恭候你们的光临。

Hotel Knowledge
新酒店人须知

(1) The four different reservations:

四种不同的点餐：

face-to-face reservation	面对面预订
Telephone Reservation	电话预订
Fax Reservation	传真预订
Internet Reservation	网上预订

No matter which kind of way the reservation is made in by the guest, you should make clear the following information: the name of the person who makes the reservation, his phone number, the time of arrival and the number of the guests.

无论客人使用哪一种预订，你都要弄清楚下列信息：预订人姓名、他的电话号码、客人抵达餐厅的时间、来用餐的人数。

(2) Someone divided the Chinese Cuisine into four major cuisines. They are: Shandong Cuisine, Guangdong Cuisine, Sichuan Cuisine and Huaiyang Cuisine.

有人把中国菜分成四大主要菜系，它们是：山东菜、广东菜、四川菜和淮扬菜。

Certainly, the Chinese Cuisine can be divided into eight cuisines. They are:

当然，也有人把中国菜划分成八大菜系，它们是：

Sichuan Cuisine	四川菜,简称川菜
Shandong Cuisine	山东菜,简称鲁菜
Cantonese Cuisine	广东菜,简称粤菜
Jiangsu Cuisine	江苏菜,简称苏菜
Fujian Cuisine	福建菜,简称闽菜
Hunan Cuisine	湖南菜,简称湘菜
Anhui Cuisine	安徽菜,简称徽菜
Zhejiang Cuisine	浙江菜,简称浙菜

(3) Some useful expressions in Food and Beverage:

餐饮部常用术语：

Food and Beverage Manager　　餐饮部经理
Chinese Restaurant Manager　　中餐厅经理
Catering/Banquet Manager　　宴会部经理
Restaurant Supervisor　　餐厅主管
headwaiter　　餐厅领班
reservation clerk　　餐厅预订员
host　　餐厅男领位员
hostess　　餐厅女领位员
waiter　　男侍应生
waitress　　女侍应生

Serving in the Restaurant

技能实训 17　餐厅用餐服务

Service Procedure 服务流程

◆ Greet the guests.
问候客人。

◆ Ask the guest if he has a reservation with the restaurant.
询问客人是否有预订。

◆ Lead the guests with the reservation to the booked table.
引领有预订的客人到预订的餐台。
Escort the guest without a reservation to choose the table that fits them.
引领无预订的客人挑选合适的餐台。

◆ Order the drinks.
点茶水。

◆ Take orders.
点餐。

◆ Serve the dishes.
上菜。

◆ Settle the bill.
结账。

◆ Say farewell.
道别。

Skill Points 技能要点

◆ When seeing the guests coming to the restaurant, the hostess greets the guests with:
"Good afternoon. Welcome to our hotel. "Then ask the guests if they have a reservation
or not. If "yes", lead them to the booked table. If "no", ask them the number of the people, and escort them to choose a table that fits them.
客人到餐厅就餐,餐厅领位跟客人打招呼:"下午好,欢迎来到我们餐厅。"问客人是否有预订。如果有,领位到预订的餐台;如果没有,询问有几位,然后引领客人挑选合适的餐台。

◆ The waitress greets the guests, pulls the chair out for the guests, unfolds napkins and puts them on the laps.

侍应生问候客人,为客人拉椅,让座,打开餐巾放在膝盖上。

◆ After the guests are seated, begin to order. First order the tea. You can ask the guests with:

客人落座,开始点餐。先点茶水,可以这样问客人:

"Would you care for drinks firstly?" or "Would you like to try…"

"请问先要茶水吗?"或"您尝一尝……吗?"

◆ Taking orders, if the guest asks you to recommend the cuisine, you can begin to recommend like the following:

点菜时,如果客人要你推荐,你可以这样开始:

Would you like to try our House Specialty?

您想尝尝我们的招牌菜吗?

Which flavor would you like/prefer, sweet or chilly?

您喜欢哪一种口味,甜还是辣?

Why not try… It is a well-known delicacy in Chinese cuisine.

为什么不尝尝……它是中国菜里的一道名菜。

◆ Pay more attention to asking the guest about his demands in detail of the order when you take the order. You can ask like that:

点餐时注意询问客人对餐点的细节要求,可以这样问:

How would you like your…

您希望我们怎样做您点的……

Are you on a special diet?

您对饮食有特别要求吗?

With ice or without ice, sir?

先生,请问加冰块还是不加冰块?

◆ Generally speaking, the dishes are served in the following orders:

一般来说,上菜的顺序如下:

The Chinese Dishes

中餐上菜

cold dishes	冷盘
wine	酒
drinks	饮料
hot dishes	热菜
soup	汤
dessert	甜点
rice or noodles etc.	米饭面条等主食
fruit	水果

But when a foreigner orders a soup in Chinese Dishes, you'd better to ask him whether to serve him the soup firstly, for the foreigners have the habit of having a soup first.

但是如果一个外国人吃中餐, 点了一份汤, 你最好问一问他是否先上汤, 因为外国人有先喝汤的习惯。

The Western Dishes

西餐上菜

appetizer/ starter	开胃品/头盘
soup	汤
main course	主菜/主盘
side dishes	副菜/副盆
dessert	甜点
drink	饮料

◆ When taking the orders in the Western Food, you have to pay special attention to asking the following.

为客人点西餐要注意问下列问题。

- How would you like your steak/ beef/ lamb?

  您喜欢怎样做您点的牛排/牛肉/羊肉?

  The guest may answer you with:

  客人可能这样回答:

well-done	全熟
medium-well	七成熟
medium	五成熟
rare	三成熟
bleu	一成熟

- When the guest orders the salad, ask him: "What kind of dressing would you like on your salad?"

  当客人点色拉时要问: "请问您喜欢哪一种色拉酱?"

French dressing	法国式酱
Italian	意大利式酱
blue chess	蓝莓酱
Thousand Islands	千岛酱

Practice 1 Serving Breakfast

实训项目 1 早餐服务

Task of Service Practice 实训任务

◆ George Brown in Room 3899 and his friends want to try some Chinese snacks for their breakfast. He doesn't know what a "bun" is, so Zhou Li informs him.

3899 房间的 George Brown 和他的朋友早餐想品尝中国的小吃,他不知道"bun"是什么意思,于是周莉为他作了介绍。

◆ They order the following: four little buns, two bowls of sweet dumplings, two bowls of Guilin rice noodles, and two glasses of soybean milk.

他们点了下列食品:四个小馒头、两碗汤圆、两碗桂林米粉,还有两杯豆浆。

◆ It totals 38 yuan. George Brown asks Zhou Li to charge it to his room bill.

共消费 38 元。George Brown 要求周莉记到他房间的账单上。

Service Practice 服务实训

Now, let's begin the practice according to *Task of Service Practice*.

请按照上述实训任务开始实训。

Model of Service Practice 实训对照

17 1 Serving Breakfast. mp3

Zhou: Zhou Li, a waitress.

Brown: George Brown, a guest.

Zhou: Good morning, welcome to our restaurant.

您早! 欢迎你们来到我们餐厅。

Brown: Good morning.

早上好。

Zhou: Please choose whichever table you like.

请随便坐。

Brown: OK. Thank you.

好的。谢谢。

Zhou: What would you like to order?

您要点什么?

Brown: We'd like to try some Chinese snacks.

我们想尝一尝中式小吃。

Zhou: Here is the menu.

给您菜单。

Brown: Bun? What's a bun?

馒头? "馒头"是什么?

Zhou: It's a kind of steamed bread, and it's very popular in China.

这是一种蒸的"面包",在中国很受欢迎。

Brown: We'll have four little buns. We had some dumplings yesterday. OK, sweet dumplings today. We want two bowls of sweet dumplings and two bowls of Guilin rice noodles as well.

我们要四个小馒头。昨天我们吃过饺子了，好，今天吃汤圆，我们要两碗汤圆，还有两碗桂林米粉。

Zhou： Which would you prefer, milk or soybean milk?

请问你们要牛奶还是豆浆？

Brown： Two glasses of soybean milk. That's all.

两杯豆浆。就这些。

Zhou： I'll repeat the order: four little buns, two bowls of sweet dumplings, two bowls of Guilin rice noodles, and two glasses of soybean milk as well. Is that right?

我重复一下您点的东西：四个小馒头、两碗汤圆、两碗桂林米粉，还有两杯豆浆。是这样吗？

Brown： Right.

是这样。

Zhou： Please wait a moment. Your order will be here soon.

请稍等。您的餐点马上送到。

Zhou： Here is your order: little buns, sweet dumplings, Guilin rice noodles and soybean milk. Please enjoy them.

这是您的餐点：馒头、汤圆、桂林米粉和豆浆。请慢用。

Brown： Bring me the bill, please.

请结账。

Zhou： Here is the bill. It totals 38 yuan. How would you like to pay?

给您账单，38 元。请问您怎样付款？

Brown： Please charge it to my room. My name is George Brown and my room number is 3899.

请算到我房间的账单上。我叫 George Brown，房号是 3899。

Zhou： Please sign your name here. Thank you. Have a good day.

请您在这儿签字。谢谢。祝您快乐！

Practice 2   Serving the Buffet
实训项目 2   自助餐服务

Task of Service Practice 实训任务

◆ The seven guests with the meal tickets are going to have the buffet. They like to sit by the window.

7 位客人拿着餐券去吃自助餐，他们想坐在窗子旁边就餐。

◆ There is the main buffet table there. The guests can get silverware and dishes there. Drinks are by the east wall. The guests can help themselves.

自助餐柜在那边，他们可以在那里取餐具和餐盘。饮料在东边靠墙处。客人可以自行取用。

Service Practice 服务实训

Now, let's begin the practice according to *Task of Service Practice*.
请按照上述实训任务开始实训。

Model of Service Practice 实训对照

17 2 Serving a Buffet. mp3

Liu： Liu Yang, a waiter.

Guest： a guest.

Liu： Good morning! Seven people?
上午好！7 位用餐，是吗？

Guest： Yes, a table for seven, please!
是的，7 个人。

Liu： May I have your meal tickets, please?
请将餐券给我好吗？

Guest： Here you are!
给你吧！

Liu： Thank you! Where would you like to sit?
谢谢！你们想坐在哪儿？

Guest： We'd like to sit by the window. It's great here!
我们想坐在窗子旁边。这儿真好！

Liu： There is the main buffet table. And you can get silverware and dishes there as well. Drinks are by the east wall. Help yourself and enjoy them.
自助餐柜在那边，您可以在那里取餐具和餐盘。饮料在东边靠墙处。请自行取用，祝用餐愉快！

Practice 3　Serving Chinese Food
实训项目3　中餐服务

Task of Service Practice 实训任务

◆ Four people with a reservation are going for the table. It is the table for four by the south window that they have reserved under the name of Abraham Jones.
四位有预订的客人前来用餐，他们以 Abraham Jones 的名字预订了靠南边窗户的四人台位。

◆ They order Longjin first. And then they ask Zhou Li to recommend some special Chinese cuisines.
他们先要了龙井茶，接着要求周莉介绍中国的特色菜。

◆ Zhou Li asks the guests which dishes they would like，light，heavy，original or spicy and hot?

周莉问客人喜欢哪一种菜，清淡可口，味重香浓，原味清香还是麻辣浓香?

◆ The guests want to try all of them.

客人们都想尝尝。

◆ Zhou Li recommends the following：fried Mandarin fish in squirrel shape，Dongpo pork，sugar candy lotus seeds，fried prawns with pepper salt，and roast Beijing duck.

周莉介绍了下列菜：松鼠鳜鱼、东坡肉、冰糖湘莲、椒盐炸明虾、北京烤鸭。

◆ Mr. Jones orders a roast Beijing duck，fried Mandarin fish in squirrel shape，sugar candy lotus seeds and fried prawns with pepper salt，eggplant with garlic sauce，stir fry gourd with garlic and Yanjing beer. He asks Zhou Li to bring them the chopsticks instead of knives and forks.

Jones 点了北京烤鸭、松鼠鳜鱼、冰糖湘莲、椒盐炸明虾、鱼香茄子、芙蓉炒丝瓜和燕京啤酒，他让周莉拿筷子而不用刀和叉子。

◆ It totals 465 yuan. Mr. Jones makes the payment by credit card.

一共是 465 元。Jones 先生用信用卡结账。

Service Practice 服务实训

Now，let's begin the practice according to *Task of Service Practice*.

请按照上述实训任务开始实训。

17 3 Serving Chinese Food. mp3

Model of Service Practice 实训对照

Wu：　Wu Jin，a hostess.

Jones：Abraham Jones，a guest.

Zhou：Zhou Li，a waitress.

Wu：　Welcome to our restaurant. Have you made a reservation?

　　　欢迎来到我们酒店，您有预订吗?

Jones：Yes，we have. Under the name of Abraham Jones.

　　　有，以 Abraham Jones 的名字订的。

Wu：　You've booked a table by the south window for four people. Is that right?

　　　您预订了靠南边窗户的四人台位，是这样吗?

Jones：Exactly.

　　　是这样。

Wu：　I'll show you to your table. This way，please. This is your table. Will this table be all right?

　　　我带您到您的餐台去，请这边走。这是您的餐台，可以吗?

Jones：Very good.

　　　很好。

Zhou：Thank you. Take your seat, please.

谢谢,请坐。

Zhou：Good morning, everyone. First, what would you like to drink?

大家早上好。先来什么茶水?

Jones：Longjing.

龙井。

Zhou：Here you are. This is our menu.

您请。这是菜单。

Zhou：Are you ready to order?

可以点菜了吗?

Jones：Yes. We want to eat Chinese food. But we don't know how to order. Could you recommend some special Chinese dishes, please?

可以了。我们想吃中国菜,但我们不知道怎样点。你可以为我们推荐一些有特色的中国菜吗?

Zhou：Certainly! Which dishes would you like, light, heavy, original or spicy and hot?

当然可以! 你们喜欢哪一种菜,清淡可口,味重香浓,原味清香,还是麻辣浓香?

Jones：We want to try all of them.

我们都想尝尝。

Zhou：Fried Mandarin fish in squirrel shape, Dongpo pork, sugar candy lotus seeds, fried prawns with pepper salt, and roast Beijing duck.

松鼠鳜鱼、东坡肉、冰糖湘莲、椒盐炸明虾、北京烤鸭。

Jones：Thank you very much! They sound great and interesting. We'd like to have a roast Beijing duck, fried Mandarin fish in squirrel shape, sugar candy lotus, and fried prawns with pepper salt. We want to get two vegetable dishes, too: seeds eggplant with garlic sauce and stir fried gourd with garlic.

非常感谢! 它们听起来很特别很有趣。我们要一只北京烤鸭、松鼠鳜鱼、冰糖湘莲和椒盐炸明虾。还要两个蔬菜,鱼香茄子和芙蓉炒丝瓜。

Zhou：What would you like to drink?

您喝点什么?

Jones：We want to try some Chinese beer.

我们想尝尝中国啤酒。

Zhou：How about Yanjing beer? It is very popular here.

燕京啤酒怎样? 这种啤酒在我们这儿很受欢迎。

Jones：We'll take it.

就要它吧!

Zhou：Anything else, sir?

先生,您还要点别的吗?

Jones：No, thank you! That's all for now.

谢谢! 先点这些。

Zhou：Shall I bring you chopsticks or knives and forks?

你们要筷子还是刀叉？

Jones：We'd like to use chopsticks.

要筷子。

Zhou：Here are your last dishes. Please enjoy.

这是最后的一道菜，请慢用。

Jones：Please give me the bill.

请结账。

Zhou：Here you are. It totals 465 yuan. How would you like to pay?

给您，一共是 465 元。请问怎样付款？

Jones：By credit card.

用信用卡结账。

Zhou：Please sign your name here. Here is your card.

请在这里签名，给您卡。

Jones：Thank you very much.

非常感谢。

Zhou：You're welcome. We hope to serve you again soon.

不用谢，欢迎您再来。

Practice 4   Serving Western Food
实训项目 4   西餐服务

Task of Service Practice 实训任务

◆ Tom Jones without a reservation is coming for the Western Food.

没有预订的 Tom Jones 前来用西餐。

◆ The orders of Mr. Jones are the following.

Jones 先生点了以下菜肴。

The appetizer：smoked salmon.

开胃菜：熏三文鱼。

The main course：two T-Bone steaks and a rump steak，medium-rare.

主菜：两份 T 骨牛排和一份牛腿排，七分熟。

Three large salads and three hamburgers，French and Thousand Island.

三大份色拉和汉堡，法式酱和千岛酱。

The vegetables：curried vegetables.

蔬菜：咖喱蔬菜。

The soup：fish soup，French style.

汤：法式鱼汤。

The dessert：Vanilla ice-cream for all.

甜点：每人一份香草冰激凌。

◆ The total is 286 yuan including 10％ service charge.

一共 286 元,10％的服务费算在内。

◆ Mr. Jones pays for it.

Jones 先生买单。

Service Practice 服务实训

Now,let's begin the practice according to *Task of Service Practice*.

请按照上述实训任务开始实训。

Model of Service Practice 实训对照

17 4 Serving West-ern Food. mp3

Wu：　Wu Jin,a hostess.

Jones：Tom Jones,a guest.

Zhou：Zhou Li,a waiter.

Wu：　Good evening. Welcome to our restaurant. Have you made a reservation?

晚上好,欢迎到我们餐厅来,请问您有预订吗?

Jones：No,we haven't.

没有。

Wu：　Three people?

是三位吗?

Jones：Right.

是的。

Wu：　This way,please. Where would you like to sit?

这边请,您想坐在哪儿?

Jones：We'd like to sit by the window.

我们想坐在窗子旁。

Wu：　How is this table?

这张餐台怎么样?

Jones：It's fine.

很好。

Wu：　Thank you. Take your seat,please.

谢谢,请坐。

Zhou：Good evening. May I take your order now?

晚上好,可以点餐了吗?

Jones：For an appetizer,smoked salmon.

来一道开胃菜,熏三文鱼。

Zhou：And,for the main course?

请问要什么主菜?

Jones：Two T-Bone steaks and a rump steak.

两份 T 骨牛排,一份牛腿排。

Zhou：How would you like your steak done?

牛排要几分熟?

Jones：Medium-well. And we'd like three large salads and three hamburgers.

七分熟。我们还要三大份色拉和汉堡。

Zhou：What kind of dressing?

要哪种酱汁?

Jones：French and Thousand Island.

法式酱和千岛酱。

Zhou：Would you like some vegetables?

要些蔬菜吗?

Jones：The curried vegetables.

咖喱蔬菜。

Zhou：What soup would you like?

要什么汤?

Jones：Fish soup,French style.

法式鱼汤。

Zhou：Anything for dessert?

需要甜点吗?

Jones：Vanilla ice-cream for all.

每人一份香草冰激凌。

Zhou：Anything else?

还需要别的吗?

Jones：No,I'm afraid that's all. Bring me the bill,please.

不,已经足够了,请结账。

Zhou：Here it is,sir. The total is 286 yuan.

给您,先生。一共 286 元。

Jones：Is the service charge included?

服务费算在内了吗?

Zhou：Yes,sir. 10% service charge. Who will pay for it?

算在内了,先生。10%的服务费。谁买单?

Jones：It's me. Here is 300 yuan.

我来。这是 300 元。

Zhou：Thank you. Here is your change. Please count it,sir.

谢谢。这是找您的钱,请点一下,先生。

Jones：Thank you for your service. Goodbye.

谢谢你的服务，再见。

Zhou：We hope to have another opportunity to serve you again.
希望能再有机会为您服务。

Practice Revision 实训回望

◆ When handling the reservation of a banquet，what information need you get?

◆ Please talk about the orders of the Chinese dishes served and West Dishes served.

◆ The Chinese cuisine is divided into four or eight major cuisines. What are they?

◆ Please talk about the differences of the four major cuisines.

◆ Please finish a list with 10 – 15 Chinese dishes in English without the teaching book.

Hotel Knowledge
新酒店人须知

(1) The Food and Beverage Department is one of the important departments of the hotel. Its working efficiency and service standard reflect the overall management of the hotel. Its service quality affects greatly the hotel's reputation and the selling of other products.
餐饮部是酒店重要的部门之一，它的工作效率和服务水准反映酒店的总体管理水准，它的服务质量不仅影响着酒店的声誉，还影响着酒店其他产品的销售。

(2) Some useful expressions in the menu：
常用菜单词汇：

roast Beijing duck	北京烤鸭
spiced peanuts	五香花生米
five flavor spiced beef	五香牛肉
green pepper and potato	青椒土豆丝
fried string beans	干煸四季豆
eggplant with garlic sauce	鱼香茄子
sichuan style bean curd	麻婆豆腐
stir fried gourd with garlic	芙蓉炒丝瓜
raised pork leg	红烧猪蹄
braised pork tendons	红烧蹄筋
stewed salt-preserved duck	桂花盐水鸭
ham with fresh bamboo shoots	鲜笋火腿
fried crisp pork slices with sugar powder	糖粉酥肉
sliced chicken in wine sauce	香糟鸡片
deep fried spring chicken	炸童子鸡
braise chicken with shallot	红葱头蒸鸡
stew chicken with chestnut	栗干焖鸡

chicken slices with bean jelly sheets	鸡丝粉皮
chicken skin with mustard sauce	芥末鸡皮
grilled young pigeon	铁扒乳鸽

Answers to "Practice Revision" 部分参考答案

◆ When handling the reservation of a banquet, what information need you get?

The company name or guest name, the expect numbers of the persons and tables, the time of the banquet, the banquet menu, the banquet budget, how to arrange the tables and seats, how to decorate the banquet hall, how to pay, and ask the guest to hand in some deposit to secure the reservation in advance.

◆ Please talk about the differences of the four major cuisines.

Generally speaking, Shandong cuisine is heavy, Guangdong cuisine is light, Sichuan cuisine is spicy and hot, while Huaiyang cuisine is famous for its cutting technique and original flavor.

Chapter Seven　Bar Service

实训模块七　酒吧服务

Unit 18
General Service

技能实训18 常规服务

Service Procedure 服务流程

◆ Greet the guest and show the way.

向客人问好,为客人引路。

◆ Take orders.

为客人点饮料。

◆ Serve wine.

上酒。

◆ Communicate with the guest.

与客人交流。

◆ Ask for the guest's opinion.

询问客人意见。

◆ Bring the bill to the guest.

为客人结账。

◆ Say goodbye to the guest.

送客人离开并致谢。

Skill Points 技能要点

◆ Pay attention to the use of polite language. When greeting the guests, hostess should always remember to ask the guests about their number, reservation information, seat preference, etc.

注意使用礼貌用语。领位员在微笑迎客的同时,应认真询问客人人数、有无预订、喜欢的位置等基本信息。

Way of Expression:

表达方法:

Have you got any reservation?

您预订了吗?

How many persons?

请问您几位？

Will this table do?

这个位置可以吗？

If the guest is not satisfied with the place, you should say: Just a moment please, I will arrange another table for you.

如客人对现有位置不满意，你应该说：请稍等，我会给您安排另外一个位置。

◆ You can use the following expressions to ask what the guest would like.

可以用以下几种方式询问客人的点餐需求。

What would you like, ladies and gentlemen?

女士们先生们，你们想点点儿什么？

Would you care for something to drink?

您想喝点什么？

May I take your order?

可以点餐了吗？

Good evening, what is your pleasure, sir?

晚上好，先生，您喜欢点什么？

Are you ready to order now?

可以点餐了吗？

◆ When you are asked for suggestions, you could say:

当客人向你征求意见时，你可以用如下表达：

Why not try...

为什么不试试……

What about...

……怎么样？

Then I would recommend...

我向您推荐……

◆ Do confirm after you get all the order information by repeating the orders. For example:

"You have ordered a sweet Martini cocktail and crisps, is that all?"

点餐后，务必重复客人所点饮品以确认。如："您点了马蒂尼甜鸡尾酒和薯片，还需要其他的吗？"

◆ Tell the guest the food and drinks will be served soon with.

告诉客人饮品马上就来的表达方式有如下几种。

Just a moment please.

请稍等。

Your order will be coming up immediately.

您的订单很快就来。

They'll be ready in a minute.

它们一会儿就能准备好。

I'll be right back.

我很快回来。

◆ According to the law, only adults are allowed to dine in the bar, if you are not sure whether the guest is over 18 years old or not, you could ask in this way:

因为法律只允许成年人进入酒吧消费,当你不确定客人是否年满18岁时,可以这样询问:

May I see your identification?

能看一下您的身份证吗?

◆ You can use the following expressions to assist the guest to pay the bill.

你可以用以下表达协助客人付账。

Just a moment please, I will calculate that for you. Thank you for your waiting, sir. Your bill comes to...

请稍等,我来为您计算一下。久等了,您的消费金额是……

Here you are, sir.

给您,先生。

There is your bill, sir.

这是您的账单,先生。

◆ When the disagreement about the bill arises, the guest may ask you about the bill details. Be sure to clarify each item politely and patiently. If you do make calculation or order wrongly, please apologize with.

当客人对账单有疑问时,会询问具体花费。一定要礼貌、耐心地说明每项花费。如果确实是计算错误或者记录错误,要立刻道歉,请使用如下表达。

I'm deeply sorry, sir. There might be some mistakes. I'll have it changed at once.

非常抱歉,可能有一些错误,我马上换掉这张单子。

I'm really sorry for the mistakes. Would you mind looking at it again?

非常抱歉出这个错误。您介意再看一下吗?

Sorry to have kept you waiting so long, sir.

抱歉让您等这么久,先生。

◆ Some guests prefer to pay cash while others may use credit card. There are also guests who hope to add the amount to the final room bill. If it is credit card, ask about the type of the card with.

有些客人选择支付现金,有些选择使用信用卡。还有一些客人希望把账单加在房费中。当用信用卡结账时,询问客人使有哪种信用卡。

What kind of card have you got, sir?

请问您使用哪种卡?

If the bill will be paid together with the room bill, ask the guests to sign the bill and write down the room number.

如果最后与房费一起支付,让客人在账单上签字并写下房间号。

Practice 1　Leading in the Guest
实训项目 1　领位

Task of Service Practice 实训任务

◆ Jane Sherlock has made the reservation with the bar of Beijing International Hotel before she comes with two friends.
  Jane Sherlock 已经在北京国际酒店的酒吧作了预订,她与两个朋友一起来到酒吧。

◆ The host greets them and leads them into the bar.
  领位问候并带他们进入酒吧。

◆ They prefer a table by the window in the non-smoking area.
  他们想坐在无烟区的靠窗座位。

Service Practice 服务实训

Now,let's begin the practice according to *Task of Service Practice*.
请按照上述实训任务开始实训。

Model of Service Practice 实训对照

18 1 Leading in the Guest. mp3

Li：　　Li Ming,a host.
Sherlock： Jane Sherlock,a guest.

Li：　　Good morning,Miss,welcome to our bar!
　　　　早上好,小姐,欢迎来到我们的酒吧。

Sherlock： Good morning.
　　　　早上好。

Li：　　Do you have a reservation?
　　　　请问您预订了吗?

Sherlock： Yes.
　　　　是的。

Li：　　May I have your name?
　　　　请问您的姓名?

Sherlock： Jane Sherlock.
　　　　Jane Sherlock。

Li：　　How many people are there in your party?
　　　　您一共几位?

Sherlock： Three.
　　　　3 位。

Li：　　Would you prefer the smoking area or the non-smoking area?

您想坐在吸烟区还是无烟区？

Sherlock：The non-smoking area please.

无烟区。

Li：This way please. Mind your step. Would you like to sit near the window or by the bar counter?

请这边来，小心脚下。您想坐在窗边还是挨着吧台？

Sherlock：Near the window, I think.

靠窗吧。

Li：Is this seat all right?

这个座位可以吗？

Sherlock：Sure, thank you very much!

可以，非常感谢。

Li：My pleasure.

不客气。

Practice 2　Taking Orders and Serving Wines
实训项目 2　点餐和送酒服务

Task of Service Practice 实训任务

◆ Two guests enter the bar in Beijing International Hotel. They are not sure what to drink and want some suggestions from the waitress.

两个客人来到北京国际酒店的酒吧。他们不知道喝点什么，请服务员推荐一些饮料。

◆ The waitress recommends a local beer —Yanjing.

酒吧服务生推荐了本地的燕京啤酒。

◆ Mr. Joseph orders a mango juice.

约瑟夫先生点了芒果汁。

Service Practice 服务实训

Now, let's begin the practice according to *Task of Service Practice*.

请按照上述实训任务开始实训。

Model of Service Practice 实训对照

Wang：　Wang Ying, a waitress.

Kate：　Kate Whitney, the first guest.

Joseph：　Mr. Joseph, the second guest.

18 2 Taking Orders and Serving Wines . mp3

Wang： Good evening, welcome to our bar. May I help you?

晚上好，欢迎光临我们的酒吧，您想喝点什么？

Kate： Yes, could you recommend something to drink?

当然，能推荐一些饮料吗？

Wang： We have soft drinks, fresh juices, mineral water and spirits. What would you like?

我们有软饮料、鲜果汁、矿泉水和酒，您想要哪种呢？

Kate： Well, beer I think.

啤酒吧。

Wang： Do you like bottled beer or draught beer?

您想要瓶装啤酒还是扎啤？

Kate： I like bottled beer.

瓶装啤酒。

Wang： Would you like a local beer or an imported beer?

想要当地啤酒还是进口的？

Kate： I want to taste some local beer. Could you recommend one for me?

我想尝尝当地啤酒。你能为我推荐一些吗？

Wang： I'm glad to do that. The most popular one in China is Yanjing. Would you like to give it a try?

很乐意为您效劳。中国最畅销的是燕京啤酒，您想品尝一下吗？

Kate： Of course, thank you.

当然，谢谢你。

Wang： And you, sir?

您呢？先生？

Joseph： I'd like to drink fresh juice, what kind do you have?

我要果汁，都有什么口味的？

Wang： We have orange, pineapple, grape, mango, peach and tomato juice.

有鲜橙、菠萝、葡萄、芒果、桃和番茄的。

Joseph： Give me a mango juice.

给我来芒果的吧。

Wang： Yes, wait a moment, please.

好的，请稍等。

Joseph： Thank you.

谢谢。

Wang： Sorry to have kept you waiting. Here is your beer and mango juice. Would you like anything else?

让您久等了。您的燕京啤酒和芒果汁。还要其他的吗？

Joseph： No, thanks.

不用了，谢谢。

Wang： You are welcome. Enjoy your drink!

不客气。请您享用吧！

Practice 3　Paying the Bill
实训项目3　结账

Task of Service Practice 实训任务

◆ Ms. Green is ready to leave and asks for the bill.
格林女士用餐完毕准备结账。

◆ The total bill is 300 RMB.
账单是300元。

◆ She lives in Room 1012 and wants to add the cost to the final bill.
她住在1012房间,希望和房费一起结。

Service Practice 服务实训

Now, let's begin the practice according to *Task of Service Practice*.
请按照上述实训任务开始实训。

18 3 Paying the
Bill. mp3

Model of Service Practice 实训对照

Green：Ms. Green, a guest.

Chen：Chen Lin, a bartender.

Green：The bill, please.
服务员,结账。

Chen：Yes, please wait a moment. Here's your bill, Miss. It is 300 yuan.
请等一下。这是您的账单,300元。

Green：What's this for?
这是哪项?

Chen：It's for the beer.
您的啤酒。

Green：I see.
哦。

Chen：How would you like to pay? We accept cash and credit cards.
您想怎样付款? 我们接受现金和信用卡。

Green：I'm a guest here. Can I put it on my hotel bill?
我住在这里,能不能和房费一起支付。

Chen：Sure. May I have your room number?
当然,请问您的房间号?

Green：Room 1012.
1012房间。

Chen：Room 1012. Could you sign your name here, please?

1012 房间,您能在这里签字吗?

Green：Sure.

当然。

Chen：Thank you. Have a good night.

谢谢您,祝您晚安。

Practice 4 Communicating with the Guest
实训项目4　与客人交流

Task of Service Practice 实训任务

◆ Mr. Sherlock is sitting at the bar counter alone and Chen Lin develops a free conversation with him while serving him the wine.

Sherlock 先生正独自在吧台饮酒,服务员陈林在为他端酒时和他交谈起来。

◆ They talk about Beijing, and their hobbies.

他们谈论到北京这座城市,以及他们的爱好。

◆ Chen Lin learns that the guest is on vacation here and they both love basketball.

陈林得知客人正在这里度假。他们都喜欢打篮球。

Service Practice 服务实训

Now, let's begin the practice according to *Task of Service Practice*.

请按照上述实训任务开始实训。

18 4 Communicating
with the Guest. mp3

Model of Service Practice 实训对照

Chen：　　Chen Lin, the bartender.

Sherlock：Mr. Sherlock, the guest.

Chen：　　Where are you from?

您来自哪里?

Sherlock：I'm from Melbourne. This is my first time in Beijing.

我从墨尔本来的,这是我第一次到北京。

Chen：　　Do you like the city?

您喜欢这座城市吗?

Sherlock：Yes, it's a very charming city, rich in culture.

是的,这是一座非常迷人的城市,文化底蕴深厚。

Chen：　　Yes, Beijing has a long history. Are you here on vacation or business?

是的,北京有很悠久的历史。您在这里度假还是公干?

Sherlock：On vacation.

度假。

Chen：If you like,I'd like to show you around. The coming Olympic Games just make it even more attractive.

如果您愿意,我可以带您逛逛这座城市。即将召开的奥运会将让这里更有吸引力。

Sherlock：That's very kind of you. I hope it won't trouble you too much.

您真是太好了。我希望不会太麻烦你。

Chen：Not at all! What do you do in your spare time? Reading,doing exercise or watching TV?

不会的。您在业余时间都做什么? 看书,运动,还是看电视?

Sherlock：I'm quite an outdoor person. I like playing basketball.

我喜欢户外运动。我喜欢打篮球。

Chen：Oh,really? Me too!

真的? 我也是。

Hotel Knowledge
新酒店人须知

(1) 星级饭店酒吧服务形式。

星级饭店,尤其是高星级饭店,一般都设有饮料部(Beverage Department),它隶属于餐饮部,分管饭店内所有酒吧。这些酒吧风格形式不同,常见的类型有大堂吧(Lobby Bar)、大堂酒廊(Lobby Lounge)、主酒吧(Main Bar)、茶室或茶廊(Tea House or Tea Lounge)、餐厅酒吧又称水吧(Soda Bar)、宴会酒吧(Banquet Bar)。盛夏时节许多饭店会应时设立环境非常宽松的露天酒吧,称为啤酒花园(Beer Garden)。

(2) Useful Expressions:

酒吧常用词汇:

on the rocks	加冰块	syrup	糖水
ice water	冰水	soft drink	软饮料
dessert wine	餐后甜酒	alcohol	"乙醇",俗称酒精
tonic water	汤力水	base	基酒
aperitifs	开胃酒	dessert wines	甜食酒
liqueurs	利口酒	gin	金酒
vodka	伏特加	tequila	特基拉
rum	朗姆酒	whiskey	威士忌
brandy	白兰地	beer	啤酒
bitter	比特苦酒	cocktail	鸡尾酒
soda water	苏打水	ginger ale	姜啤酒

Unit 19
Dealing with Unexpected Events
技能实训 19 应对突发事件

Main Services 主要服务

◆ Dealing With Complaints   处理投诉
◆ Dealing With the Drunken Guests   应对醉酒客人

Skill Points 技能要点

◆ In answer to complaints from the guest, it is very important to keep the following four things in your mind: listening, sympathizing, apologizing, and telling the guests what will be done to solve their problems.

在应对客人投诉时,要牢记四点:倾听、同情、道歉、告诉客人你们将做哪些努力。

◆ You can use the following sentences to express your willingness to help the guest.

安慰客人时可以用以下表达。

Thank you for telling us about it, sir. I'll look into the matter at once.

感谢您为我们提供这些情况,我立即去了解。

I'll speak to the person in charge and ask him to take care of the problem.

我会对负责人员讲,让他来处理这件事。

Please calm down, sir, I'll try to help you.

请您冷静,我会尽力帮助您。

Please relax, madam. I will take care of it according to your request.

请放心,夫人。我将按您的要求办。

◆ You can use the following sentences to apologize for mistakes.

向客人道歉时你可以用以下表达。

Sorry, sir, I will solve the problem for you as soon as possible.

对不起,先生,我会尽快为您解决这个问题。

I'm awfully sorry for my carelessness.

对于我的粗心我非常抱歉。

Practice 1　Handling a Complaint About Bar Service
实训项目 1　处理酒吧服务投诉

Task of Service Practice 实训任务

◆ Wang Li is practiced manager in the bar of Beijing International Hotel.
王莉是北京国际酒店酒吧的实习经理。

◆ She is asked to a guest's table. The guest is angry about the fried chips which were overcooked.
她被叫到客人桌前。客人对炸煳的薯条很不满意。

◆ Wang Li apologizes for it and gives the guest a tray of chips for free.
王莉为此道歉,并且送给客人一份免费薯条。

Service Practice 服务实训

Now,let's begin the practice according to *Task of Service Practice*.
请按照上述实训任务开始实训。

Model of Service Practice 实训对照

19　1 Handling a Complaint About Bar Service. mp3

Wang：Wang Li,a practiced bar manager.
Green：Mr. Green,a guest.

Wang：Good evening,sir. What can I do for you?
晚上好,先生,我能为您做些什么?

Green：I'm not at all happy.
我很不高兴。

Wang：Perhaps you could tell me what the problem is.
也许您可以告诉我有什么问题。

Green：It's my chips.
这份薯条。

Wang：What's wrong with them,sir?
薯条怎么了,先生?

Green：They taste bitter. They're overcooked. But when I told your waiter about it,he didn't take any notice.
吃起来是苦的,明显炸得时间长了。但是我告诉服务员的时候,他没理我。

Wang：I'm extremely sorry about that,sir. I'm sure the waiter didn't mean to be rude. Perhaps he didn't understand you correctly. I do apologize for it. I'll have the chips changed right away.
非常抱歉先生。我相信我们的服务员不是有意的。可能他不是很明白您的意思。我向您道歉,马上为您换一份薯条。

Green：Good. That's better. Do I have to pay for these?

这样好多了，我还要付钱吗？

Wang：Certainly not, sir. It's all free of charge. Please take your time and enjoy.

当然不需要，先生，这份免费。请慢慢享用。

Practice 2　Handling a Drunken Guest
实训项目2　应对醉酒客人

Task of Service Practice 实训任务

◆ Wang Li is working in the bar when three guests enter and order a bottle of whisky.

王莉正在酒吧工作，这时进来三位客人，点了一瓶威士忌。

◆ After a while, one of the guests gets drunk and begins to shout and sing.

过了一会儿，其中一个客人喝醉了，开始大唱大叫。

◆ Wang Li serves him a cup of tea and suggests his friends to take him outside for some fresh air.

王莉端上一杯茶，并建议他的朋友带他出去透透风。

Service Practice 服务实训

Now, let's begin the practice according to *Task of Service Practice*.

请按照上述实训任务开始实训。

Model of Service Practice 实训对照

19 2 Handling a
Drunken Guest
. mp3

Wang：Wang Li, a practiced bar manager.

Green：Mr. Green, a guest.

Wang：Good evening, ladies and gentlemen. Would you like a table for three? Will this table do?

晚上好，女士们先生们。您需要三人桌吗？这张可以吗？

Green：We want one far away from the band. The music is too loud.

我们想要一张离乐队远一些的，音乐太吵了。

Wang：Just a moment, please. I'll arrange another table for you.

请稍等，我给您另找一张。

Green：This is much better.

这张好多了。

Wang：May I take your order now?

能点单了吗？

Green：Let's have a bottle of whisky.

我们来一瓶威士忌。

(*One hour later, one of the guests gets drunk and begins to shout and sing.*)

(一小时后,一个客人喝醉了,开始大唱大叫。)

Wang: Here is a cup of tea. I think the gentleman may need it. It's very stuffy in here. Would you mind taking your friend outside for some fresh air, ladies and gentlemen?

这是一杯茶,我想这位先生可能需要。这里空气不太好,您可不可以带您的朋友出去呼吸新鲜空气醒醒酒,女士们先生们?

Green: We're sorry for disturbing others. He's too excited today.

很抱歉打扰其他人了,他今天太兴奋了。

Wang: It's all right, sir. Good night and have a good rest.

没关系,先生。晚安。

Hotel Knowledge
新酒店人须知

Happy Hours

The bars in the star hotels offer "happy hours" service during the off-peak time period, e. g. day time on weekdays or dinner time. The commonest means of promotion is called "buy one and get one free". During these hours, the bar tender should inform the guests of the promotions so that they could fully benefit from them.

欢乐时光

高星级酒店会在客人较少的时间段,如每天的用餐时间或周一至周四的白天,举办"欢乐时光"活动,招揽客人以便促销。最常见的促销形式是"买一赠一"。客人在"欢乐时光"时间段内光临酒吧,服务员应主动向客人介绍促销活动,避免客人在不知情的情况下消费,而不能享受到优惠。

Practice Revision 实训回望

◆ What information does the host need to get from the guests when greeting them in the bar?

◆ Why need we confirm after we get all of the orders? How can we avoid misunderstanding?

◆ If we are not sure whether the guest is over 18 years old or not, in what way can we ask about his age?

◆ How should we deal with the bill mistakes?

Case and Improvement: The Ice-cold Beer
案例与提高:冰镇啤酒

Zhang Fan is a trainee in the bar of Asian Grand Hotel. One day, an American guest, Young Smith, entered the bar and ordered something to drink. The following was the conversation between Mr. Smith and Zhang Fan.

张凡是亚洲大酒店的一名酒吧实习服务生。一天，美国客人 Young Smith 来到酒吧，点了一些饮料。以下是张凡和客人的对话。

Zhang Fan： Good evening, sir. May I help you?
晚上好，您想喝点什么？

Young Smith： Give me one ice-cold beer, please!
请给我一杯冰镇啤酒。

19 C&I The Ice-cold Beer. mp3

The guest spoke the whole sentence so fast that Zhang Fan could hardly catch every word. Certainly "ice" and "beer" are words easy to understand, so Zhang Fan took it for granted that the order was beer with ice, and served it without further confirmation with the guest.

客人说得很快，张凡没有听清楚每个词。当然她能够明白"冰"和"啤酒"这两个词，所以理所当然地认为是啤酒加冰，没有向客人确认便端着酒水上给了客人。

Zhang Fan： Is that all you want?
就要这些吗？

Young Smith： Yes.
是的。

Zhang Fan： Wait for a moment, please.
请稍等。

Later, when the guest started to drink the beer, he realized it had an ice cube in it, which made the drink much lighter. The guest was not happy about it. He asked Zhang Fan to get the beer changed. Zhang Fan realized he had made the mistake about the word "ice-cold" and apologized to the guest. She changed the beer for the guest immediately.

当客人开始饮用时，发现啤酒加了冰，味道变淡了。客人很不高兴，要求更换。张凡意识到自己在冰镇这个单词上所犯的错误，立刻道歉并为客人更换了啤酒。

Zhang Fan： I'm awfully sorry for the error, sir. This is the cold beer you ordered and this is an extra plate of popcorn. I hope you enjoy it.
对这个错误我感到非常抱歉，先生。这是您要的冰镇啤酒，这是一盘额外的爆米花。希望您喜欢。

Young Smith： That's all right.
没关系。

Case Topic 案例话题

My opinion about Zhang Fan's service in the case.
我对案例中张凡服务的看法。

Hotel Manager's Comments
酒店经理点评

（1）吧台服务员代表着酒吧和整个酒店的形象，在酒吧的运行和对外服务中担负着多种重要的角色。一名称职的吧台服务员不仅要有全面的酒品知识,还需要良好的语言交际能力及应变能力。来酒吧的客人可能来自不同的国家和地区,即便讲英语也有不同的发音讲话习惯,服务员平时要加强外语听说练习。

(2)点单时,一定要得到客人的确认(confirm),这样做能避免许多记录上的错误。如果客人语速较快,你没有听清楚,请他再重复一次,不要猜测。如果确实遇到不懂的用语,要虚心地向客人询问,不要臆断。

(3)从酒水服务常识上,能够判断出客人点单是否符合常规饮用方式。因此,酒吧服务员需要具备一定的酒类饮用常识。

Answers to "Practice Revision" 部分参考答案

◆ What information does the host need to get from the guests when greeting them in the bar?

Their number.

Reservation information.

Seat preference.

Their orders.

◆ Why need we confirm after we get all of the orders? How can we avoid misunderstanding?

When taking orders, we must confirm with the guests about their orders, so as to avoid recording mistakes. If the guest speaks very fast, don't hesitate to let him repeat. If you can't understand a specific word or phrase in the guest's sentence, honestly express your doubt and let him explain it to you. Don't guess the meaning.

◆ How should we deal with the bill mistakes?

We should help the guest clarify each item politely and patiently. Whatever mistakes in the bill they are, sincerely apologize with the following expressions:

"I'm deeply sorry, sir. There might be some mistakes. I'll have it changed at once."

"Sorry to have kept you waiting so long, sir. Would you mind looking at it again?"

Chapter Eight   Telephone

实训模块八   总机服务

Unit 20

Telephone Operator

技能实训 20　转接电话

Main Services 主要服务

◆ Making an international call.
打国际长途电话。
◆ Connecting an incoming call.
接进外来电话。
◆ Connecting an outgoing call.
帮助客人拨出电话。

Skill Points 技能要点

◆ When you receive a telephone call, firstly you should identify your hotel and say: "Good morning/afternoon/evening. This is xx Hotel. May I help you?"
当接听电话时,拿起话筒应先问候:"早上/下午/晚上好,这是××酒店,能为您效劳吗?"

◆ Finish the conversation by using a suitable closing phrase that expresses appreciation for the call.
结束电话,可用以下表达方式。

　　Thanks for calling.
　　谢谢您的来电。
　　Thank you, sir. Goodbye.
　　谢谢您,先生。再见。

You can use the following to express regret if the caller's wish could not be accommodated.
如果无法为客人效劳,可用以下表达方式。

　　We're sorry that we couldn't help you, sir.
　　很抱歉没法为您服务。
　　We look forward to another chance to serve you, sir.
　　希望下次有机会能为您效劳。

◆ If a guest wants to make a long distance call in the hotel, he can either call directly from his room or go through the operator. Calling directly is cheaper than the latter one, so the operator should get clear about the guest's request when answering his phone.

在饭店打长途电话,可以直接拨打,也可以让总机帮助拨通电话。一般情况下,采用直接拨打的方式比较便宜。接线员在接受咨询时应该问清楚客人的要求。

◆ Operator could use the following expressions instead of putting the caller through abruptly.

总机在为客人接通电话的时候切记不要太唐突、太生硬,可用下列表达方式。

Just a moment, please. I'll put you through.

请稍等,我马上帮您转接。

Please hold the line a moment. I'm putting you through to…

请别挂电话,我这就给您接过去……

Thank you for waiting, sir. Please go ahead, you're through.

让您久等了,先生。您的电话已接通,请讲。

◆ Don't leave the guests hanging on without an answer. Be alert and inform them: "Sorry, there is no answer. Would you like to leave a message?"

总机在为客人接通电话后而对方无人应答时,不要让客人空守着话机。应及时告知客人说:"很抱歉,先生。房间没有人接听。您想留言吗?"

◆ When the operator is connecting an incoming collect call from overseas, be sure to inform the guest first and then confirm whether he would like to answer or not. e. g. "This is the Hotel Operator. I have a collect call from Mr. Smith in America. Will you accept the charges?"

当总机为客人转接越洋接听人付费电话时,应先告知接听人并确认其是否愿意接听。例如:"这里是酒店总机,有一位史密斯先生从美国打来的接听人付费电话,您愿意付款吗?"

◆ When you receive a telephone call with wrong number, you should say:

对方拨错电话的时候,应采用下列应对方式。

I'm afraid you have the wrong number. This is the Beijing Hotel.

您恐怕拨错号码了。这里是北京饭店。

Practice 1 Making an International Call
实训项目 1 打国际长途

Task of Service Practice 实训任务

◆ John Smith wants to make an international call in the hotel, so he asks the hotel operator for help.

John Smith 先生想在其下榻的酒店打一个国际长途,他打电话到总机寻求帮助。

◆ The hotel operator Li Lin tells him how to make an international call in his room.

酒店接线员李琳告诉他怎样在客房直接打国际电话。

We have IDD and DDD services in our hotel. So the guest may call directly from his room. It is cheaper than going through the operator.

我们酒店提供国际直拨和国内直拨的业务,客人可以直接由客房打出去,而且比总机打出便宜一些。

Dial the country code, the area code and the number you want. The country codes are listed in the services directory in your room.

请先拨国家代码,然后是区域号码,最后是您需要的电话号码。国家代码列在您房间里的服务指南上。

Service Practice 服务实训

Now, let's begin the practice according to *Task of Service Practice*.
请按照上述实训任务开始实训。

20 1 Making an
International
Call. mp3

Model of Service Practice 实训对照

Li:　Li Lin, an operator.
Smith:　Mr. John Smith, a guest.

Li:　Good morning. This is the hotel operator. May I help you?
　　　早上好,酒店总机,能为您效劳吗?

Smith:　Yes. This is John Smith in Room 402. I'd like to make an international call.
　　　我是402房间的John Smith。我想打一个国际长途。

Li:　Mr. Smith. We offer IDD and DDD services in our hotel, so you may call directly from your room. It is cheaper than going through the operator.
　　　史密斯先生,我们酒店提供国际直拨和国内直拨的业务。您可以直接由客房打出去,这样比经由总机打出便宜一些。

Smith:　Oh, would you please tell me how to do that?
　　　哦,你能告诉我该怎么打吗?

Li:　Certainly, sir. Please dial the country code, the area code and the number you want. The country codes are listed in the services directory in your room.
　　　当然可以,先生。请先拨国家代码,然后是区域号码,最后是您需要的电话号码。国家代码列在您房间里的服务指南上。

Smith:　I see. Thanks a lot.
　　　我明白了,非常感谢。

Li:　You're welcome, sir.
　　　不客气,先生。

Practice 2　Connecting an Incoming Call
实训项目2　外线电话的处理(接进)

Task of Service Practice 实训任务

◆ Mr. Wang calls switchboard operator of Beijing Hotel to speak with Mr. Winston in

Room 213.

王先生打电话到北京饭店找 213 房间的 Winston 先生。

◆ The operator should deal with two situations.

总机需应付两种情况。

Practice A：The line is busy.

实训 A：房间电话占线。

Practice B：This incoming call is connected well.

实训 B：电话接通。

Service Practice 服务实训

Now，let's begin the practice according to *Task of Service Practice*.

请按照上述实训任务开始实训。

Model of Service Practice 实训对照

20 2 Connecting an Incoming Call A. mp3

Wang：Mr. Wang Han，a caller.

Li：Li Lin，an operator.

Practice A

实训 A

Wang：Is this the Beijing Hotel?

是北京饭店吗？

Li：Yes，it is. May I help you?

是的，能为您效劳吗？

Wang：Yes. Could you put me through to Room 213，please?

请帮我接通 213 房间好吗？

Li：Certainly，sir. Just a moment，please.

好的，先生，请稍等。

（*After a while*）

（过了一会儿）

Li：I'm sorry. The line is busy. Would you like to hold on or call back?

抱歉，先生，电话占线。您愿意继续等待还是等会儿打来？

Wang：OK，I'll call back later. Thank you.

我等会儿打来吧，谢谢。

20 2 Connecting an Incoming Call B. mp3

Li：You're welcome，sir.

不客气，先生。

Practice B

实训 B

Li：Good morning. Beijing Hotel. May I help you?

早上好,北京饭店,能为您效劳吗?

Wang: I'd like to speak with Mr. Winston in Room 213, please.

我想找 213 房间的 Winston 先生接电话。

Li: How do you spell his name please?

请问他的姓名怎么拼?

Wang: W-I-N-S-T-O-N.

W-I-N-S-T-O-N。

Li: Could you repeat that, please?

请再重复一遍,好吗?

Wang: W-I-N-S-T-O-N.

W-I-N-S-T-O-N。

Li: Please hold the line, and I'll put you through.

请别挂电话,我这就给您接过去。

(*After a while*)

(过了一会儿)

Li: Thank you for waiting, sir. Please go ahead, you're through.

让您久等了,先生。您的电话已接通,请讲。

Practice 3   Connecting an Outgoing Call
实训项目 3   外线电话的处理(打出)

Task of Service Practice 实训任务

◆ Mike Smith wants to make a local call and a domestic long distance call in the hotel, so he asks the hotel operator for help.

迈克·史密斯先生想在其下榻的酒店打市内电话和国内长途,他打电话到总机寻求帮助。

◆ Practice A: The hotel operator explains to him in detail how to call directly from his room. We offer IDD and DDD services in our hotel. For calls outside Beijing, please dial "0" first and then the area code and the number you want. For calls inside Beijing, please dial "0" first and then the number you want.

实训 A:酒店总机详细地告诉他怎样在客房内直接拨打。我们酒店提供国际直拨和国内直拨的业务。打国内长途,请先拨"0",然后拨区域号码和您需要的电话号码。打北京市内电话,请先拨"0",再拨您需要的电话号码。

Practice B: The hotel operator helps to connect the call for the guest.

实训 B:酒店总机帮客人接通电话。

Service Practice 服务实训

Now, let's begin the practice according to *Task of Service Practice*.

请按照上述实训任务开始实训。

Model of Service Practice 实训对照

20 3 Connecting an Outgoing Call A. mp3

Li： Li Lin, an operator.

Smith： Mr. Mike Smith, a guest.

Practice A

实训 A

Li： Good morning. This is the hotel operator. May I help you?

早上好,酒店总机,能为您效劳吗?

Smith： Yes. I'd like to make a long distance call to my friend in Guangzhou. What should I do?

我想给我广州的朋友打一个长途电话,该怎么打呢?

Li： We offer IDD and DDD services in our hotel. You can call directly if you like.

我们酒店提供国际直拨和国内直拨的业务。如果您愿意,可以直拨。

Smith： Oh, would you please tell me how to dial directly?

哦,你能告诉我该怎么拨吗?

Li： Please dial "0" first and then the area code and the number you want.

请先拨"0",然后拨区域号码和您需要的电话号码。

Smith： I see. Well, what about calls inside Beijing? I'd like to call to Dong Dan Street.

我明白了,那么打北京市内电话呢? 我想打到东单大街。

Li： For calls inside Beijing, please dial "0" first and then the number you want.

请先拨"0",再拨您需要的电话号码。

Smith： Fine. Thanks a lot.

好的,非常感谢。

Li： You're welcome, sir.

不客气,先生。

20 3 Connecting an Outgoing Call B. mp3

Practice B

实训 B

Li： Good morning. This is the hotel operator. May I help you?

早上好,酒店总机,能为您效劳吗?

Smith： Yes. I'd like to make a long distance call to Guangzhou. Could you place the call for me?

我想打一个长途电话到广州。能不能帮我打通这个电话?

Li： Certainly, sir. I'd be glad to help you. What number are you calling, please?

好的,先生。很乐意为您效劳。请问您要打的电话号码是多少?

Smith： 8502-7665.

8502-7665。

Li： Would you please tell me to whom you'd like to speak?

请问您想和谁通话?

Smith：Mr. Wang Tao.

王涛先生。

Li：Do you want to make a pay call or a collect call?

您想打主叫付费电话还是对方付费电话？

Smith：A pay call, please.

主叫付费电话。

Li：May I have your name and room number, please?

请告诉我您的姓名和房间号码好吗？

Smith：Yes, my name's Mike Smith and I'm in Room 324.

好的，我叫 Mike Smith，住 324 房间。

Li：Thank you, sir. Could you hang up, please? I'll call you back as soon as I can.

谢谢。请先挂断，我会尽快给您回电话。

Hotel Knowledge
新酒店人须知

（1）While dial IDD, please dial the hotel code, international prefix, country code, area and subscriber number continuously, with no pause (exceeding 10 seconds), making you ensure that your dialing will not be interrupted.

打国际电话时，请将酒店代码、国际字冠、国家代码、地区代码和用户号码一次拨完，中间不要停顿（停顿时间不要超过 10 秒），以免造成呼叫中断。

（2）After completing your call, please see to it that the receiver is properly placed on the telephone hook. Otherwise the hour-meter will work continuously.

打完电话后请将电话挂好，否则电话将会继续计时。

Unit 21

Other Services

技能实训 21　其他服务

Main Services 主要服务

◆ Connecting room-to-room calls.
内线通话。
◆ The morning call.
叫醒电话。
◆ Leaving the message.
电话留言。

Skill Points 技能要点

◆ When the guest isn't in, the visitor can leave a message on the phone or leave a written message at the front desk.
当客人外出时,来访客人既可以通过电话留言,也可以直接到前台手写留言条。

◆ For a complete telephone message, the following information should be recorded.
记录完整的电话留言应该注意以下信息。

- Name of the person called and his room number.
  客人(即接电话人)姓名和房间号。
- Name of the caller and company.
  打电话人的姓名及其公司名称。
- The caller's telephone number and extension.
  打电话人的电话号码及其分机号。
- The caller's city.
  打电话人所在城市。
- The message.
  留言内容。
- The action requested and promised.
  打电话人要求的注意事项。

- The date and time of the call.

  打电话的日期及具体时间。

◆ In some hotels, the operators are not allowed to tell the caller about the guest's information, including his room number. So the operator could answer the call as following："I'm afraid I can't help you due to the regulations."

有的酒店禁止告诉查询人有关部门房客的情况,包括房号。这时可以回答查询人:"很抱歉,按规定我不能帮您这么做。"

◆ Some guidelines for good telephone conversation:

总机在接听客人电话时应注意:

- Try to visualize the person you are talking to. It is necessary to maintain a pleasant tone. Put a smile in your voice.

  试着想象和你通话的客人就在面前,说话时如平常般殷勤、恳切。

- Listen attentively and, if necessary, ask the caller to repeat.

  认真接听电话内容,如果有必要,请客人再重复一遍。

- Be patient and attentive.

  接听电话时既要耐心又要专心。

- Always answer the phone promptly before the second ring.

  通常电话铃响第二声之前就要快速拿起电话。

- Afterwards, hang up gently (don't bang down the phone abruptly).

  通话结束后,轻轻地挂断电话(切忌很生硬地摔电话)。

Practice 1   Connecting Room-to-Room Calls
实训项目1   客房间的通话

Task of Service Practice 实训任务

◆ Mr. Zhang wants to call his friend in room 501, but he doesn't know how to do that. The operator tells him to dial "1" first, then the room number directly from a house phone(In some hotels, guests need to dial "9" first).

张先生想给住在 501 房间的朋友打电话,但不知道该如何打。酒店总机告诉他先拨"1"再打内线直拨房号即可(注:有些酒店需先拨"9")。

◆ Mr. Zhang wants to check another guest Mike Smith's room number by name through operator. The operator refuses his request according to the hotel regulations.

张先生想通过总机查寻客人 Mike Smith 的房号,总机按照酒店规定委婉地拒绝其要求。

Service Practice 服务实训

Now, let's begin the practice according to *Task of Service Practice*.

请按照上述实训任务开始实训。

Model of Service Practice 实训对照

Li： Li Lin, an operator.

Zhang： Mr. Zhang Bin, a guest.

21 1 Connecting
Room-to-Room Calls
A. mp3

Practice A
实训 A

Li： This is the hotel operator. May I help you?

酒店总机，能为您效劳吗？

Zhang： Yes. I'd like to call my friend in his room. What should I do?

我想打电话到朋友的房间，该怎么打呢？

Li： Do you know the room number?

请问您知道房间号码吗？

Zhang： Yes, it's 501.

知道，501 房间。

Li： From a house phone, please dial "1" first, then the room number. And there is no charge for house calls.

打内线，请先拨"1"再拨您要的房间号码。内线电话不收费。

Zhang： I see. Thank you.

我明白了，谢谢。

Li： You're welcome, sir.

不客气，先生。

Practice B
实训 B

21 1 Connecting
Room-to-Room Calls
B. mp3

Zhang： Operator, may I have Mike Smith's room?

总机，请帮我接通 Mike Smith 的房间好吗？

Li： May I have the guest's last name?

能告诉我客人的姓吗？

Zhang： It's Smith, S-M-I-T-H.

Smith, S-M-I-T-H。

Li： Just a moment, please. I'll connect the line for you... I'm sorry, nobody is answering the phone.

请稍等，我这就为您转接……先生，很抱歉，房间没有人接听。

Zhang： Would you tell me the room number?

那你能告诉我他的房间号码吗？

Li： I'm afraid I can't help you due to hotel regulations. Would you like to leave him a message?

很抱歉，按规定我不能帮您这么做。您需要给他留言吗？

Zhang： Could you try again, please?

你能再试一次吗?

Li： …I'm sorry there is still no reply.

……抱歉,还是没有人接听。

Zhang： That's all. Thanks a lot.

那算了吧。谢谢。

Li： We look forward to another chance to serve you,sir.

先生,希望下次有机会能为您效劳。

Practice 2   Wake-up Call
实训项目 2   预订叫醒电话

Task of Service Practice 实训任务

◆ Mrs. Anna Chen asks the operator for the morning call.

酒店客人陈安娜女士向总机预订早叫服务。

◆ Practice A：The operator offers the guest a computer wake-up service.

实训 A：总机向客人提供计算机叫醒服务。

Practice B：The operator offers the guest an operator wake-up service.

实训 B：总机向客人提供人工叫醒服务。

Service Practice 服务实训

Now,let's begin the practice according to *Task of Service Practice*.

请按照上述实训任务开始实训。

Model of Service Practice 实训对照

Li： Li Lin,an operator.

Chen： Mrs. Anna Chen,a guest.

21 2 Wake-up Call
A. mp3

Practice A

实训 A

Li： Good evening. This is the Hotel Operator. May I help you?

晚上好,酒店总机,能为您效劳吗?

Chen： I'm leaving for Britain tomorrow morning. Will you please give me a wake-up call in the morning?

我明天早晨要出发去英国。早上请电话叫我起床好吗?

Li： Certainly,ma'am. At what time?

好的,夫人。几点?

Chen: At around 6:30 a.m.

大约 6 点半。

Li: We have a computer wake-up service. Please dial 5 first and then 0630 for the time. There must be five digits in the final number.

我们有计算机叫醒服务。请先拨 5,然后拨时间 0630。所拨的号码总共必须是五位数。

Chen: 50630. I see.

50630。哦,我明白了。

Li: That's right, ma'am. Our computer will record the time and your room number.

对了,夫人。我们的计算机将会记录您的叫早时间和房间号码。

Chen: Thank you.

谢谢。

Li: You're welcome, ma'am. Good night.

不客气,夫人。晚安。

Practice B

实训 B

21 2 Wake-up Call B. mp3

Chen: Operator. I wonder if your hotel has wake-up call service.

总机,我想请问你们酒店是否有叫早服务。

Li: Yes, Anyone who stays in our hotel can ask for the service. Would you like a wake-up call?

有的,夫人。每位住店客人都可以要求叫早服务。您需要吗?

Chen: Yes. I'd like to be woken up at 6:30 tomorrow morning.

是的,我想明天早晨 6 点半把我叫醒。

Li: What kind of call would you like, by phone or by knocking at the door?

您要哪种叫醒服务,电话叫醒还是敲门叫醒?

Chen: By phone, please. I don't want to disturb my neighbors.

电话叫醒,我不想吵醒别人。

Li: Sure. Let me confirm your name and room number.

好的。我需要确认你的姓名和房间号码。

Chen: Anna Chen in Room 345.

Anna Chen,住 345 房间。

Li: Mrs. Chen in Room 345, tomorrow morning at 6:30. OK, we'll give you a call in the morning. Anything else I can do for you?

陈女士,345 房间,明天早晨 6 点半需要叫醒。好的,我们明早 6 点半给您打电话。还有什么事需要我做的吗?

Chen: Nothing. thank you.

没有了。谢谢。

Li: You're welcome, ma'am, Good night.

不客气,夫人。晚安。

Practice 3　Taking the Message
实训项目 3　电话留言

Task of Service Practice 实训任务

◆ Mr. Tom Miles wants to speak to Mr. Smith in Beijing Hotel. But Mr. Smith happens to be out. So the operator suggests him leaving a message.

Tom Miles 先生打电话到北京饭店找 Smith 先生。碰巧 Smith 先生不在,总机建议他电话留言。

◆ The operator should confirm the following information:the caller's name,address,telephone number and message.

总机在电话留言中确认来电者的姓名、地址、电话及留言内容等信息。

Service Practice 服务实训

Now,let's begin the practice according to *Task of Service Practice*.
请按照上述实训任务开始实训。

Model of Service Practice 实训对照

21 3 Taking the Message. mp3

Li：　Li Lin,an operator.

Miles：　Mr. Tom Miles,a caller.

Li：　This is Beijing Hotel. May I help you?

北京饭店,能为您效劳吗?

Miles：Yes,could you put me through to Mr. Smith in Room 234,please?

请帮我接通 234 房间的 Smith 先生好吗?

Li：　Certainly,sir. Just a moment,please.

好的,先生,请稍等。

(*One minute later*)

(一分钟后)

Li：　I'm sorry,sir. Nobody is answering the phone. Would you like to leave a message for him?

很抱歉,先生。房间没有人接听。您想留言吗?

Miles：OK. I'm calling from Beijing Hai Xing Engineering Company. Next Tuesday we will hold a conference in Xi Yuan Tower. Please tell him to call back at 6632-4564.

好的。我从北京海星工程公司打来。下个星期我们将要在西苑饭店举行一个会议。请转告他回电话到 6632-4564。

Li： May I have your name?

能告诉我您的姓名吗?

Miles： Yes, this is Tom Miles.

我是 Tom Miles。

Li： Could you repeat your phone number, please?

请再重复一下您的电话号码好吗?

Miles： It's 6632-4564.

6632-4564。

Li： OK. Thank you. We will inform him as soon as possible when he comes back.

谢谢。客人回来后我们会尽快通知他。

Miles： Thanks a lot.

非常感谢。

Li： You're welcome, sir.

不客气,先生。

Practice Revision 实训回望

◆ When the operator is connecting an incoming collect call from overseas for the guest, what does he need to do?

◆ What should the operator pay attention to when recording a complete telephone message?

◆ Why are the telephone skills and abilities of dealing with varied situations especially essential for the operators?

◆ What kind of English ability does the operator in the hotel need to have?

Hotel Knowledge
新酒店人须知

Useful Expressions：

常用词汇：

IDD(International Direct Dial) 国际直拨电话

DDD(Domestic Direct Dial) 国内直拨电话

station-to-station call	叫号电话	outside call	外线电话
person-to-person call	叫人电话	internal call	内线电话
morning call/wake-up call	叫醒电话	local call	市内电话
collect call	对方付费电话	long distance call	长途电话
pay call	主叫付费电话	coin call	投币电话
international call	国际电话	domestic call	国内电话
credit card call	信用卡电话	emergency call	急救电话

switchboard	电话总机	telephone directory	电话指南
operator	话务员	area code	区号
telephone number	电话号码	extension number	分机号码
incoming/outgoing calls	打进/打出电话	dial	拨电话

Case and Improvement：The Hotel Operator Refused to Serve Her Guest
案例与提高：酒店总机拒绝为客人服务

Mr. Zhou would like to speak with the guest in Room 921, so he called the hotel operator and claimed that he wanted the guest for the very urgent matter. The operator put him through to the Room, but the line was busy. The operator told Mr. Zhou and asked him to wait a moment. Then the operator tried many times, but the line was still busy all the time. Gradually a long time wait and the operator's unchanging reply made Mr. Zhou very annoyed and impatient. He took it for granted that the operator was unwilling to serve him, so he got angry and yelled at her rudely. Though the operator felt wronged and didn't quarrel with Mr. Zhou, she showed her disapproval by refusing to put him though to Room 921 until the line in Room 921 was not engaged any more. Finally, Mr. Zhou complained to the hotel about the operator's service. And the operator was punished for her attitude towards the guest.

　　周先生给饭店总机打电话,要求接到 921 房间,称有急事找客人。但是,房内客人正在通电话,电话长时间占线,总机话务员为周先生转接了几次仍然占线。由于周先生听不到占线的声音,每次电话打到总机时,总机话务员只能告诉周先生占线,由于等的时间太长,而且话务员总是称占线,周先生便以为总机话务员不愿意为他转电话,便开始对总机话务员发火,说了一些不堪入耳的话。总机话务员感到十分委屈,虽然没有与周先生争吵,但向周先生表示将不再接他的电话,并在 921 客人挂断电话后仍然拒绝为周先生接通电话。最终导致周先生向饭店投诉。经过调查,饭店对总机话务员进行了相应的处罚。

Case Topic 案例话题

My opinion about the operator's service in the case.
我对案例中总机服务的看法。

> **Hotel Manager's Comments**
> **酒店经理点评**

　　为客人接通电话是总机话员义不容辞的工作职责,无论遇到什么情况都不应该拒绝客人转接电话的要求。在上述案例中,总机话务员虽然受到客人的误解,但不应该采取极端措施,变有理为无理。

　　(1) 话务员本可以在周先生发火之前向其做些解释,也许能得到周先生的理解,或者可以通过总机插入功能先打断一下921房间的客人,告知周先生有急事给他打电话。总机话务员也许怕打扰921房间的客人而未这么做,最终使问题的性质发生了变化。

(2)周先生在不了解真实情况下对总机话务员说了一些不适当的话,说明他素质不高。但是,总机话务员作为饭店的员工应该具备相应的素质,正确地控制自己的情绪,不能以牙还牙,拒绝客人的要求,以致损坏了饭店的形象。

(3)饭店的客人来自各个阶层,文化素养有很大差异,有的素质高,有的素质低,有的情绪变化无常,如何与不同性格的客人处理好关系是饭店员工应该上好的一课。应对客人的技巧在员工上岗前的培训中已经有过训练,但是在实际工作中有些员工缺乏应用技巧,把握不好时机,导致意想不到的问题发生。

Answers to "Practice Revision" 部分参考答案

◆ Why are the telephone skills and abilities of dealing with varied situations especially essential for the operators?

Because unlike the face-to-face talk, speaking on the phone is easy to cause misunderstanding if the switchboard operators' response is not appropriate.

◆ What kind of English ability does the operator in the hotel need to have?

The operators in the hotel need to complete the following services in English: connect calls for guests, provide wake-up and messages services, show guests how to use IDD and DDD, answer guests' inquiries, and page a guest etc. The above services require the operator not only to have a good knowledge of telephone skills, but also to have an ability of high level English.

Chapter Nine   Business Center（Ⅰ）

实训模块九   商务中心服务（一）

Unit 22
Secretarial Services

技能实训 22　文秘服务

Service Procedure 服务流程

◆ Greet the guest.
　　欢迎客人光临。

◆ Ask for the requirements in detail.
　　详细询问客人的具体需求。

◆ Introduce the services and answer the guest's questions.
　　介绍服务项目，回答客人问题。

◆ Take notes and confirm.
　　作记录，并确认。

◆ Ask the guest give his contact method and show the room card to confirm the name and the room number.
　　请客人告知联系方式并出示房卡以确认姓名，房间号。

◆ Promise to contact the guest immediately after accomplishment.
　　承诺完成后，立即联系客人。

◆ Fill in the fee schedule and ask for the way of payment.
　　填写收费明细单，弄清支付方式。

◆ Ask for signing or paying.
　　请客人签字或付费。

◆ Make a record of the service and put the document in a file.
　　做好服务记录并存档。

Skill Points 技能要点

◆ Inspect the equipment in advance and prepare for the work every day. Check the boxes of the copier and the printer regularly to see if there are enough papers of various sizes.
　　每天提前检查设备，做好准备工作。经常查看复印机和打印机盒内是否有足够的常用型号纸张。

◆ When the guest enters the Business Center, you should stand up with smile, greet the guest to show courtesy and respect, and ask what you can do for him. If you are busy with phone or another guest, please seat the guest first and tell him you will attend to him as soon as possible. After the service, you must keep the guest's name in mind so that you can recognize him next time.

当客人走进商务中心,你应该微笑着站起来,向客人表示礼貌和尊重,并询问有什么可以帮他的。如果你正在打电话或给其他客人提供服务,你可以请客人先坐下等候,并告诉客人,你会尽快为客人服务。提供服务后,你必须用心记住客人的名字,以便客人下次来的时候,你能认出来。

◆ You need to specify the printer settings to the guest in advance, such as suitable paper, color, orientation, size, version number, single or double-side, reduction or enlargement scale, number of sheets, and other relevant issues before printing. Show the sample and make a confirmation before printing in order to avoid misunderstanding.

打印前,需向客人详细说明打印设置,包括使用的纸张、颜色、方向、尺寸、版数、单双面、缩小或放大比例和张数等相关事宜。在打印前要先出示样本并确认,以免发生误会。

◆ Before copying, you should count the pages first and make sure what kind of paper will be used, and then make a sample for the guest in order to check the effect of the copier. Only when the guest makes the confirmation, a batch copy can be made. After binding and counting, start charging a fee for the service. The steps of the copying are as follows: lift the cover of the copier, place the original with face down on the platen glass, gently put off the cover, put the paper required in the tray, select the setting function of single or double-side, reduction or enlargement scale, number of sheets and so on, press the "start" button.

在复印前,你应该先数清页码,确认使用哪种纸张,然后复印一份样本给客人检查复印效果。只有在客人确认之后,才能批量打印。装订和确认数目后,再收取服务费用。复印的步骤如下:打开复印机盖,把原件正面朝下放至面盘上,轻轻盖上盖子,把需要的纸放在纸盘上,选择单面或双面,缩小或扩大,复印份数等,然后按"开始"按钮。

◆ When providing plastic lamination service, you should confirm the lamination size, choose the right lamination plastic, turn on the lamination machine for preheating(put it on 65℃), part the plastic and put the photo or paper in the middle. When the machine is ready(the light turns red), put the photo with plastic into the lamination machine.

提供塑膜服务时,你应该确认客人过塑的文件或者照片的尺寸,选择合适的过胶膜,将过塑机预热(将其温度调节至 65℃),将过胶膜打开,将纸张或者照片放在中间并调好。当机器预热结束后(红色指示灯变亮),将带有胶片的纸张放入过塑机。

◆ Fee schedule should include the following items: room number, guest name, specification, number of sheets, unit and total price.

收费明细需要包括下述内容:房间号、客人姓名、规格、张数、单价和总价。

◆ Any information in the documents of the guest should be treated in strict confidence. Any discarded file or electronic file left should be destroyed on the spot after the service.

客人的文件应该被严格保密。任何不用的纸质或电子文件都应该在服务完成后当场销毁。

Practice 1 Printing and Copying
实训项目1 打印和复印

Task of Service Practice 实训任务

◆ Mr. Andrew Jones，a guest of Room 2615 is going to print a two-page file and make 100 double-sided copies of it with white A4 paper in half an hour.

2615号房的客人Andrew Jones先生，想要在半小时内打印一个两页的文件，并用A4纸双面复印100份。

◆ Lu Yue helps Mr. Jones to insert the page number in the upper right hand corner，change the margin from 2cm to 1.5cm，and print the file double-sided. And then make 100 double-sided copies.

陆月帮助Jones先生在右上角插入页码，将页面边缘从2厘米调整至1.5厘米，并双面打印。然后双面复印100份。

◆ It is at the price of 3 yuan per single-sided piece，5 yuan per double-sided piece for copying，and 5 yuan per single-sided piece and 8 yuan per double-sided piece for printing in black and white.

单面复印3元一张，双面复印5元一张，单面黑白打印5元一张，双面黑白打印8元一张。

Service Practice 服务实训

Now，let's begin the practice according to *Task of Service Practice*.
请按照上述实训任务开始实训。

22 1 Printing and
Copying. mp3

Model of Service Practice 实训对照

Lu：   Lu Yue，a receptionist of the Business Center.

Jones：Andrew Jones，a guest of Room 2615.

Lu：   Good morning. Welcome to the Business Center. What can I do for you?
          早上好，欢迎您来到商务中心。请问有什么需要吗？

Jones：Good morning. Can you help me to print a file and make a batch copy?
          早上好。你们能帮助我打印一份文件并且批量复印吗？

Lu：   Sure.
          当然可以。

Jones：How much do you charge?

怎么收费的?

Lu： It depends on what kind of paper you choose. Here are the samples of the paper.

这取决于您选的纸张。这是纸张的样本。

Jones：I prefer white A4 paper.

我要白色 A4 纸。

Lu： Here is the price list. It is at the price of 3 yuan per single-sided piece，5 yuan per double-sided piece for copying，and 5 yuan per single-sided piece and 8 yuan per double-sided piece for printing in black and white.

这是价目单。单面复印 3 元一张，双面复印 5 元一张，单面黑白打印 5 元一张，双面黑白打印 8 元一张。

Jones：Oh，it's much higher than the prevailing price.

哦，这比市价高很多啊。

Lu： 20％ quantity discount is allowed for over 100 pieces for each item. How many pieces would you like to have?

如果每项超过 100 份的话，会有 20％的数量折扣。您要多少份呢?

Jones：I'd like to print a two-page file and make 100 copies of it.

我想打印一份两页的文件，并复印 100 份。

Lu： Single or double-sided pieces do you need?

您需要单面还是双面?

Jones：Double-sided pieces. I'm in urgent need of them. Can you finish it in half an hour?

双面。我急需这些材料。你能在半个小时内完成吗?

Lu： No problem. Double-sided print a two-page file and make 100 copies of it in half an hour，is that right?

没问题。在半小时内双面打印一个两页的文件，并双面复印 100 份，对吗?

Jones：Yes，that's right.

是的，没错。

Lu： Where is the electronic file?

电子版文件在哪儿呢?

Jones：In my flash disk. Here you are.

在我的 U 盘里。给你。

Lu： Let's print it first. Do you have any specific requirements?

我们先打印这个文件。您还有什么具体要求?

Jones：Will you page the file up for me in the upper right hand corner，and adjust the margin from 2cm to 1.5cm.

请你在右上角编上页码，并把页边距从 2 厘米调整到 1.5 厘米好吗?

Lu： The page number is inserted in the upper right hand corner. And the margin is adjusted from 2cm to 1.5cm. Please have a look at the preview. May I print it now?

在右上角插入页码。把页边距从 2 厘米调整到 1.5 厘米。请您看一下预览效果。我现在可以打印吗？

Jones： Yes.

可以。

Lu： Are you satisfied with the printing effect?

您对打印效果满意吗？

Jones： Good job.

不错。

Lu： Would you like to save it in your flash disk?

您需要在 U 盘中保存它吗？

Jones： Yes, please.

好的。

Lu： Here's your flash disk. Then I'd like to make one copy for you. Please have a look. How about the printing color?

这是您的 U 盘。那我给您复印一份。您看看，这墨色可以吗？

Jones： That's OK. How much?

挺好。多少钱？

Lu： According to the fee schedule, 100 double-sided pieces for copying with 20% discount and one double-sided piece for printing, the total is 408 yuan. Would you like to pay cash or charge to your room bill?

根据账单明细，双面复印 100 张有 20% 的折扣，双面打印 1 张，总额是 408 元。您是付现金还是记入您房间的账单？

Jones： To my room bill.

记账。

Lu： Would you like to show me your room card?

请您出示一下房卡？

Jones： Here you are.

给你。

Lu： Mr. Jones, your room number is 2615. Here's your room card. Would you like to sign for the bill?

Jones 先生，您的房间号是 2615。给您房卡。请您签下单吧？

Jones： Sure. How long it will last?

好的。需要多长时间？

Lu： About 10 minutes.

大概 10 分钟。

Jones： Would you like to send them to my room as soon as possible?

你能尽快送到我的房间吗？

Lu： I'd like to. I'll have them sent to your room in 20 minutes. Thank you for coming.

好的。我会派人在 20 分钟之内将这些文件送至您房间。感谢您的光临。

Practice 2   Scanning and Photo Processing
实训项目 2   扫描和图像处理

Task of Service Practice 实训任务

◆ Mr. Andrew Jones, a guest of Room 2615 is going to scan a photo and do some photo processing.

2615 号房的客人 Andrew Jones 先生, 想要扫描一张照片, 并做些图像处理。

◆ According to the requirements of Mr. Jones, Lu Yue scans a photo in 360dpi, make a red-eye removal and adjust the luminance and the contrast, and then she saves it as *My Family*. jpg under the root directory in the flash disk. Finally, she color prints it in 12 inches Glossy Photo Paper and laminates it.

按照 Jones 先生的要求, 陆月以 360dpi 的分辨率为他扫描一张照片, 并对照片进行去红眼、调整亮度和对比度的图像处理; 接着以"*My Family.jpg*"作为文件名将照片存储在 U盘的根目录下; 最后, 她用 12 英寸光面相纸彩打并塑封了照片。

◆ The price is at 15 yuan per piece for scanning, 30 yuan per piece for color printing and 30 yuan per piece for laminating.

价格是扫描每张 15 元, 彩打每张 30 元, 塑封每张 30 元。

Service Practice 服务实训

Now, let's begin the practice according to *Task of Service Practice*.
请按照上述实训任务开始实训。

22 2 Scanning and Photo Processing. mp3

Model of Service Practice 实训对照

Lu：   Lu Yue, a receptionist of the Business Center.

Jones：Andrew Jones, a guest of Room 2615.

Lu：   Good afternoon, Mr. Jones. Welcome to the Business Center. Can I help you?
下午好, Jones 先生。欢迎您来到商务中心。请问有什么需要吗?

Jones：Would you like to help me with scanning a photo and doing some photo processing?
你能帮我扫描照片, 并且作图像处理吗?

Lu：   I'd like to.
我很愿意。

Jones：Here is the photo.
照片给你。

Lu：   Where would you like to save it?
您想将照片存在哪里?

Jones：Under the root directory in this flash disk.

　　　　　　存在这个 U 盘的根目录里。

Lu： OK. What kind of picture resolution would you like to set?

　　　　好的。您想设定什么样的分辨率呢?

Jones： Oh,what do you recommend?

　　　　哦,你建议多少好呢?

Lu： If you print it,360dpi will be enough.

　　　　如果你要打印它的话,360pdi 的分辨率就可以了。

Jones： OK with me,you're the boss.

　　　　我没问题,听你的。

Lu： It's done. How about this?

　　　　好了。您看这个怎么样?

Jones： Well done.

　　　　真不错。

Lu： What would you like to do with it by means of Photoshop?

　　　　通过 Photoshop 软件,您想怎么处理这个照片呢?

Jones： Can you remove the red eyes caused by the flash?

　　　　你能去掉由于闪光灯产生的红眼吗?

Lu： Sure.

　　　　可以。

Jones： Well,it seems to be too dark. Could you please make adjustment of the luminance and the contrast?

　　　　嗯,看上去似乎太暗了。能调整下亮度和对比度吗?

Lu： Is that OK with you now?

　　　　您看现在这样行吗?

Jones： Good job.

　　　　真棒。

Lu： Which type do you prefer,JPG or GIF?

　　　　您想用哪种文件格式,JPG 还是 GIF?

Jones： JPG,please.

　　　　JPG。

Lu： How would you like to name it?

　　　　您想给文件起什么名字?

Jones： I'd like to name it "*My Family*".

　　　　文件名就叫"我的家庭"吧。

Lu： Would you like to save it under the root directory in your flash disk?

　　　　您需要在 U 盘的根目录中保存它吗?

Jones： Yes,please.

　　　　好的。

Lu： Do you need to print it?

您需要打印吗？

Jones： Yes, I'd like to color print it in 12 inches of Glossy Photo Paper and laminate it.

好的, 我要用 12 英寸的光面照片纸彩打然后塑封。

Lu： Do you think the photo looks good in the preview?

您看打印预览效果如何？

Jones： Fine.

挺好。

Lu： Well, let's print it. Wait a moment. Are you satisfied with the printing effect?

好的, 我们开始打印了。请稍等。您对这打印效果满意吗？

Jones： I'm quite satisfied with it.

我很满意。

Lu： Here is your flash disk. Please take it well. Then, I'd like to laminate it for you over there. Just a moment, please.

这是您的 U 盘。请收好。那么, 我去那边给您塑封。请稍等。

Jones： OK.

好的。

Lu： Well, it's done. Would that be all right?

好了, 完成了。您看行吗？

Jones： Good job. How much do you charge?

不错。多少钱啊？

Lu： According to the fee schedule, it is 15 yuan per piece for scanning, 30 yuan per piece for color printing and 30 yuan per piece for laminating. The total is 75 yuan. Would you like to pay cash or charge to your room bill?

根据账单明细, 扫描每张 15 元, 彩色打印每张 30 元, 塑封每张 30 元, 总额是 75 元。您是付现金还是记入您房间的账单？

Jones： To my room bill.

记账。

Lu： Mr. Jones, is Room 2615 yours?

Jones 先生, 您是 2615 号房吗？

Jones： Yes.

是的。

Lu： Would you like to sign for the bill?

请您签下单。

Jones： Sure. Thank You.

好的。谢谢你。

Lu： You're welcome. Hope to see you again.

不用谢。欢迎您下次光临。

Practice 3　Arranging Translation and Interpretation
实训项目3　安排笔译和口译

Task of Service Practice 实训任务

◆ Mr. Andrew Jones, a guest of Room 2615 is going to have a 20 000-word English file translated into Chinese in three days. And he also needs an Chinese-English interpreter to help him negotiate with his clients during the weekends.

2615号房的客人Andrew Jones先生，需要将一份2万字的英语文件在三天内翻译成中文，他还需要一位中英翻译周末陪同他去与客户谈判。

◆ Lu Yue helps Mr. Jones with an English-Chinese translation service and recommends a Chinese-English interpreter to accompany him.

陆月为Jones先生安排英译中服务，同时推荐一位中英口译陪同。

◆ It is at the price of 400 yuan per thousand words for a professional English-Chinese translation within 20 000 words in 3 days plus 15% surcharge. It will be charged 1 500 yuan per hour for negotiation purpose plus 15% surcharge.

将2万字以内的文件三天内由英文翻译成中文，收费每千字400元，另外加收15%服务费。以商务谈判为目的的翻译每小时收费1 500元，另外加收15%服务费。

Service Practice 服务实训

Now, let's begin the practice according to *Task of Service Practice*.
请按照上述实训任务开始实训。

Model of Service Practice 实训对照

22 3 Arranging
Translation and
Interpretation. mp3

Lu：　　Lu Yue, a receptionist of the Business Center.

Jones：　Andrew Jones, a guest of Room 2615.

Lu：　　Good morning, Mr. Jones. Welcome to the Business Center again. May I help you?
　　　　早上好，Jones先生，欢迎您再次来到商务中心。有什么需要我帮助吗？

Jones：　Morning, Miss Lu. Can you help me find someone to translate the English file into Chinese?
　　　　早上好，陆小姐。你能帮我找个人把英语文件翻译成中文吗？

Lu：　　Of course. What kind of file do you need to translate?
　　　　当然可以。您想翻译什么类型的文件呢？

Jones：　A legal document. How much do you charge?
　　　　法律文件。怎么收费呢？

Lu：　　When do you need it? And how many words are there in the file?

您什么时候需要呢？文件一共多少字呢？

Jones： I'm in urgent need of it in 3 days. And there're almost 20 000 words in it.

我三天内急需这个文件。大约有 2 万字。

Lu： Here is the price list. It is at the price of 400 yuan per thousand words for a professional English-Chinese translation within 20 000 words in 3 days plus 15％ surcharge.

这是价目单。三天内完成 2 万字以内的英译中，收费每千字 400 元，额外加 15％ 服务费。

Jones： Why do you charge 15％ surcharge?

为什么要加收 15％ 的费用呢？

Lu： As there isn't a suitable professional translator in our hotel, we have to contact the translation company to arrange one for you. The company gives us special offers for professional translation. The 15％ surcharge is the commission of our hotel.

我们酒店没有合适的专业翻译，我们需要和翻译公司联系为您安排一位。这个翻译公司以特价向我们酒店提供专业翻译。15％额外费用是我们酒店收取的佣金。

Jones： Oh, I see. I'm also willing to find a Chinese-English interpreter to help me negotiate with the clients during the weekends. How to charge?

哦，我明白了。我还需要请一位中英文口译，来协助我在本周末与客户进行的谈判。怎么收费呢？

Lu： The interpreter will be paid by hour. It will be charged 1 500 yuan per hour for negotiation purpose plus 15％ surcharge.

口译是按小时收费的。商务谈判口译每小时收费 1 500 元，另外加收 15％服务费。

Jones： When can I have a personal interview with the interpreter?

我什么时候与这位翻译面谈呢？

Lu： I'll contact the translation company and arrange the interview for you as soon as possible. Mr. Jones, would you still like to charge to your room bill?

我会尽快联系翻译公司安排这次面谈的。Jones 先生，还是记入您的房间账单吗？

Jones： Yes, to my room bill.

是的，记账。

Lu： Would you like to sign for the form? It will be charged after the interview.

请您在这个表格签字。在您和翻译面谈后再收费。

Jones： Sure.

好的。

Lu： How can I contact you?

我怎么联系您呢？

Jones： My cell phone number is 13889298225.

我手机号是 13889298225。

Lu： 13889298225，is that right?

13889298225，对吗?

Jones： Yes.

对的。

Lu： I'll inform you as soon as possible.

我会尽快通知您的。

Jones： That's fine. Thank you.

好的，谢谢您。

Lu： You are welcome. Hope to see you again.

不客气。下次再见。

Hotel Knowledge
新酒店人须知

◆ The responsibilities of the secretary at the business center are as follows：make the office in order and clean，be familiar with Business Center services，procedures，regulations and equipments，use and maintain the facilities at the business center，provide secretarial services，be responsible for up-to-date filing system for the Business Center and report to the supervisor of the Business Center.

商务中心的文员的工作职责如下：保持办公区域的有序和整洁；熟悉商务中心的所有服务项目、服务流程、服务规定和服务设备；使用和维护商务中心的设施；提供文秘服务；负责更新商务中心的档案系统；向商务中心主管进行汇报。

◆ The appliances at the Business Center include copier，printer，computer/desktop，scanner，binding machine，shredder，fax machine，lamination machine，telephone，calculator，and so on.

商务中心使用的设备主要包括复印机、打印机、计算机、扫描机、装订机、碎纸机、传真机、塑封机、电话、计算器等。

◆ The main secretarial services at the Business Center include English and Chinese typing，black & white printing，color printing，scanning，black & white copy，color copy，transparency，binding，laminating，translation and interpretation.

商务中心的秘书服务主要包括：中英文打字、黑白打印、彩印、扫描、黑白复印、彩色复印、胶片影印、装订、塑封、笔译和口译等服务。

◆ Settlement can be done in cash，by credit card or charged to the guest's room bill. When charging in cash，you should fill in the fee schedule，get the guest's signature and give the guest receipt or invoice after settlement. When charging by credit card，you should fill in the fee schedule，make sure the amount is correct，swipe a credit card，obtain the guest's signature on the voucher and give the guest receipt or invoice. When charging to the room bill, you should confirm the guest's room number and name, fill in the fee schedule and get the guest's signature on the bill, and charge to the guest's room bill.

费用可以以现金、银行卡结算,也可以计入房间账单。当以现金结算时,你需要填写收费明细单,让客人签名,现金结算完毕后给客人提供收据或发票。当以信用卡结算时,你应该填写收费明细单,确认后刷卡,让客人在刷卡单上签名,将信用卡回执和发票给客人。当采用计入房间账单方式收费时,先确认顾客房间号和姓名,填写收费明细单,请客人在账单上签名,然后将费用计入房间账单。

Unit 23

Express Service

技能实训 23　快递服务

Service Procedure 服务流程

◆ Greet the guest.

欢迎客人光临。

◆ Ask the guest about his service needs.

询问客人的服务需求。

◆ Make clear the courier address and the approximate time.

弄清快递地址及快递大概时间要求。

◆ Take notes and confirm.

做记录，并确认。

◆ Ask the guest to give contact method and show the room card to confirm the name and the room number.

请客人告知联系方式并出示房卡以确认姓名和房间号。

◆ Promise to contact the guest immediately after sending or receiving.

承诺发送或接收后立即联系客人。

◆ Fill in the fee schedule and ask the way of payment.

填写收费明细单，询问支付方式。

◆ Ask for signing or paying.

请客人签字或付费。

◆ Contact the guest immediately after sending or receiving.

接收或发出后立即联系客人。

◆ Make a record of the service and put the document in a file.

做好服务记录并存档。

Skill Points 技能要点

◆ If the guest wants to send packages by express service, you should get the relevant information of the packages and the receiver's address. Confirm if there is any fragile item, valuable item or any special requirements on handling the package. Introduce the different express services of the different courier companies for the guest's reference. Weigh the package and ask the guest to fill in the express application form. Confirm the total charges with the guest and promise to ask the courier company to take it as soon as possible.

如果客人想要用快递寄送包裹,你应该了解包裹的相关信息,收件人的地址。并确保包裹里是否有易碎物品,昂贵物品以及处理包裹时的特殊要求。向客人介绍不同快递公司的不同快递服务以供客人参考。称量包裹的重量,然后请客人填写快递申请单。和客人确认总价格,并承诺尽快让快递公司收取包裹。

Practice　Sending and Receiving Packages
实训项目　发送和接收包裹

Task of Service Practice 实训任务

◆ Mr. William Swift, a guest of Room 3100 is going to send a 2-kilogram package, with a Barbie Doll in it as his daughter's birthday gift to Shanghai by EMS overnight express service.

3100 号房的客人 William Swift 先生,想要用 EMS 的第二天到达服务发一个装有芭比娃娃的 2 公斤重的包裹去上海,作为他女儿的生日礼物。

◆ Lu Yue helps Mr. Swift to wrap the gift with light pink wrapping paper with red rose pattern on it. She makes a bowknot with a colorful string. M-size transport package is also used for protection from damage. She asks EMS to take the package. At the same time, she receives another package from Hong Kong for Mr. Swift.

陆月用带有红色玫瑰图样的淡粉色包装纸来为 Swift 先生包装礼物。她还用彩带打了一个蝴蝶结。为避免损坏,还用了中号的运输包装盒。她让 EMS 公司取走包裹,同时,她收到了从香港寄给 Swift 先生的另外一个包裹。

◆ Wang Na sends the package received to Mr. Swift's room.

王娜把收到的包裹送到 Swift 先生的房间。

◆ The gift wrapping charges 50 yuan. The M-size transport packing is 30 yuan and the overnight express costs 60 yuan per kilogram.

礼物包装收费 50 元,中号运输包装收费 30 元,第二日送达快递费是每公斤 60 元。

Service Practice 服务实训

Now, let's begin the practice according to *Task of Service Practice*.
请按照上述实训任务开始实训。

Model of Service Practice 实训对照

23 Sending and Receiving Packages . mp3

Lu：　Lu Yue, a receptionist of the Business Center.
Swift：William Swift, a guest of Room 3100.

Wang： Wang Na, a housekeeper of the Housekeeping Center.

Lu： Good morning, Mr. Swift. Welcome to the Business Center. What can I do for you?

早上好,Swift 先生。欢迎您来到商务中心。请问有什么需要吗?

Swift： Good morning. Would you like to help me to send a package to Shanghai?

早上好。你能帮我往上海发个包裹吗?

Lu： Sure. Is there anything valuable or breakable in it?

当然可以。请问是否有贵重物品或易碎物品?

Swift： No, there isn't. It's just a Barbie Doll as a birthday gift to my daughter. Can you wrap it for me?

不,都没有。只是给我女儿的生日礼物芭比娃娃。请您帮我包装一下好吗?

Lu： Of course. What color does your daughter like?

当然可以。您女儿喜欢什么颜色?

Swift： Pink and rosy.

粉色和玫瑰色。

Lu： How about this kind of wrapping paper? Light pink wrapping paper with red rose pattern on it.

这种包装纸可以吗? 有红色玫瑰花图案的淡粉色包装纸。

Swift： I believe that she would like it.

我相信她会喜欢的。

Lu： Do you like to make a bowknot with this colorful string?

您想用这个彩色包装带打个蝴蝶结吗?

Swift： That's great.

太好了。

Lu： Which do you prefer for the transport package for protection from damage, S, M or L-size?

为避免损坏,运输包装您想用哪种,小号,中号还是大号?

Swift： M-size is enough.

中号。

Lu： Which courier company do you choose, DHL or EMS?

您选哪家快递公司,是中外运敦豪或是邮政特快专递?

Swift： EMS is OK.

就 EMS 吧。

Lu： There are two services, overnight and three-day delivery.

有两种方式,明天送达或三天送达。

Swift： Tomorrow is my daughter's birthday. I'd like to choose the service of overnight.

明天就是我女儿的生日,明天送达。

Lu： Would you like to fill in the express application form?

请您填写快递申请单。

Swift： OK. How much does it cost?

好的。多少钱?

Lu： According to the fee schedule, the gift wrapping charges 50 yuan. The M-size transport packing is 30 yuan and the overnight express costs 60 yuan per kilogram. The weight of the package is 2 kilograms. So the total is 200 yuan. Would you like to pay cash or charge to your room bill?

根据账单明细,礼物包装收费 50 元。中号运输包装收费 30 元,明日送达快递费是每公斤 60 元。您的包裹 2 公斤重。总计收费 200 元。您是付现金还是记入您房间的账单?

Swift： To my room bill.

记账。

Lu： Mr. Swift. Is your room number 3100?

Swift 先生,您的房间号是 3100 吗?

Swift： Yes, it is.

是的。

Lu： Would you like to sign for the bill?

请您签单好吗?

Swift： Sure. If there is any express for me, please send it to my room.

好的。如果有给我的传真,请给我送到我的房间。

Lu： I'd like to. I'll have it sent to your room as soon as possible if there is any express. I'll ask the EMS to take this package immediately.

好的。如果有任何快递,我会尽快找人送给您的。我马上让 EMS 来取件。

Swift： Bye.

再见。

Wang： Good afternoon, Mr. Swift. I am Wang Na of the Housekeeping Center.

下午好,Swift 先生。我是客房服务中心的王娜。

Swift： Good afternoon, Miss Wang.

王小姐,下午好。

Wang： Miss Lu Yue at the Business Center asked me to tell you that the EMS has taken your package and the package will reach Shanghai tomorrow morning. And there is another package from Hong Kong for you. Here you are.

商务中心的陆月让我告诉您,EMS 已经取走了您的包裹,您的包裹明天早上到达上海。还有一个从香港发给您的包裹。给您。

Swift： Oh, that's great. I'm looking forward to it for a few days. Thanks a lot. Is it free for receiving the packages?

啊,太好了。我等这个包裹好几天了。非常感谢。收包裹免费吗?

Wang： Yes, the receiving packages service is free. Would you like to sign here to confirm that you have received the package?

是的,收包裹服务免费。请您在这里签字,确认您收到了包裹,好吗?

Swift: That's OK.

好的。

Wang: If you need anything else, please contact us. See you.

如果您有任何需要,请联系我们。再见。

Swift: See you.

再见。

Hotel Knowledge

新酒店人须知

◆ The express application form includes name and address of the courier company, types of express service, sender's name, contact method and address, receiver's name, contact method and address, details of contents, weight and dimensions, indication of insurance required, and guest signature.

快递申请表包括快递公司的名字和地址;快递服务项目;发件人的姓名,联系方式和地址;收件人的姓名,联系方式和地址;邮寄物品详情;重量和体积;保险说明;客人签字。

Chapter Ten   Business Center（Ⅱ）

实训模块十　商务中心服务（二）

Unit 24
Tickets Booking Services

技能实训 24　票务服务

Service Procedure 服务流程

◆ Greet the guest.

欢迎客人光临。

◆ Ask the specific requirements of booking the ticket.

询问订票的详细要求。

◆ Take notes and confirm.

做记录,并确认。

◆ Ask the guest to give the contact method and show the room card and ID card or passport.

请客人告知联系方式,出示房卡、身份证或护照。

◆ Promise to contact the guest immediately after booking.

承诺票订到后,立即联系客人。

◆ Fill in the fee schedule and ask the way of payment.

填写收费明细单,询问支付方式。

◆ Ask for signing or paying.

请客人签字或付费。

◆ Send the ticket to the guest's room when receiving the ticket.

当收到票时,将票送到客人的房间。

◆ Make a record of the service and put the document in a file.

做好服务记录并存档。

Skill Points 技能要点

◆ As booking ticket online enters the mainstream, it is necessary for the Business Center to offer the booking ticket online services, especially for the foreign guest who is not familiar with the Chinese interface of some booking websites.

随着网上订票已经成为主流,尤其是对那些不熟悉某些网站中文界面的外国客人来说,商务中心提供网上订票服务就是十分必要的了。

◆ When booking the air ticket, you should get the detailed requirements of the guest first, confirm the information, check the airline information online to find a suitable flight which is acceptable to the guest, and contact the airline online or by phone to book the ticket and get the confirmation from the airline. Show the confirmation with details including flight number, aircraft model, departure and arrival time, airports and terminals, and so on.

订机票的时候，你应该了解客人的详细需要，确认信息，网上查询航班信息，找到一个可以被客人接受的航班，通过网络或电话联系航空公司订票，从航空公司获取确认信息。向客人出示详细的确认信息，包括航班号、航班机型、抵离时间、机场和航站楼等。

◆ When booking the group tickets, it is necessary for the Business Center to establish a good cooperative relationship with all kinds of ticket agencies in order to do the best services for the hotel guests.

订团体票的时候，商务中心应该和各类订票机构维持良好的合作关系，以便为酒店客人提供最好的服务。

Practice 1　Booking Air Tickets Online
实训项目 1　网上订机票

Task of Service Practice 实训任务

◆ Mr. Alan Hansen, a guest of Room 6805, is going to book a first-class air ticket from Beijing to Shanghai in the morning on Dec. 24, and a first-class return ticket from Shanghai to Beijing in the afternoon on Dec. 30.

6805 号房的客人 Alan Hansen 先生，想要订一张 12 月 24 日从北京飞往上海的头等舱机票和一张 12 月 30 日从上海到北京的头等舱返程票。

◆ Bai Xue helps Mr. Hansen to check the airline information online and book the air tickets of CA1501 and CA1532. CA1501 is to take off from T3 Terminal of Beijing Capital International Airport at 8:30 and arrive at T2 Terminal of Shanghai Hongqiao International Airport at 10:40 on Dec. 24. The aircraft model is Boeing 777. CA1532 is to take off from T2 Terminal of Shanghai Hongqiao International Airport at 13:55 and arrive at T3 Terminal of Beijing Capital International Airport at 16:15 on Dec. 30. The aircraft model is Airbus A330.

白雪帮助 Hansen 先生在网上查找航班信息，帮他订了 CA1501 航班和 CA1532 航班的机票。CA1501 预计 12 月 24 日上午 8:30 从北京首都国际机场 T3 航站楼起飞，10:40 到达上海虹桥国际机场 T2 航站楼。机型是波音 777。CA1532 预计 12 月 30 日下午 13:55 从上海虹桥国际机场 T2 航站楼起飞，16:15 到达北京首都国际机场 T3 航站楼。机型是空客 A330。

◆ The air tickets charge 4 790 yuan , plus 240 yuan for fuel surcharge, 100 yuan for airport tax and 40 yuan for insurance premium. Mr. Hansen pays by Air China Phoenix Miles Card. And the booking service is free for the hotel guest.

机票收费 4 790 元的，加上 240 元燃油附加费，100 元机场税费和 40 元保险费。Hansen 先生用国航凤凰知音卡付款。住店客人免收订票费。

Service Practice 服务实训

Now, let's begin the practice according to *Task of Service Practice*.
请按照上述实训任务开始实训。

24 1 Booking Air
Tickets Online. mp3

Model of Service Practice 实训对照

Bai： Bai Xue, a receptionist of the Business Center.
Hansen： Mr. Alan Hansen, a guest of Room 6805.

Bai： Good morning. Welcome to the Business Center. What can I do for you?
早上好，欢迎您来到商务中心。请问有什么需要吗？

Hansen： Good morning. Would you like to help me to book air tickets online?
早上好。你能帮我在网上订机票吗？

Bai： Sure. May I have your room card?
当然可以。您能出示一下房卡吗？

Hansen： Here you are.
给你。

Bai： Mr. Hansen. Your room number is 6805. May I have your detailed requirements?
Hansen 先生，您的房间号是 6805。您能告诉我您的具体要求吗？

Hansen： I'd like to book a first-class air ticket from Beijing to Shanghai in the morning on Dec. 24 and a first-class return ticket from Shanghai to Beijing in the afternoon on Dec. 30.
我想要订一张 12 月 24 日从北京飞往上海的头等舱机票和一张 12 月 30 日从上海到北京的头等舱返程票。

Bai： Which airline do you prefer? Do you have special requirments for the aircraft model?
您想要乘坐哪家航空公司的航班？您对机型有要求吗？

Hansen： I have joined the FFP of China Air and I have the Phoenix Miles Card of Air China. Any aircraft model in China Air can be accepted.
我已加入国航的常客计划，我有国航凤凰知音卡。国航的任何机型都可以。

Bai： Just a moment please. A first-class air ticket from Beijing to Shanghai in the morning on Dec. 24 and a first-class return ticket from Shanghai to Beijing in the afternoon on Dec. 30. Is that right?
您稍等。一张 12 月 24 日上午从北京飞往上海的头等舱机票和一张 12 月 30 日下午从上海飞往北京的头等舱返程票。是这样吗?

Hansen：Yes.

是的。

Bai：There are 5 flights available in the morning on Dec. 24. The flights will take off at 6:30,7:30,8:30,9:30 and 10:30 respectively. The first-class prices of the flights are the same, 2 490 yuan. Which one do you like to take?

12 月 24 日上午有五架航班有票,起飞时间分别是 6:30、7:30、8:30、9:30 和 10:30。这些航班的头等舱票价相同,都是 2 490 元。您想乘坐哪个航班?

Hansen：8:30 looks good,neither very early nor very late. How about the return flight?

8:30 那班看上去不错,既不早,也不晚。返程航班情况如何?

Bai：There are 4 flights available in the afternoon on Dec. 30. The flights will take off at 13:55,14:55,16:55 and 17:55 respectively. The first-class price of the 13:55 flight is 2 300 yuan,while the other three are the same, 2 490 yuan. Which one would you like to take?

12 月 30 日下午有四架航班有票。起飞时间分别为 13:55、14:55、16:55 和 17:55。13:55 的航班头等舱票价是 2 300 元,而其他三架航班的头等舱票价相同,都是 2 490元。您想乘坐哪个航班?

Hansen：I'd like to choose 13:55.

我选 13:55 的航班。

Bai：CA1501 is to take off from T3 Terminal of Beijing Capital International Airport at 8:30 and arrive at T2 Terminal of Shanghai Hongqiao International Airport at 10:40 on Dec. 24. The aircraft model is Boeing 777. CA1532 is to take off from T2 Terminal Shanghai Hongqiao International Airport at 13:55 and arrive at T3 Terminal of Beijing Capital International Airport at 16:15 on Dec. 30. The aircraft model is Airbus A330. Are you sure about that?

CA1501 预计 12 月 24 日上午 8:30 从北京国际机场 T3 航站楼起飞,10:40 到达上海虹桥国际机场 T2 航站楼。机型是波音 777。CA1532 预计 12 月 30 日 13:55 从上海虹桥国际机场 T2 航站楼起飞,16:15 到达北京国际机场 T3 航站楼。机型是空客 A330。可以吗?

Hansen：Sure.

确定。

Bai：Do you need any insurance?

您需要保险吗?

Hansen：Yes,please.

我需要。

Bai：The total is 5 170 yuan,including 4 790 yuan for air tickets,240 yuan for fuel surcharge,100 yuan for airport tax and 40 yuan for insurance premium. Would you pay by your credit card?

总价是 5 170 元,包括 4 790 元的机票费,240 元燃油附加费、100 元机场税费和 40 元保险费。您是用信用卡付款吗?

Hansen：Yes, by my Air China Phoenix Miles Card.

是的，用我的国航凤凰知音卡付款。

Bai：Would you like to login in first?

请您先登录。

Hansen：OK. Is that all right?

好的。可以了吗？

Bai：May I have your passport number and telephone number?

请说下您的护照号码和电话号码好吗？

Hansen：Here is my passport. My cellphone number is 13681795786.

这是我的护照。我的手机号是 13681795786。

Bai：Would you like to enter your password of payment?

请您输入支付密码好吗？

Hansen：Is that OK?

可以了吗？

Bai：It's done. Do you get the short message from the China Air?

完成了。您收到国航的短信了吗？

Hansen：Not yet.

还没呢。

Bai：I'd like to print the confirmation for you?

我给您打印确认函吧。

Hansen：Thank you.

谢谢。

Bai：Here is the confirmation. You can print the tickets at the airport or go aboard by passport directly.

这是确认函。您可以在机场打印机票，或直接凭护照登机。

Hansen：That's OK. Oh, I get the short message. How much for the booking service?

好的。哦，我收到短信了。订票服务收多少钱啊？

Bai：It is free for our hotel guest. Would you like to sign here for the service?

酒店的客人免费。请您签字好吗？

Hansen：OK. Thanks a lot. See you.

好的。多谢。再见。

Bai：See you.

再见。

Practice 2　Ordering Group Tickets
实训项目 2　订购团体票

Task of Service Practice 实训任务

◆ Mr. Gregory Meyer, a guest of Room 3780, is going to order group tickets for *New Year's*

China Tour of Orchestras National de Lyon which is to celebrate 50 years of Sino-French Diplomatic Relations. It will be held at National Grand Theater on Jan. 4.

3780 号房的 Gregory Meyer 先生想要预订 1 月 4 日为庆祝中法建交五十周年在国家大剧院举办的里昂国立管弦乐团新年音乐会中国巡演的团体票。

◆ Bai Xue，a receptionist of the Business Center，books 15 tickets at the price of 450 yuan per ticket for Mr. Meyer. It is free to deliver the ticket in Beijing，and payment can be done after receiving the tickets.

商务中心的接待员白雪以每张 450 元的价格为 Meyer 先生订了 15 张票。北京地区免费送票，票到付款。

◆ Mr. Meyer is also going to book 15 HST(High Speed Train)tickets on Jan. 24.

Meyer 先生还想订 15 张 1 月 24 日的高铁票。

◆ Bai Xue tells him the train ticket can be booked only 20 days in advance. It's not the right time for booking. And it is difficult to book the ticket in the coming Spring Festival travel rush. She will try her best to book it for Mr. Meyer as soon as the sales start. But she can't promise to succeed in booking.

◆ 白雪说火车票提前 20 天才开始售票。现在不是订票时间。即将到来的春运期间预订高铁票是很难的。火车票一开始发售她就会尽快为 Meyer 先生订票，但她不能保证一定能够成功。

Service Practice 服务实训

Now，let's begin the practice according to *Task of Service Practice*.
请按照上述实训任务开始实训。

24 2 Ordering
Group Tickets. mp3

Model of Service Practice 实训对照

Bai： Bai Xue，a receptionist of the Business Center.

Meyer：Gregory Meyer，a guest of Room 3780.

Bai： Good morning. Welcome to the Business Center. What can I do for you?
          早上好。欢迎您来到商务中心。请问有什么需要吗?

Meyer：Good morning. Can you help me to book group tickets for shows?
          早上好。你能帮我订到演出的团体票吗?

Bai： Sure. Which show do you like to see?
          当然可以。您想看什么演出呢?

Meyer：I'd like to book tickets for New Year's China Tour of Orchestras National de Lyon. It is to celebrate 50 years of Sino-French Diplomatic Relations and will be held at National Grand Theater on Jan. 4.
          我想订里昂国立管弦乐团新年音乐会中国巡演的票。这个巡演是为庆祝中法建交五十周年而举办的，1 月 4 日在国家大剧院上演。

Bai： How many tickets do you need?

您需要几张票？

Meyer： 15 tickets.

15 张票。

Bai： Which price do you choose，200，300，500，650，760，880 or 1 080 yuan?

您选什么价位的，是 200、300、500、650、760、880 还是 1 080 元的？

Meyer： I prefer 15 tickets at 500 yuan. Is there any discount for group tickets?

我想要 15 张 500 元的票。团体票有折扣吗？

Bai： I'd like to contact the ticket agency to inquire. Just a moment please.

我可以联系票务公司咨询一下。请您稍等一下。

Meyer： That's OK.

好的。

Bai： The ticket agency gives you 10% discount for group tickets. Are you sure to book?

票务代理可以给团队票打九折。您确定订票吗？

Meyer： That's great. I'd like to book.

太好了。我订票。

Bai： Would you like to show me your room card?

您能出示房卡吗？

Meyer： Here you are.

在这儿呢。

Bai： Mr. Gregory Meyer in Room 3780，books 15 tickets at 450 yuan per ticket for New Year's China Tour of Orchestras National de Lyon held at National Grand Theater on Jan. 4. Is that right?

3780 号房的 Gregory Meyer 先生预订 15 张 1 月 4 日在国家大剧院上演的里昂国立管弦乐团新年音乐会中国巡演 450 元价位的团体票。对吗？

Meyer： That's right.

对。

Bai： May I have your cellphone number?

请问您的手机号？

Meyer： 13668976534.

13668976534。

Bai： It's all done. The tickets will be delivered tomorrow. It is free to deliver the ticket in Beijing，and payment can be done after receiving the tickets. I'd like to contact you then and have the tickets sent to your room as soon as possible.

全订好了。北京地区免费送票，票到付款。我会尽快联系您，并让人把票送到您的房间。

Meyer： Thanks a lot. Would you like to help me with HST group tickets to Shanghai?

多谢。你能再帮我订去上海的高铁团体票吗？

Bai： Which day's tickets would you like?

您要订哪天的票呢?

Meyer：15 HST tickets on Jan. 24.

15 张 1 月 24 日的高铁票。

Bai：The train tickets can be booked only 20 days in advance. It's not the right time for booking. We can pay attention to it in advance. But as you know, it is difficult for us to book the HST ticket in the coming Spring Festival travel rush. We'll try our best to book for you as soon as the sales start. But we can't promise to succeed in booking.

火车票提前 20 天才开始售票。现在不是订票时间。我们会为您提前关注此票。不过您也知道,即将到来的春运高铁票是很难订的。火车票一开始发售我们就会尽快为您订票,但我们不保证一定能订到。

Meyer：Yeah,I see what you mean.

是的,我明白你说的情况。

Bai：Would you like to provide the detailed information including the names and IDs or passport numbers of your group?

您能提供您的具体需求和团队成员的姓名、身份证号或护照号等详细信息吗?

Meyer：Of course. I'll give the specific information to you tomorrow. How much for the booking service?

好的,我明天给你具体信息。订票服务多少钱?

Bai：The booking service is free for our hotel guest. Would you like to sign here for confirmation?

我们酒店的客人享受免费订票服务。请您在这里签字以便确认好吗?

Meyer：That's OK.

好的。

Bai：If you need anything else,please contact us. See you.

如果您有任何需要,请联系我们。再见。

Meyer：See you.

再见。

Hotel Knowledge
新酒店人须知

◆ Bank of China-Air China Phoenix Miles Credit Card offers the basic functions and standard services of Bank of China Credit Card. In addition, with the credit card, passengers can enjoy air mileage accumulation and other Phoenix Miles membership services. As soon as the accrued mileage reaches the required level, the passenger can get free trips or free class upgrades.

中国银行-国航凤凰知音卡可以提供中国银行信用卡的基础功能和标准服务。另外,乘客使用此卡可以享有航空里程累积和其他凤凰知音成员的服务项目。当乘客累积的里程数达到所需要求,乘客可以获得免费旅程和免费升舱服务。

◆ The best 3 airlines in China are as follows:

中国排名前三的航空公司如下:

Air China(CA)　中国国际航空公司

China Eastern Airlines(MU)　中国东方航空公司

China Southern Airlines(CZ)　中国南方航空(集团)公司

◆ The ticket agencies for shows on line in China are as follows:

中国网上演出票务代理如下:

http://www.t3.com.cn/中演票务

http://www.damai.cn/大麦网

http://www.228.com.cn/永乐网

◆ http://www.12306.cn is the only official website authorized for booking train tickets online.

12306 铁路客户服务中心是唯一授权的网上预订火车票官方网站。

◆ During the Spring Festival travel rush hour, the train ticket is in great demand and difficult to book. It is necessary for the Business Center to make a good plan to help the guest in advance. If there is no possibility to book the ticket, you'd better tell the guest about it in advance and suggest the guest to change the itinerary or means of transport.

春运期间,火车票需求量大,很难订到,因此商务中心提前做好预案很重要。如果不能订到票,最好提前告知客人情况,并建议客人调整行程或改乘其他交通工具。

Unit 25
Office Facilities Services
技能实训 25　办公设施服务

Service Procedure 服务流程

Renting Meeting Room and Equipment
出租会议室及设备

◆ Greet the guest.

　问候客人。

◆ Find out what the guest wants to get.

　了解客人需求。

◆ Introduce the relative information to the guest.

　介绍相关信息。

◆ Get the following information from the guest.

　从客人处获取下列信息。

　　The name and telephone number of the guest.

　　客人姓名和电话号码。

　　The date and time of the meeting, the number of the attendees and the type of the meeting.

　　会议召开的日期和时间、参会人数及会议类型。

　　The detailed requirements for the meeting room and equipments.

　　对会议室及设备的具体要求。

　　The way of payment.

　　付款方式。

◆ Make a record and confirm the above information with the guest.

　做好记录并与客人确认上述信息。

◆ Charge the guest the deposit, give him the receipt.

　收取客人押金，交给客人押金收据。

◆ Express the best wishes.

　向客人表达良好祝愿。

Providing Internet Services

提供互联网服务

◆ Get to know the problems of using the Internet by the telephone and come to the guest's room as soon as possible.

通过电话得知客人使用网络时遇到的问题,尽快赶到客人所在的房间。

◆ Listen to the guest and learn the problems when using the network.

倾听客人陈述,了解客人在网络使用中出现的问题。

◆ Answer the guest's technical questions and give the solution to the problems.

回答客人提出的技术问题,并为客人提供解决方案。

◆ Extend the wishes to the guest when there is no question about the network and then leave the room.

网络运行正常,向客人表达祝愿后离开。

Skill Points 技能要点

◆ Make sure to remind the guest of keeping the receipt of deposit well when renting the equipments.

出租设备时务必要提醒客人保管好押金收据备用。

◆ The staff at the Business Center should check the rental situation of meeting room and equipment, ensure that the guest's needs can be met, and then make final confirmation with the guest.

商务中心员工应查询会议室及设备的租用情况,确定可满足客人需求后再与客人做最后的确认。

◆ After confirming the guest's rental, the staff should arrange the meeting room and equipment immediately.

确认客人的租用要求后,应立即为客人布置会议室、安装调试会议设备。

◆ Make sure that the equipment is trouble-free before renting. Tell the guest the usage of the equipment and the matters needing attention.

出租设备前务必检查确认设备无故障。告知客人设备的使用方法及注意事项。

◆ There should be a technician standing by while the guest uses the meeting room or equipment. Once there is something out of order, the technician should provide with technical support immediately, to make the meeting going on smoothly.

客人使用会议室及设备过程中,须安排技术人员随时待命,一旦出现故障马上给予技术支持,以保证会议的顺利进行。

◆ After using the meeting room or equipment, the staff should check it up together with the guest. If there is no problem with the room or equipment, let the guest sign the name and take back the receipt of deposit and then settle the bill.

会议室和设备使用完毕后,要与客人一同进行检查,确认没有问题后让客人签字,收回客人押金收据,最后完成结账程序。

◆ When answering the guest's question about the use of network, the staff should explain the charge method of network patiently and remind the guest to get off from the Internet promptly, so as not to cause unnecessary losses.

接受客人关于网络使用情况的问询时,工作人员须耐心地向客人解释上网计费的方法,提醒客人及时下线,以免造成不必要的损失。

◆ Demonstrate how to access the Internet personally if the guest can't make it.

如客人无法领会网络的接入要领,则亲自为客人示范。

Practice 1　Renting Meeting Room and Equipment
实训项目 1　出租会议室及设备

Task of Service Practice 实训任务

◆ Mr. Green comes to the Business Center. He wants to rent a meeting room and equipments.

Green 先生来到商务中心,想要租用会议室及会议设备。

◆ Bai Xue, the receptionist of the Business Center receives him. She introduces the service information to Mr. Green.

商务中心接待员白雪热情地接待了 Green 先生。她向 Green 先生介绍了出租服务的有关信息。

◆ The following information about the meeting:

有关会议的信息如下:

This is the annual meeting of A&B Company, which will be held on Dec. 31, from 10 a. m. to 6 p. m. , and the number of attendees is about 40.

这是 A&B 公司的年会,会议准备于 12 月 31 日早 10 点至下午 6 点召开,参会人数是 40 人左右。

The meeting room should be equipped with enough tables and chairs, HD projector, LED screen, computer, stereo equipments and necessary lighting equipments. The broadband access services and tea break services should be provided during the meeting. There should be buffet lunch at noon.

会议室要配备足够的桌椅、高清投影仪、LED 电子屏幕、计算机、音响设备和必要的灯光设备。会议室内要求提供宽带接入服务,会议期间提供茶歇,中午提供自助午餐。

◆ Bai Xue recommends No. 1 Meeting Room to Mr. Green. The rental fee is 3 500 yuan a day, including a full set of meeting facilities and tea break services both in the morning and afternoon. The buffet lunch at noon should be booked additionally. It has both Chinese and Western styles, and the price is 50 yuan per person.

白雪推荐 Green 先生租用酒店的一号会议室。会议室的租赁费用是 3 500 元一天,包括全套会议设备及上、下午茶歇服务。中午的自助午餐需额外预订,分中式和西式两种,标准是每人 50 元。

◆ Mr. Green books No. 1 Meeting Room and Chinese buffet lunch.

  Green 先生预订一号会议室和中式自助午餐。

◆ Mr. Green chooses to pay with the check finally and pays 1 000 yuan in cash as the deposit.

  Green 先生选择最后用支票付账，并支付了 1 000 元现金作订金。

◆ Mr. Green's cellphone number is 13912340808.

  Green 先生的手机号是 13912340808。

◆ Bai Xue confirms the renting information with Mr. Green and gives him the receipt of deposit.

  白雪与 Green 先生确认租用信息，并将订金收据交给 Green 先生。

◆ Bai Xue expresses the best wishes to Mr. Green and reminds him to come to the hotel earlier that day and check the operation of the equipments in advance.

  白雪向 Green 先生表达良好祝愿，提醒他会议当天提前来酒店调试会议设备。

Service Practice 服务实训

Now, let's begin the practice according to *Task of Service Practice*.

请按照上述实训任务开始实训。

25 1 Renting Meeting Room and Equipment. mp3

Model of Service Practice 实训对照

Bai：   Bai Xue, a receptionist of the Business Center.

Green：Mr. Green, a guest at the Business Center.

Bai：   Good morning, sir. Welcome to the Business Center of our hotel. Can I help you?

       早上好，先生。欢迎光临本酒店商务中心。需要我为您服务吗？

Green：Yes. I'm David Green from A&B Company. I'd like to rent a meeting room with equipmentsat your hotel for the annual meeting of our company.

       是的。我是 A&B 公司的 David Green。我想为我们公司开年会租用贵酒店的会议室和会议设备。

Bai：   All right, Mr. Green. We have different types of meeting rooms and various equipments for you to choose. Could you tell me when you will hold the meeting and how many people there will be?

       好的，Green 先生。我们酒店有各种规模的会议室及不同种类的会议设备供您选择。请问您想什么时候租，参会人员有多少？

Green：Our annual meeting will be held on 31 of December, from 10 a. m. to 6 p. m. , and the number of attendees is about 80.

       我们公司的年会准备于 12 月 31 日早 10 点至下午 6 点召开，参会人数是 80 人左右。

Bai：   I got it. What meeting equipments do you need?

       我知道了。您需要什么样的会议设备？

Green：Briefly, I think the meeting room should be equipped with enough tables and chairs, HD projector, LED screen, computer, stereo equipments and necessary lighting equipments. We also need the broadband access services and tea break services during the meeting. By the way, do you provide buffet lunch at noon?

简单来说,我认为会议室要配备足够的桌椅、高清投影仪、LED 电子屏幕、计算机、音响设备和必要的灯光设备。我们还需要在会议室内提供宽带接入服务,会议期间提供茶歇。对了,顺便问一下,贵酒店中午可以提供自助午餐吗?

Bai：According to what you said, I recommend you to rent No. 1 Meeting Room of our hotel. It can accommodate 100 people, equipped with a full set of advanced meeting facilities and can meet your requirements perfectly. The rental fee is 3 500 yuan a day, including a full set of meeting facilities and tea break services both in the morning and afternoon. We do provide buffet lunch, but it needs to be booked additionally. We have both Chinese and Western styles of buffet and the price of them is both 50 yuan per person.

按照您所说的,我推荐您租用本酒店的一号会议室。该会议室可以容纳 100 人,配备有全套先进的会议设备,完全可以满足您的要求。会议室的租赁费用是一天 3 500 元,包括全套会议设备及上、下午的茶歇服务。本酒店可以提供自助午餐服务,但是需要您额外预订。我们有中式和西式两种自助餐,价格均是每人 50 元。

Green：Let me think …I can accept your offer. We'd like to book Chinese buffet lunch on that day.

让我想想。你的报价可以接受。我们那天就预订中式自助午餐吧。

Bai：Thank you, Mr. Green. So what about your payment? Would you like to pay in cash or by card?

谢谢您,Green 先生。那么请问您的付款方式? 是付现金还是刷卡?

Green：I'd like to pay with our company's check.

我想用公司支票付账

Bai：That's OK, Mr. Green. Would you mind paying 1 000 yuan in cash as a deposit?

没问题。您介意预付 1 000 元现金作为订金吗?

Green：Of course not. Here you are, 1 000 yuan.

当然不介意。这是 1 000 元。

Bai：Thank you, sir. May I have your cellphone number, please?

谢谢您,先生。请问您的电话号码?

Green：Yes. My cellphone number is 13912340808.

我的手机号码是 13912340808.

Bai：OK, Mr. Green. Let me confirm the information with you. You will rent No. 1 Meeting Room for A&B Company at our hotel on Dec 31, from 10 a. m. to 6 p. m. The number of attendees will be 80. The meeting services include a full set of meeting equipments and tea break services in the morning and the afternoon. Chinese buffet lunch for 80 people will be served on that day. Your cellphone number is

13912340808. You have paid a deposit of 1 000 yuan. Is that right?

好的,Green 先生,我来跟您确认一下您的信息。您要为 A&B 公司租用我们酒店的一号会议室,时间是 12 月 31 日早 10 点至下午 6 点。参会人数是 80 人。会议室服务包括全套会议设备及上、下午两顿茶歇。当天提供 80 人的中式自助午餐。您的手机号码是 13912340808。你已预付订金 1 000 元。对吗?

Green: That's completely right.

完全正确。

Bai: OK, sir. This is the receipt of the deposit for you. Please keep it well. By the way, please come to our hotel earlier that day and check the operation of the meeting equipmentswith our staff. Hope you have a good day. Thank you for your coming.

好的,先生。这是给您的订金收据,请妥善保管。顺便说一下,请您当天上午提早到酒店和我们的工作人员调试会议设备。祝您一天愉快。感谢您的光临。

Practice 2 Accessing the Internet
实训项目 2 接入互联网

Task of Service Practice 实训任务

◆ Ms. Wells in Room 914 calls the service counter of the Business Center, asking about how to access the WLAN by her own laptop.

914 客房的 Wells 女士给商务中心服务台打电话,询问是否可以用自己的笔记本电脑连接酒店的无线网络。

◆ Wang Yang, a staff at the Business Center receives her call, and tells her that the WLAN at the hotel is charged by time.

商务中心工作人员王洋在电话里告诉客人酒店的无线网络是计时收费使用的。

◆ The fee of the WLAN is 2 yuan per hour and 45 yuan per day. The login name and password for accessing the WLAN needs to be applied at the Business Center in advance. The fee will be charged together with room rate when checking out.

使用无线网络每小时收费 2 元,每天 45 元。接入无线网需要提前向商务中心申请登录名及密码。上网费会在结账退宿时和房费一并收取。

◆ Ms. Wells applies to access the WLAN which is charged by day.

Wells 女士申请开通按天收费的无线网络。

◆ Wang Yang helps her with the application and sends the information of login name and password to her room.

王洋为 Wells 女士办理上网手续,并将用户名和密码信息送至客房。

◆ Ms. Wells asks Wang Yang to demonstrate for her how to do operation on her own laptop.

Wells 女士要求王洋为其示范如何用自己的笔记本电脑进行操作。

◆ Wang Yang helps Ms. Wells complete the program of Internet access.

王洋协助 Wells 女士完成了接入程序。

◆ Wang Yang extends the wishes to Ms. Wells and leaves the room.

王洋向客人表达美好祝愿并离开。

Service Practice 服务实训

Now, let's begin the practice according to *Task of Service Practice*.

请按照上述实训任务开始实训。

25 2 Accessing the
Internet. mp3

Model of Service Practice 实训对照

Wang：Wang Yang, a staff at the Business Center.

Wells：Ms. Wells, a hotel guest.

Wang：Good afternoon, Business Center. Can I help you?

下午好,这里是商务中心。可以为您服务吗?

Wells：Yes. I'm the guest in Room 914. I'm asking about how to access the WLAN of the hotel by my own laptop.

是的。我是914房间的客人。我打电话来是想问问怎么能用我的笔记本电脑上网?

Wang：Thank you for calling, madam. We provide wired and wireless network access services both at the lobby and in rooms. If you'd like to access the WLAN, you have to pay for it beforehand.

感谢您的来电,女士。酒店大堂及各个房间均提供有线和无线网络接入服务。如您想接入无线网络,需预先付费。

Wells：Well, what about the charge fee of it? How can I pay for it?

那么,无线网络的使用费用是多少? 我怎样付费呢?

Wang：The fee of the WLAN is 2 yuan per hour and 45 yuan per day. The login name and password for accessing the WLAN needs to be applied at the Business Center in advance. The fee will be charged together with room rate when you check out.

使用无线网络每小时收费2元,每天45元。接入无线网需要提前向商务中心申请登录名及密码。上网费会在结账退宿时和房费一并收取。

Wells：I'd like to apply for it by day.

我要申请按天收费的无线网络。

Wang：OK, madam. Please wait a moment. I'll help you do application and send the login name and password to your room right now.

好的,女士。请稍等。我马上为您办理申请手续,并将用户名和密码信息送至您的房间。

(*After a while*)

(过了一会儿)

Wang：Excuse me, madam. May I come in?

打扰了,女士。我可以进来吗?

Wells： Come in，please.

请进。

Wang： Good afternoon，madam. I'm from the Business Center. I'm coming to give/send you the login name and password for the WLAN access.

下午好，女士。我是商务中心的。我来给您送上网的用户名和密码。

Wells： Thank you very much. Let me see…Sorry to trouble you again，but I really don't know how to get it done on my laptop. Could you please give me a hand to demonstrate the operation for me?

太谢谢你了。让我看一下……非常抱歉又麻烦你，但我实在是不知道怎么用我自己的笔记本电脑进行操作。你能给我示范一下吗？

Wang： No problem，madam. Just follow me，please. Turn on your laptop. There is a small Internet connection icon in the bottom right-hand task bar at the laptop screen. Click on the "WiFi Connection" icon. A list of available networks should appear. Find a wireless network named "Hotel-WLAN" and click on it to connect. Open your Internet web browser. Enter the login name and password I have given you into the dialogue boxes on the welcome page of our hotel web site. Thus you can go on the Internet now. I have to remind you that the timing of the WLAN begins from zero o'clock every day. If you don't plan to use the WLAN on the second day，make sure to click the button of "offline" before zero o'clock，so as not to cause unnecessary losses.

没问题。请跟着我操作。打开您的笔记本电脑。在笔记本电脑的屏幕右下角任务栏有一个小的网络连接图标。单击"无线网络连接"图标，会出现一个可用网络列表。找到一个名为"Hotel-WLAN"的无线网络，单击加入。打开您的网络浏览器，在我们酒店网站的欢迎页面对话框里输入我给您拿来的登录名和密码，您就可以上网了。我得提醒您无线网络每天从零点开始计时，如果第二天不打算使用网络，务必在零点前单击"下线"，以免导致不必要的损失。

Wells： I got it. Thank you for your great help.

这下我明白了。谢谢你给我的帮助。

Wang： It's my pleasure. If you have any problems when using the network，just call the Business Center to find me and I am ready to serve you at any time.

这是我的荣幸。如果您上网时还有什么问题，就给商务中心打电话找我，我随时准备为您服务。

Hotel Knowledge
新酒店人须知

(1) Common forms of meeting：

常见的会议形式：

teleconference	远程电话会议
video conference	视频会议、电视会议

net meeting　　　　　　　网络会议

（2）Some useful terms about network:

常用网络术语

setup	安装	uninstall	卸载
click	单击	double click	双击
right click	右击	icon	图标
command	命令	menu	菜单
debug	调试	restart	重新启动
password	口令	code	密码
tool bar	工具条	status bar	状态条
LAN	局域网	WLAN	无线局域网
Internet	互联网	Browser	浏览器
website	网站	Search Engine	搜索引擎
Online	在线	Offline	下线
laptop	笔记本	desktop	台式机
netbook	上网本	ultra book	超极本

（3）The staff at the Business Center should know the types of office equipments and basic usage of them.

商务中心工作人员应了解办公设备的种类和基本使用方法。

The staff at the Business Center should inquire the rental situation of meeting room and equipments,ensure that the guest's needs can be met,and then make the final confirmation with the guest.

商务中心工作人员应根据客人的租用需求,查询会议室及设备的租用情况,确定可满足客人需求后再与客人做最后的确认。

Practice Revision 实训回望

◆ Can you list 10 kinds of services provided by the Business Center?

◆ What is the procedure of a shift in the Business Center?

◆ Can you list the steps of booking air ticket online?

◆ Can you list the steps of providing internet service?

Case and Improvement:Fail to ask the guest to sign the renting agreement
案例与提高:未让客人签订租用协议

Ms. Shaw,a hotel guest who just checked in,hopes to rent a laptop to write her thesis. He comes to the Business Center to inquire about this. Jack,one staff member is on shift.

肖女士,一位刚刚办理入住手续的客人,希望租用一台手提电脑写论文。她来到商务中心询问这一事宜。酒店员工杰克正当值。

Jack receives Ms. Shaw warmly andpolitely. He informs Ms. Shaw the brands of computer the hotel can offer. Apart from that, he tells her the deposit for renting a computer and service charge as well as ways of payment.

杰克热情礼貌地地接待了肖女士并告知她酒店提供的计算机品牌,以及租用计算机需要支付的押金、服务费用及支付方式。

As required by the hotel, the renting agreement must be signed by Ms. Shaw. Butunfortunately, Jack forgets to ask Ms. Shaw to sign it and submit the deposit due to carelessness.

按照酒店要求,肖女士需要签署一份租用协议。但是由于粗心,杰克忘了让肖女士签协议并提交押金。

Jack provides Ms. Shaw with the whole set of computer equipment. After one day's renting, Ms. Shaw returns the laptop she rented the day before without the power cable. Jack requires her to compensate for the loss. But she refuses because there is no written agreement to support Jack's assertion.

杰克把全套计算机设备交付给肖女士使用。肖女士在租用一天后,返还了计算机,但是电源线遗失了。杰克要求她赔偿损失。但是肖女士拒绝了这一主张,因为她主张杰克没有给她数据线,并且认为没有任何书面协议能证明杰克的说辞。

Case Topic 案例话题

My opinion about the above service case.
我对以上案例的看法

Hotel Manager's Comments
酒店经理点评

这个案例中,商务中心的杰克由于工作的失误,导致没有和顾客签订计算机租用协议,数据线遗失,顾客拒绝赔偿,给酒店带来了负面影响和一定的经济损失。

（1）Jack should be responsible for the loss of the power cable and compensate for it. 杰克应该对电源线的遗失负责并赔偿损失。

（2）The staff members of the hotel should continue to learn the regulations of the hotel and be clear of their duties, proving guests with standard service. 酒店员工应该继续学习管理规定,清楚地明晰个人职责,为客人提供规范服务。

（3）The hotel should strengthen the management of its business and training of its staff. 酒店应该加强对业务的管理和员工的培训。

Answers to "Practice Revision" 部分参考答案

◆ What is the procedure of a shift in the Business Center?

1. Sign in.

2. Handover and make a record in the handover book.

3. Dust the table,turn on the power and inspect all the equipments.

4. Scan the virus for the computer,fill in the paper in the machine,ensure the equipment keep good function.

5. Read the handover book and follow up the things.

6. Double check the cash float and all kinds of tickets.

7. Check the E-mail,and ensure every hour must be checked one time.

8. Provide various kinds of services and meet the requirements of the guest.

9. Charge for the services.

10. Input the specific information in the computer.

11. Make records of follow up things in the handover book.

12. Handover with the next shift.

13. Print the report.

14. Sign out.

◆ Can you list the steps of providing internet service?

1. Ask the specific requirements of internet services.

2. Show the price list.

3. Lead the guest to workstation.

4. Help the guest login in.

5. Ask the guest if he needs any help.

6. Confirm the time with the guest.

7. Charge for the services.

8. Make a record.

Chapter Eleven Health and Recreation

实训模块十一 康乐服务

Unit 26

Health Care Services

技能实训 26　保健服务

Service Procedure 服务流程

◆ Greet the guest.
问候客人。
◆ Find out what the guest wants to get.
了解客人需求。
◆ Introduce the relative information to the guest.
介绍相关信息。
◆ Confirm the health care items the guest has chosen and make the record.
确认客人选择的保健项目并作记录。
◆ Provide health care services to the guest.
为客人提供保健服务。
◆ Ask the way of payment and settle account for the guest.
询问付款方式并为客人办理结账手续。
◆ Give best wishes to the guest.
致以良好祝愿。

Skill Points 技能要点

◆ Try to be polite during service, and always keep smiling.
服务要有礼貌,时刻面带微笑。
◆ Communicate with the guest patiently, and try to learn about the needs of him.
耐心地与客人沟通,了解客人的保健需求。
◆ In the process of service, the therapist should answer the guest's questions in detail, and recommend the appropriate products and services for the guest according to his age, job, and health, etc.
进行服务过程中,理疗师应耐心详细地回答客人提出的各种问题,并根据客人的年龄、职业、健康度等为客人推荐合适的产品和服务。

◆ Therapist should apologize immediately and improve the way of service as soon as possible, when the guest is unsatisfied with the service. Never dispute with the guest in any case.

如果客人对服务表示不满,理疗师应马上致歉并尽快改进服务方法。在任何情况下,不得与客人发生争执。

Practice 1　Enjoying Spa Treatment
实训项目 1　享受温泉水疗

Task of Service Practice 实训任务

◆ The guest Mrs. Smith wants to enjoy a Spa treatment at the Spa Center of the hotel.
酒店客人 Smith 夫人来到温泉水疗中心,想做一次温泉水疗。

◆ Li Hong, a Spa therapist in the Spa Center receives her.
水疗中心的水疗师李红接待了她。

◆ Mrs. Smith gets sore on her body and feels tired.
Smith 夫人身体酸疼,感到疲劳。

◆ Li Hong recommends "*the whole body relief therapy by aroma oil massage*" and explains the details of this treatment.
李红推荐"香薰精油全身减压按摩疗法",并详细解释了这个疗法的具体内容。

◆ The whole treatment includes bathing, exfoliation and body oil massage, totally 2 hours, and costs 550 yuan.
整个过程包括沐浴、去角质和全身精油按摩,大概两个小时,费用共 550 元。

◆ Mrs. Smith pays the bill by a charge card when the Spa is finished.
Spa 做完后,Smith 夫人通过签单卡付账。

Service Practice 服务实训

Now, let's begin the practice according to *Task of Service Practice*.
请按照上述实训任务开始实训。

Model of Service Practice 实训对照

26 1 Enjoying Spa Treatment. mp3

Li：　Li Hong, a Spa therapist.
Smith：　Mrs. Smith, a hotel guest.

Li：　Good evening, madam. Welcome to the Spa Center. What can I do for you?
　　　晚上好,女士。欢迎来到温泉水疗中心。我能为您做什么?
Smith：　I would like to have a Spa treatment here.

我想在这儿做一次水疗。

Li：Please sit down here,madam. Take off your shoes and put on the slippers,firstly.

请坐,女士。请您先脱掉鞋子换上拖鞋。

Smith：OK.

好的。

Li：I am a Spa therapist here. Please call me Li. How are you feeling these days?

我是这里的水疗师,请叫我小李。您最近感觉如何?

Smith：Not very good. My whole body gets sore recently and I always feel tired. Would you please recommend some suitable treatment for me?

不太好。我最近总是觉得浑身酸痛,容易疲劳。你能给我推荐一个适合的项目放松一下吗?

Li：If so,I'd like to recommend *"the whole body relief therapy by aroma oil massage"*. This treatment selects specific plant essential oils for the whole body lymphatic drainage massage,together with relaxing music,pleasant aroma and healthy herbal tea,to reach the effect of relaxation and relief.

根据您的症状,我向您推荐"香薰精油全身减压按摩疗法"。这个项目是选取专门的植物精油进行全身的淋巴排毒按摩,同时配合轻松愉悦的音乐、怡人的香薰及养生花草茶,可以达到放松心情、舒缓压力的功效。

Smith：That sounds pretty good. How long does one treatment last and how much is it?

听起来不错。请问做一次需要多长时间,费用是多少?

Li：The whole treatment includes bathing,exfoliation and body oil massage,totally two hours. It costs 550 yuan in all.

整个过程包括沐浴、去角质、全身精油按摩,大概两个小时,费用一共是 550 元。

Smith：OK. I'll get it.

好的。我就选择这个吧。

Li：Please follow me to the bathing room. The bathing services in our hotel include hot spring,sauna and steam bath. You can choose any treatment you like to try,but please don't stay in the hot spring or sauna too long. If you feel uncomfortable, please tell me as soon as possible. Hope you enjoy it.

请您随我到浴室。我们酒店的洗浴服务可提供温泉浴、桑拿和蒸气浴。您可以选择你喜欢的洗浴方式,但是请您不要在温泉浴或桑拿房中待太长时间。如果感到不舒服,请立即通知我。祝您愉快。

Smith：OK,thank you for reminding me.

好的,谢谢你的提醒。

(*After bathing*)

(沐浴完毕后)

Li：Next,I will do exfoliation for your body. We will use a plant gel for exfoliation, which can remove the aged layer of skin mildly and make the skin smooth and dedicate again.

接下来，我将为您做全身的去角质护理。我们选用的是一种植物凝胶去角质产品。这款产品可以温和、彻底地清除身体老化角质，使肌肤恢复光滑、细腻。

Smith：All right.

好的。

(After exfoliation treatment)

（去角质护理之后）

Li：Please put on this robe and disposable underwear for you. This is lavender tea. It can help eliminate fatigue and tension. Please enjoy it.

请换上为您准备的睡袍及一次性内衣。这是薰衣草花茶。它可以帮助消除疲劳和紧张，请品尝。

Smith：Thank you very much.

太谢谢了。

Li：OK, we'll start with the whole body lymphatic drainage massage. I'll choose a compound essential oil containing lavender, eucalyptus, orange flower and chamomile. I'll use lymphatic drainage massage technique combined with magical detoxification efficiency of essential oil, to improve your lymph circulation, accelerate metabolism and enhance the immune function of your body.

好了，我们要开始进行全身的淋巴排毒精油按摩了。我给您选择的是薰衣草、尤加利、橙花和洋甘菊的复方精油。我会利用淋巴引流手法结合排毒精油的神奇功效，改善您的淋巴循环系统，加速新陈代谢，提高您身体的免疫功能。

Smith：Marvelous!

太好了。

Li：Please lie on the bed, close your eyes and enjoy the beautiful music and pleasant aroma. Let's begin. Your skin will be full of energy and your body will be relaxed after the Spa treatment.

请您躺在床上，闭上眼睛，享受优美的音乐和怡人的香气吧。我们要开始了。相信做完 Spa 之后，您的皮肤会显得健康有活力，您全身都会感到轻松舒服。

Smith：Good. That's what I want.

太棒了，正是我想要的。

Li：For your enjoyable massage, please turn off your cellphone. If you feel any uncomfortable during the treatment, please let me know. The whole treatment is about one hour.

为了使您更好地享受您的按摩护理，请您关掉手机。如果您在护理期间有任何不适，请告诉我。整个护理过程大约一个小时。

Smith：I see.

我知道了。

Li：Are you comfortable? How is the pressure? If you like stronger or softer, please let me know.

您舒服吗？力度怎么样？如果您想力度重点儿或轻点儿，请告诉我。

Smith：I feel very comfortable. Maybe stronger is better.

我觉得挺好的。可能再重点儿会更好。

(*After about one hour*)

(大约一个小时后)

Li：Excuse me, madam. I have finished the treatment. Did you enjoy your treatment?

您好, 女士。这次的水疗结束了。您对这次水疗满意吗?

Smith：Very good. I enjoy it very much. Thank you for your service.

非常好。我很享受这次的水疗。谢谢你为我服务。

Li：My pleasure. How would you like to pay?

很荣幸为您服务。请问您怎么结账?

Smith：I'm here for a meeting. I'll pay by a charge card.

我是会议客人, 用消费签单卡结账。

Li：Could you please show me your room card and charge card? This is your bill. Please sign your name here.

好的, 请您出示房卡和签单卡。这是您的账单, 请您在上面签字。

Smith：OK. Here you are.

好的。给你。

Li：Thank you for your coming. Hope you have a good stay in our hotel.

感谢您的光临。祝您在酒店过得愉快。

Smith：Thank you for your service.

感谢你的服务。

Practice 2   Experiencing Chinese Physiotherapy
实训项目 2　体验中医理疗

Task of Service Practice 实训任务

◆ Mr. Smith wants to enjoy a Chinese physiotherapy treatment at the Chinese Physiotherapy Center, for he suffers from headache and insomnia

Smith 先生想在中医理疗中心做一次中医理疗, 因为他头痛失眠。

◆ Chen Lin, a therapist in the Chinese Physiotherapy Center receives him and makes a self-introduction.

理疗中心的女理疗师陈琳接待了他, 并做自我介绍。

◆ Chen Lin recommends *Tui Na* to Mr. Smith and makes a brief introduction about it, and then does foot massage and *Tui Na* for him on the head, hands and feet.

陈琳推荐并简要介绍了中医推拿, 接着为其做了泡脚, 头部、手部和足部推拿。

Tui Na is a Chinese ancient medical treatment dating back 4 000 years ago. In all realms of Chinese medicine, pain is viewed as a form of imbalance that can be alleviated through reopening meridians, or pathways, to blocked energy. *Tui Na* targets the 12 meridians, six Yin and six Yang, found in the arms and legs, with deep massage. There are three techniques commonly used in Tui Na, such as *An Mo*, *Dian Xue* and *Zheng Gu*. The benefits of *Tui Na* include relaxation of body, improvement of blood circulation, and prevention of illness. Acupoint massage can also treat many diseases. Regular *Tui Na* on several acupoints on the head, hands and feet can alleviate the symptoms of headache and insomnia.

推拿是一种中国古代的治疗方法，历史可以追溯到4 000年前。在中医领域，疼痛被视为一种不平衡，可以通过打通被阻塞的经络或通路来缓解。推拿针对位于胳膊和腿部的6阴6阳12条经脉，进行深层按摩。常用的推拿手法有按摩、点穴和正骨。推拿有利于放松身体，改善血液循环，预防疾病。穴位按摩也可以治疗很多的疾病，对头部、手部和足部的几处穴位进行定期的推拿按摩都可以缓解头痛失眠的症状。

◆ Mr. Smith pays the bill to his room account when the treatment is finished.
理疗结束后Smith先生将账单计入房费。

Service Practice 服务实训

Now, let's begin the practice according to *Task of Service Practice*.
请按照上述实训任务开始实训。

26 2 Experiencing Chinese Physiotherapy. mp3

Model of Service Practice 实训对照

Chen：Chen Lin, a therapist.
Smith：Mr. Smith, a guest.

Chen：Good evening, sir. Welcome to the Chinese Physiotherapy Center. Can I help you?
晚上好，先生。欢迎来到中医理疗中心。我能为您做什么？

Smith：I would like to try a Chinese physiotherapy treatment here.
我想在这儿尝试一下中医理疗。

Chen：Let me introduce myself to you. I'm Chen, the therapist here. What kind of Chinese physiotherapy treatment would you like to try?
我先介绍一下我自己，我是这里的理疗师小陈。请问您想体验哪个理疗项目？

Smith：Sorry, I have no idea about Chinese physiotherapy treatment. Would you please introduce it for me?
抱歉，我对中医理疗不太了解，能给我简单介绍一下吗？

Chen：Would you tell me what is troubling you on your body now?
能告诉我您哪儿不舒服吗？

Smith：I am suffering from insomnia recently, and I always feel headache.
我最近总是失眠，头也觉得有点疼。

Chen：You are right to choose the traditional Chinese physiotherapy treatment. *Tui Na* can effectively ease your insomnia and headache.

您选择中医理疗是对的。用推拿的办法可以有效缓解失眠和头痛症状。

Smith：That's great. So what is *Tui Na*?

那太好了。那么到底什么是推拿？

Chen：*Tui Na* is a Chinese ancient medical treatment dating back 4 000 years ago. In all realms of Chinese medicine, pain is viewed as a form of imbalance that can be alleviated through reopening meridians, or pathways, to blocked energy. *Tui Na* targets the 12 meridians, six *Yin* and six *Yang*, found in the arms and legs, with deep massage. There are three techniques commonly used in *Tui Na*, such as *An Mo*, *Dian Xue* and *Zheng Gu*. The benefits of *Tui Na* include relaxation of body, improvement of blood circulation, and prevention of illness.

推拿是一种中国古代的治疗方法，历史可以追溯到 4 000 年前。在中医领域，疼痛被视为一种不平衡，可以通过打通被阻塞的经络或通路来缓解。推拿针对位于胳膊和腿部的 6 阴 6 阳 12 条经脉，进行深层按摩。常用的推拿手法有按摩、点穴和正骨。推拿有利于放松身体，改善血液循环，预防疾病。

Smith：Is medicine such as oils, gels or lotions applied on the body during *Tui Na*.

推拿时会在身体上涂抹诸如油、啫喱或者液体之类的药物吗？

Chen：No. *Tui Na* depends on therapist's hands, not medicine.

不需要。推拿主要靠技师的手法，而不是药物。

Smith：Need I remove all my clothes for a *Tui Na* massage?

我需要在推拿时脱掉衣服吗？

Chen：No, you needn't. Loose cotton clothes are thin enough to receive light finger pressure through.

不需要。手指的力道可以经由轻薄宽松的棉质衣服透入身体。

Smith：I always suffer from insomnia and headache. Which parts of body would you do *Tui Na* for me?

我经常头痛失眠，需要在哪些部位做推拿？

Chen：Meridians in traditional Chinese medicine is amazing. Acupoint massage can treat many diseases. There are a lot of acupoints in our body. Regular *Tui Na* on several acupoints on the head, hands and feet can alleviate the symptoms of headache and insomnia. Today, I'll do a *Tui Na* for you. You can experience its magic effect on your body.

中医穴位是很神奇的，穴位按摩可以治疗很多的疾病。人的身体有很多穴位，对头部、手部和足部的好几处穴位进行定期的推拿按摩都可以缓解头痛失眠的症状。我今天给您做一次推拿，您可以体验一下它的神奇效果。

Smith：All right. I can't completely understand the theory of the traditional Chinese physiotherapy treatment, but I am willing to have a try.

好吧。尽管我还不太能够理解中医理疗的原理，但我愿意尝试一下。

Chen：Please sit down here, and I'll do foot massage for you. Please soak your feet firstly.

请您坐在这里,我来给您做足疗。做足疗之前请您先泡脚。

Smith：OK.

好的。

Chen：During the foot soaking, please close your eyes, and I'll do massage to you on your head and hands. Massage toward acupoints on head and hands is a good way to ease your tension and helpful for sleeping.

在您泡脚的时候,请您闭上眼睛,我来给您做头部和手部按摩。按摩头部和手部的穴位可以很好地缓解紧张情绪,非常有助于睡眠。

(*After 30 minutes*)

(30分钟之后)

Chen：It's finished. How do you feel?

头部和手部按摩做完了。您感觉如何?

Smith：So comfortable. I almost fell asleep.

好舒服呀,我差点睡着了。

Chen：Next part is foot massage. I'll do massage toward some acupoints on your feet, which are related to your symptoms of headache and insomnia. It's about 30 minutes. Please let me know if you feel hurt.

接下来是足疗的部分了。我会针对您失眠头痛的症状重点对足部的几处穴位进行按摩。时间大概是30分钟。如果您觉得疼就告诉我。

Smith：Sure.

好的。

Chen：Foot massage is over, sir. what do you think of the Chinese physiotherapy treatment?

足疗做完了,先生。您觉得中医理疗有效果吗?

Smith：It's really very comfortable. My headache seems reduced, and I had a nap just now. I haven't slept so sweetly for a long time.

真的很舒服。我的头好像不太疼了,而且刚才还打了一个盹儿。好久没有睡得这么香了。

Chen：That's good. It has more effect to take Chinese physiotherapy treatment regularly.

那就好。中医理疗要定期做才更有效果。

Smith：I'd like to. Thank you for your advice.

我会的。谢谢你的建议。

Chen：That's right. May I ask how you would like to pay, sir?

不客气。先生,请问您怎么结账?

Smith：Charge it to my room account, please. My room number is 5213.

请挂在我的房账上吧。我的房间号是5213。

Chen：Please show me your room card, sir. I've got to record it. Would you please sign your name on the bill?

先生,请您出示您的房卡。我需要记录一下。请您在账单上签字。

Smith：Sure. Here you are.

　　　好的，给你。

Chen：Thank you for your coming. Welcome to experience Chinese physiotherapy again in a few days.

　　　谢谢您的光临。欢迎您过几天再来体验中医理疗。

Smith：I'll be back.

　　　我一定再来。

Hotel Knowledge
新酒店人须知

（1）The term of Spa is derived from the name of the town of Spa, Belgium, whose name is known back to Roman times. A Spa treatment is non-medical procedure to help the health of the body. Typical Spa treatments include：aromatherapy, bathing? or soaking in hot spring, hot tub, cold tub, mud bath, sauna and steam bath, body wraps, facials, massage, nail care, skin exfoliation, yoga and meditation, waxing, the removal of body hair with hot wax.

Spa 一词源自比利时一个以温泉著称的名叫 Spa 的小镇，小镇的名字最早可追溯到古罗马时代。Spa(温泉水疗)是一种有助人体健康的非医疗过程。典型的 Spa 疗法包括：芳香疗法、沐浴(如温泉浴、热水浴、冷水浴、泥浆浴、桑拿浴、蒸气浴)、身体裹敷、面部护理、按摩、指甲护理、去角质、瑜伽冥想、蜡纸脱毛。

（2）Traditional Chinese Physiotherapy treatment is well known in the following types, such as *Tui Na* (Manipulation), *Gua Sha* (Skin scraping), fire cupping, foot massage, acupressure and acupuncture.

传统中医理疗有以下几种治疗方法：如推拿、刮痧、拔火罐、足疗、点穴和针灸。

（3）Therapist should make up lightly, with neat and decent clothes.

保健技师宜化淡妆，衣着干净得体。

（4）Don't make or answer personal calls, or leave the guest alone during the service.

服务客人时不接打私人电话，不离开客人。

（5）Therapist should know Chinese or Western knowledge about health care and learn the effects and contraindications of various health care methods.

保健技师应了解中西保健知识，了解各种常见护理方法的功效及其禁忌症。

（6）Therapist should serve the guest in a good mood, and let him or her feel warm and comfortable.

保健技师应以轻松愉悦的心情为客人服务，让客人感到温暖、舒适。

（7）Therapist should do health care slowly and regularly. Ask about the guest's feelings to adjust the treatment at any time.

技师的动作宜缓慢，有规律。应随时询问宾客的感受以调整护理手法。

Fitness Services

技能实训 27　健身服务

Service Procedure 服务流程

◆ Greet the guest.
问候客人。

◆ Find out what the guest wants to get.
了解客人需求。

◆ Introduce the relative information to the guest.
介绍相关信息。

◆ Confirm the fitness items the guest chose and make the record.
确认客人选择的健身项目并作记录。

◆ Lead the guest to the fitness site.
引领客人到达健身场所。

◆ Introduce the way to use fitness facilities and remind the guest the points for attention.
介绍健身设施的使用方法及注意事项。

◆ Ask the way of payment and settle account for the guest.
询问付款方式并为客人办理结账手续。

◆ See the guest off and give great wishes.
目送客人离开并致以良好祝愿。

Skill Points 技能要点

◆ Try to be polite during service, and always keep smiling.
服务时要讲礼貌,时刻面带微笑。

◆ Communicate with the guest patiently, try to learn about the needs of him.
耐心地与客人沟通,了解客人的需求。

◆ Know clearly the price and the way to charge each fitness item.
了解各个健身项目的价格和计费方式。

◆ Practice how to give first aid to the guest in an accident.

掌握急救知识,在客人发生意外时给予紧急救护。

Practice 1 Having a Swim
实训项目 1 游泳

Task of Service Practice 实训任务

◆ The guest Mr. Black wants to go swimming at the Fitness Center.

酒店客人 Black 先生想来健身中心游泳。

◆ Liu Yuan,a receptionist at the service counter receives Mr. Black. She makes records,
gives him the key of the locker and shows him to the locker room.

服务台接待员刘媛接待了 Black 先生。她做好登记,交给 Black 先生更衣柜钥匙然后引领
他到达更衣室。

◆ Zhang Qiang,a staff in the locker room shows Mr. Black to his locker No. 811 and
answers his questions about the temperature of the water, the size and depth of the
swimming pool. Zhang Qiang also suggests Mr. Black to do some warm-up exercises
before swimming and serves him a dry towel.

更衣室员工张强为 Black 先生找到了 811 号更衣柜,并回答了 Black 先生有关泳池和水温
的问题。张强还建议 Black 先生在游泳前做好热身运动,并递给 Black 先生一条干毛巾。

◆ Zhao Ming,a life guard of swimming pool introduces himself to Mr. Black and tells him
not to dive in the pool on our left because the water is so shallow that you may hurt your
head.

泳池救生员赵明向 Black 先生做自我介绍并告之不能在左手边的泳池跳水,因为水较浅,
可能会碰伤头部。

◆ Mr. Black asks for help when his calf muscles have a sudden cramp during swimming.
Zhao Ming gives him first aid.

Black 先生游泳的时候小腿突然抽筋,紧急呼救。赵明为其提供了紧急救护。

Service Practice 服务实训

Now,let's begin the practice according to *Task of Service Practice*.
请按照上述实训任务开始实训。

27 1 Having a
Swim. mp3

Model of Service Practice 实训对照

Liu：Liu Yuan,a receptionist.

Black：Mr. Black,a guest.

Zhang：Zhang Qiang,a staff in the locker room.

Zhao：Zhao Ming,a life guard of swimming pool.

Liu: Welcome to the Fitness Center, sir. What can I do for you?

欢迎来到健身中心。请问我能为您做些什么?

Black: I'd like to go swimming. What do you charge?

我想游泳。请问怎么收费?

Liu: Are you a hotel guest? The swimming pool is free for hotel guests.

请问您是酒店的住客吗? 我们的游泳池对酒店客人是免费的。

Black: That's great. I am the guest of your hotel.

太好了,我就是酒店的客人。

Liu: Would you please show me your room card? I have to fill in this form.

麻烦您出示房卡,我需要登记一下。

Black: Sure. Here is my room card.

好的。这是我的房卡。

Liu: Sorry for waiting so long. This is the key to your locker. Please return it before you leave.

不好意思,让您久等了。这是您的更衣柜钥匙。游泳完毕后请将钥匙交回这里。

Black: OK, thanks.

好的。谢谢。

Liu: Male locker room is on the 2nd floor. Please turn left and go upstairs by elevator. Hope you enjoy your play here.

男更衣室在二楼,请您左转乘电梯上楼。祝您玩得愉快。

(*After Mr. Black has arrived at the locker room*)

(Black 先生来到更衣室后)

Zhang: Welcome to the locker room, sir. May I have your locker number?

先生,欢迎来到更衣室,请问您的更衣柜号码是多少?

Black: Let me see. It's No. 811.

我看一下。是 811 号。

Zhang: Locker No. 811 is in the third row. Please go this way.

811 号更衣柜在第三排。请这边走。

Black: OK. What about the temperature of the water?

好的。游泳池水温是多少?

Zhang: Our swimming pool maintains constant temperature of 29℃ all year round.

我们的泳池是恒温的,常年保持 29℃。

Black: How big and how deep is the pool?

泳池有多大,多深?

Zhang: We have two pools. One is standard size with 50 meters long, 21 meters wide and 1.8 meters deep. The other one is irregular, with the depth from 0.9 to 2 meters.

我们有两个泳池,一个是标准泳池,长 50 米,宽 21 米,水深 1.8 米。另一个泳池是不规则泳池,水深从 0.9 米到 2 米。

Black：Oh, I see. I'm not good at swimming and maybe shallow water is better.

哦，我知道了。我的游泳技术不太好，还是选择在浅水区好一点。

Zhang：Don't worry about it. The life guard nearby is ready to help you whenever you need.

请您放心，我们有救生员随时在旁边做好帮助您的准备。

Black：That's great.

那太好了。

Zhang：You'd better do some warm-up exercises before swimming in order to avoid muscle cramps.

您最好在游泳前做做热身运动，以防肌肉抽筋。

Black：OK, I will.

好的，我会的。

Zhang：This is a bath towel for you. Hope you have a good time here.

这是为您准备的浴巾。祝您在这里玩得愉快。

Zhao：Welcome to swim here, sir. I'm the life guard. You can call me Zhao. If you are in trouble, I'm ready to help you at any time.

欢迎您来这里游泳，先生。我是救生员，您可以叫我小赵。如果您遇到麻烦，我随时准备帮助您。

Black：Thank you, Zhao. By the way, where is the shallow water area?

谢谢你，小赵。顺便问一下，哪里是浅水区？

Zhao：The pool on our left is from shallow to deep. Please don't dive in this pool. The water isso shallow, you may hurt your head.

我们左手边的泳池是由浅及深的。请您不要在这个泳池跳水，因为水较浅，您可能会碰伤头部。

Black：I got it. Thank you for mentioning that.

好的。谢谢你的提醒。

Zhao：Not at all. Hope you have a wonderful time here.

不用谢。祝您在这儿玩得愉快。

（*After 10 minutes*）

（10 分钟之后）

Black：Ouch! Mr. Zhao, help me! I've got a muscle cramp on my right calf.

哎哟，小赵，快来帮帮我。我的右小腿抽筋了。

Zhao：I'm here, sir. Let me see your calf. Don't worry about it. Please sit down on the beach chair. Relax your muscles, keep your foot flat and stretch your right leg as much as you can. Let me do massage on your calf. Maybe the warm-up exercises before swimming are not enough.

先生，我来了。让我看一下您的小腿。别担心，请坐在椅子上。放松肌肉，保持脚平放，尽量伸直您的右腿。我给您做一下小腿按摩。也许是游泳前的热身运动不够充分。

Black： It happened maybe because I did less exercises recently.

也可能是因为我最近运动比较少的缘故。

Zhao： May I bring you a dry towel, sir?

需要我给您拿条干浴巾吗, 先生?

Black： Yes, I do need a towel. That's very kind of you.

是的, 我确实需要一条浴巾。太谢谢你了。

Zhao： You're welcome. You'd better have a rest here. What do you like to drink, tea or mineral water?

不用谢。您最好在这儿休息一下吧。您想喝点什么, 茶或是矿泉水?

Black： Mineral water is OK.

矿泉水就可以了。

Zhao： Here is the mineral water. How are you feeling now, sir? Is your calf still painful?

这是您的矿泉水。先生, 您现在感觉如何? 您的小腿还疼吗?

Black： I feel better now. Thank you for your first aid, Mr. Zhao. Without you, I even didn't know what to do just now.

我现在感觉好多了。小赵, 谢谢你的急救。当时如果没有你, 我都不知道该怎么办了。

Zhao： It's my pleasure to help you. Please make sure to do enough warm-up exercises before swimming next time.

能帮到您是我的荣幸。请下次务必充分热身之后再下水游泳。

Black： That's for sure.

一定。

Practice 2　Playing Bowling
实训项目2　打保龄球

Task of Service Practice 实训任务

◆ Mr. White and his friends are meeting guests. They want to play bowling.

　White 先生和朋友们是会议客人。他们想打保龄球。

◆ Pang Wei, a staff at the Bowling Alley introduces the price list.

　保龄球馆的服务员庞伟介绍了球馆的消费价目表。

◆ Mr. White shows their charge cards to Pang Wei.

　White 先生向庞伟出示了他们的签单卡。

◆ Meeting guests are allowed to play 5 rounds of bowling and each of them is given a bottle of drink for free.

　　会议客人可以免费打5局保龄球, 并可免费获赠一瓶饮料。

会议客人每人可以免费打 5 局球，并附赠一瓶饮料。

◆ Mr. White and his friends play 5 rounds.

White 先生和朋友们打了 5 局球。

◆ Mr. White asks Pang Wei to turn on 2 lanes and set trios for each lane.

White 先生要求庞伟开 2 条球道，每条球道设置成三人赛。

Service Practice 服务实训

27 2 Playing Bowling. mp3

Now，let's begin the practice according to *Task of Service Practice*.

请按照上述实训任务开始实训。

Model of Service Practice 实训对照

Pang：Pang Wei，a hotel staff.

White：Mr. White，a meeting guest.

Pang：Good evening. Welcome to the bowling alley. Can I help you?

晚上好。欢迎光临保龄球馆。我可以帮您吗？

White：Yes. My friends and I would like to play bowling here. How would you like to charge?

是的。我和朋友们想打保龄球。这里怎么收费呢？

Pang：The charge is by the lane，200 yuan per hour or 20 yuan for a round. Are you staying in our hotel now，sir?

我们是按球道收费的。每条球道每小时 200 元或者每局 20 元。先生，您目前是住在本酒店吗？

White：Yes，we are. All of us are attending the meeting here.

是的。我们所有人都在这里参加会议。

Pang：Since you're meeting guests，do you have charge card?

既然您是会议客人，请问您有签单卡吗？

White：Yes，we have.

是的，我们有签单卡。

Pang：Fine. Would you mind showing me your charge card，please? Thank you for waiting. According to the agreement with the organizing committee，every one of you can play 5 rounds of bowling and enjoy a bottle of soft drink for free.

好的。麻烦您出示一下您的签单卡好吗？感谢您的耐心等待。根据之前与会务组的签单协议，您和您的朋友每人可以在此免费打 5 局保龄球，并享受一瓶免费饮料。

White：That's great. We'd like to play 5 rounds.

太好了。那我们就打 5 局吧。

Pang：Would you please change your shoes into bowling shoes over there? You'd better do some exercises to warm up before playing.

请您在那里把鞋子换成保龄球鞋。您最好在打球前先活动一下热热身。

White： All right. Please turn on 2 lanes, and set trios for each lane.

好的。请帮我们开 2 条球道，每条道都设为三人赛。

Pang： No problem. I'll get it ready at once. By the way, there are the towels and drinks for you on the table.

没问题。我马上去准备好。另外，给您准备的毛巾和饮料都已经放在桌子上了。

White： Thank you very much.

非常感谢。

Pang： You're welcome. Have a nice time!

不用谢。祝您玩得愉快。

Hotel Knowledge
新酒店人须知

（1）A fitness center(also known as a health club, fitness club, and commonly referred to as a gym)is a place which houses exercise equipment to meet the demand of the guest on the physical exercise in a hotel. It mainly includes badminton, tennis, golf, shuffle board, table tennis(Ping-Pong), snooker, bowling, gym, swimming, etc. Different hotels provide different items according to their own conditions.

健身中心（也称健康俱乐部、健身俱乐部，通常也被称为健身房）是酒店为满足客人进行体育锻炼的需要而设立的服务区域。健身中心通常设有羽毛球、网球、高尔夫球、沙狐球、乒乓球、斯诺克、保龄球、健身、游泳等项目。不同酒店根据自身情况设置不同的项目。

（2）Staff at the Fitness Center should be familiar with the basic rules of sports and know the operation of sport facilities.

健身中心工作人员应该熟悉各项体育运动的基本规则，了解运动设施的操作规程。

（3）Staff at the Fitness Center should learn some knowledge about the maintenance of simple breakdowns.

健身中心工作人员应该了解简单故障的维修办法。

（4）The points for attention at Fitness Center：

健身中心行为守则：

Do wear sport shoes before entering the sport field.

进入运动场地前请换好运动鞋。

Do wipe up your sweat off after using the equipment.

使用运动器械后请擦去器械上的汗水。

Do learn proper operation of equipment.

请正确操作运动器械。

Do pay attention to personal hygiene.

请注意个人卫生。

Do keep the gym and locker room clean.

请保持健身房及更衣室清洁。

Do warm up before doing exercises.

请在运动前充分热身。

Do take care of your own child.

请照管好自己的孩子。

Don't get drunk before entering the sport field.

请勿醉酒后进入运动场地。

Don't dive without gauging the depth.

请勿在未知深度的泳池跳水。

Don't smoke.

请勿吸烟。

Don't spit.

请勿随地吐痰。

(5) Key words related to fitness services：

健身服务有关术语：

gym	健身房	swimming trunks	泳裤
ball games	球类运动	swimming cap	泳帽
shuffle board	沙狐球	swimming goggles	泳镜
table tennis	乒乓球	amount of exercises	运动量
snooker	斯诺克	physician scale	体重秤
bowling	保龄球	upright cycle	直立式单车
squash	壁球	rowing ergo meter	划船练习器
diving	跳水	overhead press	推肩练习器
jog	慢跑	chest press	推胸练习器
yoga	瑜伽	abdominal	腹肌练习器
climber	台阶器	dumbbell	哑铃

Unit 28

Entertainment Services

技能实训 28　娱乐服务

Service Procedure 服务流程

◆ Greet the guest.

问候客人。

◆ Find out what the guest wants to do.

了解客人需求。

◆ Introduce the relative information to the guest.

介绍相关信息。

◆ Confirm the entertaiment items the guest chose and make the record.

确认客人选择的娱乐项目并作记录。

◆ Lead the guest to the entertainment place.

引领客人到达娱乐场所。

◆ Introduce the way to use facilities and remind the guest the points for attention.

介绍娱乐设施的使用方法及注意事项。

◆ Ask the way of payment and settle account for the guest.

询问付款方式并为客人办理结账手续。

◆ See the guest off and give best wishes.

目送客人离开并致以良好祝愿。

Skill Points 技能要点

◆ Try to be polite during service, and always keep smiling.

服务时要讲礼貌,时刻面带微笑。

◆ Communicate with the guest patiently, try to learn about the needs of him.

耐心地与客人沟通,了解客人的需求。

◆ The waiter should knock at the door 3 times, wait for 3 seconds and then enter the room, saying "Excuse me. Sorry to disturb you".

服务员应先敲门三下，等待三秒后再进入包间，并说"对不起，打扰了"。

◆ The waiter should face the guest and close the door softly when leaving the room.
服务员离开包间时应面对客人退出，轻声关门。

◆ Patrol the room regularly, clean the table and take away the used tableware.
定期进包间巡视，清理台面垃圾并回收用过的餐具。

Practice 1 Chess & Card Services
实训项目 1 棋牌服务

Task of Service Practice 实训任务

◆ The guest in Room No. 116, Mr. Brown and his Chinese friends want to play board games at the BG Bar of the Entertaining Center.
酒店 116 房的客人 Brown 先生和他的中国朋友想在娱乐中心桌游吧玩桌游。

◆ Huang Ying, a receptionist at the service counter receives them. Huang introduces many kinds of board games to them.
服务台接待员黄莺接待了他们。她为客人介绍了多种桌上游戏。

◆ Mr. Brown wants to try playing mahjong.
Brown 先生想尝试一下麻将。

◆ The price of the room equipped with automatic mahjong table is 10 yuan per hour.
设有自动麻将桌的包间价格是每小时 10 元。

◆ Mr. Brown plans to play for 4 hours.
Brown 先生打算玩 4 个小时。

◆ Mr. Brown orders a pot of chrysanthemum tea and 4 bottles of orange juice.
Brown 先生点了 1 壶菊花茶，4 瓶橙汁。

◆ The bill is charged into the oom account.
账单计入房账。

◆ Huang leads them to the room No. 6. She gives best wishes to them and closes the room door when leaving.
黄莺引领他们进入 6 号包间，送上良好祝愿并为客人关上房门后离开了。

Service Practice 服务实训

Now, let's begin the practice according to *Task of Service Practice*.
请按照上述实训任务开始实训。

28 1 Chess & Card Services. mp3

Model of Service Practice 实训对照

Huang：Huang Ying, a receptionist at the BG Bar.

227

Brown：Mr. Brown, a guest.

Huang：Welcome to the BG Bar, sir. What can I do for you?

　　　　欢迎来到桌游吧。我能为您做些什么？

Brown：I'm wondering what kinds of board games you are serving.

　　　　我想知道您这里有什么桌上游戏。

Huang：We serve many kinds of board games, such as chess, Chinese chess, Chinese checkers, weiqi, mahjong and cards.

　　　　我们为客人提供国际象棋、中国象棋、中国跳棋、围棋、麻将、纸牌等多种桌上游戏。

Brown：My Chinese friends want to teach me how to play mahjong.

　　　　我的中国朋友想教我打麻将。

Huang：I'd like to introduce the room equipped with automatic mahjong table to you. The rental charge of it is 10 yuan per hour. Could you please tell me how long you are going to play?

　　　　我想向您推荐设有自动麻将桌的包间，租金是每小时 10 元。您能告诉我您打算玩多长时间吗？

Brown：We are going to play for 4 hours.

　　　　我们打算玩 4 个小时。

Huang：What drinks would you like?

　　　　请问您想喝点什么？

Brown：A pot of chrysanthemum tea and 4 bottles of orange juice.

　　　　1 壶菊花茶，4 瓶橙汁。

Huang：Would you mind telling me the way of payment?

　　　　请问您怎么结账？

Brown：Charge it into my room account.

　　　　挂到我的房账上。

Huang：May I have your room number, please?

　　　　请问您的房间号是多少？

Brown：It's No. 116.

　　　　116 房间。

Huang：Wait a moment, sir. Let me make a record. Thank you for waiting. Room No. 6 with automatic mahjong table is ready for you.

　　　　请稍等，先生。我需要做一下记录。感谢您的等待。带自动麻将桌的 6 号包间已经为您准备好了。

Brown：That's cool.

　　　　太棒了。

Huang：Please go with me. You're here in Room No. 6. A pot of chrysanthemum tea and 4 bottlesof orange juice are here on the table.

　　　　请随我来。6 号包间到了。1 壶菊花茶、4 瓶橙汁给您放在桌子上了。

Brown：Thank you very much.

谢谢。

Huang：The power of the table is turned on now. Shuffle and roll of dice are done automatically. If there are any problems with the automatic mahjong table or anything you want，please dial "01" for service counter.

麻将桌的电源已经打开了。洗牌和掷骰子都是自动完成的。如果自动麻将桌有问题或者您需要什么，请拨"01"到服务台。

Brown：OK. We got it.

好的。知道了。

Huang：I have to remind you that gambling is absolutely prohibited in our hotel. Wish you have a good time here.

我得提醒您，本酒店绝对禁止赌博行为。希望您在这里玩得愉快。

Brown：Thank you for reminding us.

谢谢你的提醒。

Practice 2   Singing in KTV
实训项目 2   KTV 服务

Task of Service Practice 实训任务

◆ The hotel guest，Mr. Henry and his friends want to sing at the KTV of the Entertaining Center.

酒店客人 Henry 先生及其朋友要在酒店娱乐中心的 KTV 唱歌。

◆ Zhou Wei，a receptionist at the KTV receives them and introduces the price list of KTV.

KTV 接待员周伟接待了 Henry 先生，并介绍了 KTV 的价位。

◆ There are 5 people and they want a medium-sized box.

他们一共是 5 个人，想要一间中型包厢。

◆ Mr. Henry orders a dozen of beer，a nut flatter and a fruit platter.

Henry 先生点了一打啤酒，一份坚果拼盘和一份水果拼盘。

◆ After 2 hours，Mr. Henry calls for the service to settle the bill.

2 小时后，Henry 先生呼叫服务要结账。

◆ Mr. Henry pays the bill by credit card.

Henry 先生用信用卡结账。

Service Practice 服务实训

Now，let's begin the practice according to *Task of Service Practice*.

请按照上述实训任务开始实训。

Model of Service Practice 实训对照

28 2 Singing in KTV. mp3

Zhou：Zhou Wei, a receptionist at the service counter of KTV.

Henry：Mr. Henry, a hotel guest.

Zhou：Good evening, ladies and gentlemen. Welcome to the KTV of our hotel. What can I do for you?

女士们先生们晚上好。欢迎来到本酒店 KTV。我能为你们做点什么？

Henry：My friends and I would like to sing here. Do you have spare boxes here?

我和我的朋友想在这里唱歌，还有空余的包房吗？

Zhou：Yes, we have a lot of spare boxes with different size and different price. Could you tell me how many people there are with you?

是的，我们还有许多不同大小和价位的包房。请问您有几位？

Henry：We have 5 people here.

我们有 5 个人。

Zhou：I recommend you with the medium-sized box. It can hold 4 to 6 people and is 150 yuan per hour.

我推荐您选中包。中包可以容纳 4 至 6 人，每小时 150 元。

Henry：That's what we want. We'll take it.

那正是我们想要的。就订这个吧。

Zhou：Fine. Please go with me. Your box is No. 206 on the 2nd floor. Sir, we're here. Wait a moment. Let me open the KTV equipment for you. This is the menu for drinks and snacks. Would you like something to eat?

好的。请跟我来。您的包房是 206 号，在 2 楼。先生，我们到了。请稍等，我来打开 KTV 设备。这是酒水和小食菜单。请问您想点些什么？

Henry：We'd like a dozen of cold beer, a nut flatter and a fruit platter.

我们点一打冰啤酒，一份坚果拼盘和一份水果拼盘。

Zhou：OK. I'll bring to you right now.

好的，我马上送来。

（*After a moment*）

（过了一会儿）

Zhou：Excuse me, sir. A dozen of cold beer, a nut flatter and a fruit platter are served now. What else do you want?

打扰了，先生。一打冰啤酒，一份坚果拼盘和一份水果拼盘给您送来了。您还想点别的吗？

Henry：We're not sure how to order songs on the computer. Would you mind demonstrating for us?

我们不太会在计算机上点歌。你介意给我们示范一下吗？

Zhou： Of course not. There are over 5 000 new and old Chinese or English songs in our song system, so there should be something for everyone. Generally you can search for English songs alphabetically and also you can do it according to the language, the name of singers and the song's category, etc. The system allows you to type the key words on the keyboard, as well as hand-write it on the screen. For example, if you want to order "Jingle Bell", you can type the song name into the search bar, as well as find it in the category of "Christmas Songs", and also it can be found in the song list of Carpenters. Do you get it? By the way, there is a button for service staff on the operation panel. If you have something unclear or when you want to order something else, just click the button and I will come to help you. Hope you have a fun.

当然不介意。我们的点歌系统有超过5 000首中英文新歌和老歌，所以每个人都可以找到要点的歌。一般来说，您可以通过字母顺序搜索英文歌曲，也可以按照语种、歌手姓名及歌曲类别点歌。您既可以在键盘上键入歌曲关键词，也可以通过屏幕手写来点歌。比如说，如果想点"铃儿响叮当"，您可以在搜索栏键入歌名，也可以在"圣诞歌曲"类中找到，还可以在卡朋特的歌曲列表里找到。这下您明白了吗？对了，顺便说一下，控制面板上有呼叫服务的按钮。如果您还有什么不明白的或者还想点什么东西，就按那个按钮，我会来帮您的。祝您玩得愉快。

Henry： Thank you for your help. I finally figure it out.

多谢帮助。我终于搞清楚了。

(After 2 hours)

(2小时后)

Henry： Anybody here. I'd like to settle the bill.

有人在吗？我要结账。

Zhou： Sir, this is your bill. Please check it. The total is 496 yuan, including 300 yuan for the box, 80 yuan for the beer, 68 yuan for the nut flatter and 48 yuan for the fruit flatter. Would you like to pay it in cash or by credit card?

先生，这是您的账单。麻烦您看一下。包厢费300元，啤酒80元，坚果拼盘68元，水果拼盘48元，总共是496元。请问您是付现金还是刷卡？

Henry： Let me see. I'd like to pay by credit card.

让我看一下。我用信用卡结账吧。

Zhou： OK. Would you please show me your card and swipe it on the POS?

好的。请出示您的信用卡并在刷卡机上刷卡。

Henry： Sure, here you are.

好的，给你我的卡。

Zhou： Sir, we charged you 496 yuan from your card. Please sign your name here on this receipt. Thank you for your coming and wish you have a good night.

先生,我们从您的信用卡刷了496元,麻烦您在这张小票上签字。感谢您的光临,祝您度过一个愉快的夜晚。

Hotel Knowledge
新酒店人须知

(1) Generally speaking, board games(BG)refer to all the games that can be played by some people on the table or face-to-face platform. Different from sports or video games, board games pay more attention to exercises on way of thinking, ability of language expression and EQ(emotional intelligence), and do not rely on electronic equipment or electronic technology, so they are also referred to as "unplugged" games. Mahjong, chess, poker, *Werewolf*, and *Killers of the Three Kingdoms* all belong to the category of board games.

桌上游戏简称"BG"或者"桌游",从广义上来讲,"桌游"是指一切可以在桌面上或者某个多人面对面的平台上玩的游戏。与运动或者电子游戏不同,"桌游"更注重对思维方式、语言表达能力及情商的锻炼,并且不依赖电子设备及电子技术,因此它也被称为"不插电游戏"。麻将、象棋、扑克、"杀人游戏""三国杀"都属于"桌游"的范畴。

(2) Mahjong, a game that originated in China, is commonly played by four players. The game is widely played throughout Eastern and South Eastern Asia and has a small following in Western countries. Similar to the Western card games, mahjong is a game of skill, strategy and calculation and involves a certain degree of chance. Mahjong is usually played with 144 tiles bearing Chinese characters and symbols. Each player begins by receiving thirteen tiles. In turn players draw and discard tiles until they complete a legal hand using the fourteenth drawn tile to form four groups(melds)and a pair(head). The winner is the first player to hole four sets and a pair of like tiles.

麻将是一种起源于中国的四人游戏,在东亚和东南亚地区广泛普及,在一些西方国家也有出现。与西方的纸牌游戏类似,麻将是一种需要技巧、策略和计算同时也包含一定随机性的游戏。麻将通常由带有中国图案和符号的144张牌组成。每个玩家首先拿到13张牌,然后不断摸牌打牌,直到能够让手中的牌和第14张牌凑成4组顺子和1对将,就算"和牌",即为获胜。

(3) When the guest is in entertainment, the waiter should exit the room, and stand in place, waiting for the guest's order at any time.

客人娱乐期间,服务员应退出房间,站在适当的位置,随时听候客人的吩咐。

(4) Contact maintenance staff to maintain the equipment immediately when it is out of order. Replace the room and apologize to the guest right away if the equipment can't be repaired in a short time.

包间娱乐设备出现故障后应马上联系维修人员维修,短时间内无法修好的应马上为客人更换包间,并向客人道歉。

Practice Revision 实训回望

◆ Can you list the points for attention at the Fitness Center?

◆ What are the pool emergency procedures?

◆ What should we pay attention to when serving Spa treatment?

Case and Improvement：Who Will Pay the Bill
案例与提高：谁来买单

One day at 2 a. m. , Zhou Yang, one of the staff at the Entertainment Center found 4 guests in Chess Room 105 getting out of the room. It seemed that they were going to leave. This room began to be charged from around 4 p. m. previous day. There were 5 guests at first and one of them left at 7 p. m. , who told Zhou Yang that he would pay the bill from 4 p. m. to 9 p. m. , and the rest bill should be paid by the guests inside the room. Zhou Yang immediately made the bill of 5 hours. The guest paid it and left directly.

一天凌晨 2 点, 娱乐中心服务员周扬发现 105 号棋牌室的 4 位客人走出了房间, 似乎是要离开了。这间房是前一天下午 4 点左右开始计时消费的。本来有 5 位客人, 其中一位在当天晚上 7 点左右离开, 并且告诉周扬, 他负责将此房间的消费时间从下午 4 点买到晚上 9 点, 其余的由留在里面的客人负责。周扬当即打出了 5 个小时的账单, 客人付账后直接离开了。

Seeing the guests leaving, Zhou Yang immediately took the remaining unpaid bill of 5 hours with her and asked the guests politely："Excuse me, are you leaving now? Could you tell me who would pay the bill?" A guest walking in front of them said："The gentleman behind us. " Zhou Yang waited until the last guest getting out and said："Sir, please check here. " The guest looked at Zhou Yang questioningly and asked："Our room has been paid, hasn't it?" Zhou Yang said："There was a guest who has paid the bill before, but only paid the bill from 4 p. m. to 9 p. m. Another bill of 5 hours hasn't been paid yet. " The guest said angrily："It's not true. It should have been paid already. " Zhou Yang explained to the guest, and showed the bill that has been paid previously to the guest, feeling hurt. But the guest refused to pay and insisted to leave, saying："Neither my friend nor you told me about it. How can I believe what you said?"

看到客人准备离开, 周扬立刻拿着剩余未付的 5 个小时的消费账单上前礼貌地询问客人："请问各位是要离开了吗? 请问哪位客人买单呢?"走在最前面的一位客人说："后面的那位先生结账。"周扬于是等到最后面的先生走出来时说："先生, 请这边结账。"客人疑惑地看着周扬说："我们房间的单不是已经有人买了吗?"周扬说："是有一位客人之前买了单, 不过只是从下午 4 点买到晚上 9 点, 还有 5 个小时的单没买呢。"客人气愤地说："哪有这种事, 应该是全买了的。"周扬跟客人解释, 并拿出了先前已经付过的账单给客人看, 感觉非常委屈。可是客人就是不答应买单, 并执意要离开, 并且说："我的朋友没跟我说, 你当时也没跟我说, 我怎么能够相信你说的话呢?"

Case Topic 案例话题

My opinion about Zhou Yang's service in the case.

我对案例中周扬提供的服务的看法。

> ### Hotel Manager's Comments
> ### 酒店经理点评

（1）酒店中以时间计算消费的娱乐项目，一般都会提示客人消费的起始时间和计时收费方法，以便客人能够在娱乐时对大致的消费金额做到心中有数。此案例中的关键是：提前离开的客人没有告知房内的客人已付和未付账单的情况，周扬也没能将 105 号棋牌室已付和未付账情况，及时告知仍留在房内的其他客人，由此造成了误会。如果当时周扬能及时告知房内继续消费的客人，就不会出现这样的纠纷了。

（2）发现客人情绪激动，执意拒付账单时，周扬应马上通知当班的娱乐部经理。当班经理应马上赶到现场，向客人诚恳地道歉，并耐心向客人说明情况，请求客人与之前已付账离开的客人联系，查证此事。同时可以采用送果盘或减免账单金额的办法安抚客人的情绪，挽回给客人留下的不良印象。

（3）娱乐中心工作人员应加强服务技能和服务态度的培训，将发生工作失误的可能性减小到最低；在对客服务中时刻注意保持礼仪和风度，客人情绪激动时要保持冷静，绝对不能与客人发生争执。如与客人无法沟通时，应马上向上级报告，请求上级出面解决问题。

Answers to "Practice Revision" 部分参考答案

◆ Can you list the points for attention at the Fitness Center?

(1) Do wear sport shoes before entering the sport field.

(2) Do wipe up your sweat off after using the equipment.

(3) Do learn proper operation of equipment.

(4) Do pay attention to personal hygiene.

(5) Do keep the gym and locker room clean.

(6) Do warm up before doing exercises.

(7) Do take care of your own child.

(8) Don't get drunk before entering the sport field.

(9) Don't dive without gauging the depth.

(10) Don't smoke.

(11) Don't spit.

◆ What are the pool emergency procedures?

(1) Alert Swimmers

As soon as a pool emergency arises, lifeguards are supposed to give a long and steady blast of their whistles to alert patrons in the pool.

（2）Clear Pool Area

After lifeguards have captured the attention of patrons, they must calmly instruct swimmers to clear the pool in an orderly fashion immediately. Lifeguards are supposed to direct patrons to a designated area.

（3）Maintain Order

When an emergency strikes, particularly in a public swimming area, confusion can lead to panic. Lifeguards or other responsible parties must maintain a sense of order among the crowd.

（4）Rescue the Victim

Lifeguards need to remove the victim of the accident from the pool. If the victim is still alive, lifeguards may need to administer CPR or other first aid. If more than one lifeguard is present, one may execute the rescue while the other evacuates the area.

（5）Call for Assistance

Lifeguards need to instruct someone to call for assistance—perhaps a 911 call that will lead to the arrival of emergency medical personnel.

（6）Alert Authorities

After the emergency ends, lifeguards need to alert the appropriate authority figures, who can be people such as property owners or managers, group leaders or parents.

（7）File a Report

Lifeguards need to complete an emergency incident report. Such reports can help the authorities as they investigate the incident and as they consider whether changes are needed in pool safety rules.

◆ What should we pay attention to when serving Spa treatment?

Each service provided by the spa should have an established procedure when administered to the guest. Guidelines vary based on the specific treatment. Manicure and pedicure workers must be sure to sterilize all equipment. Estheticians must monitor the guest to ensure that he is not having an allergic reaction. Massage therapists must make sure that the guest is comfortable in the process of massage.

Chapter Twelve   Convention and Exhibition Services

实训模块十二   会展服务

Unit 29
Convention Service

技能实训 29　会议服务

Main Services 主要服务

Services before the meeting
会前服务

◆ Book the meeting.
预订会议。

◆ Discuss the service details for the meeting.
讨论会议服务细节。

◆ Show the meeting planner the facilities of the meeting and the decoration of the meeting hall.
带领会议策划人查看会议所需设施的配置和会场布置。

Services during and after the meeting
会议期间和会后服务

◆ Register for the conference.
为会议报到。

◆ Routine Service.
会议常规服务。

◆ Return the rental equipment.
归还租借的设备。

◆ Payment.
结账。

Skill Points 技能要点

Booking the meeting
预订会议

◆ Pay special attention to getting the following information from the meeting planner.
要注意从会议策划人那里了解下列信息。

What size of the conference or how many participants.

会议规模或参加会议的人数。

What kind of conference or what kind of function room.

会议类型或所需具有何种功能的会议室。

The special demands for the meeting facilities.

对会议设施的特殊要求。

The special demands for the meeting service.

对会议服务的特殊要求。

The time of the conference.

会议的时间。

The number of the rooms needed.

房间数。

◆ Introduce the facilities and services of the hotel according to the information above.

根据上述信息向会议策划人介绍酒店的会议设施和服务。

◆ Get the name of the meeting planner and his telephone number and the date of the discussion about the service details for the conference.

获得会议策划人的姓名、电话号码及商讨会议服务相关细节的日期。

Discussing the service details for the meeting

讨论会议服务细节

◆ Confirm

确认

The number of the participants.

与会人数。

The number and the size of the conference rooms (including big conference hall, small meeting room and exhibition room).

所需的不同大小的会议室间数(包括：会议大厅、小会议室和展室)。

The facilities for the meeting.

所需的会议设施。

◆ Discuss

讨论

The arrangements and demands for catering for the meeting.

会议餐饮安排和要求。

The demands in detail for the meeting services and meeting facilities.

会议服务的细节要求及对会议设施的要求。

◆ Establish

确定

The number of the rooms and the room rates.

房间数和房价。

The food and beverage rates.

餐饮费用。

Practice 1　Reserving a Conference
实训项目 1　预订会议

Task of Service Practice 实训任务

◆ Mr. Harry Carter is a convention planner, whose telephone number is 00492785261. They plan to hold a meeting in the hotel, so he wants to speak to the person in charge. Zhao Jun says that she is the Convention Service Manager of the hotel.

Harry Carter 先生是一位会议策划人,他的联系电话号码是 00492785261。他们计划在这家酒店召开会议,他想和负责这项工作的人谈一谈。赵君说她就是酒店的会议服务经理。

◆ The Conference Center of the hotel has just been equipped with full simultaneous interpretation facilities. There are two large conference halls in the hotel. One can be seated for 300 people; the other can hold 500 attendees. Beside the largest conference hall, there are five small meeting rooms which can hold 60 people and a small exhibition room for display purpose.

酒店的会议中心配置了全套的同声传译设备。酒店共有两个大会议厅,一个能坐 300 人,另外一个可以坐 500 人。在最大的会议厅旁边有五个小的能容纳 60 人的会议室,还有一个可用于陈列展品的小展室。

◆ The conference will be held from May 20 to 26. It is an international teaching seminar. It is expected that 300 people will attend the conference. They need to book a largest conference hall, 5 small meeting rooms and an exhibition room. They plan to introduce some advanced equipment of teaching to the delegates. They also need to reserve 180 standard rooms.

会议于 5 月 20 日至 26 日在酒店召开。这是一次国际教学研讨会,预计有 300 人参加。需要订一个大的会议厅和 5 个小的会议室,还要一个展室,他们计划向与会代表介绍一些先进的教学设备。他们还需要订 180 个标准间。

◆ Mr. Harry Carter hopes to get the information in detail about the services of the hotel and the price list of the services in order to make a good plan for the conference. Zhao Jun will send him the Service Guidance, the price list of the service in the hotel, and a plan of the actual conference center. She asks Mr. Carter to switch on his fax machine and give her a signal.

为了制订好会议计划,Harry Carter 先生希望获得酒店各种服务以及服务价目表的详细信息。赵君将传真本酒店的服务指南和服务价目单及一张会议中心的平面图,她要求 Carter 先生打开传真机,给她一个信号。

◆ Mr. Carter will come to the hotel to have a discussion of some details with Zhao Jun on May 15.

Carter 先生将于 5 月 15 日到达酒店,就一些细节问题再同赵君协商。

Service Practice 服务实训

Now, let's begin the practice according to *Task of Service Practice*.
请按照上述实训任务开始实训。

Model of Service Practice 实训对照

29 1 Reserving a
Conference. mp3

Zhao：Zhao Jun, Convention Service Manager.

Carter：Harry Carter, a convention planner.

Zhao：Good morning. can I help you?

早上好,有什么需要我帮助的吗?

Carter：Good morning. We want to hold a meeting in your hotel. May I speak to the person in charge?

早上好。我们想在你们酒店里举行会议,我可以和负责这项工作的人谈一谈吗?

Zhao：I'm our hotel's Convention Service Manager. My name is Zhao Jun. What kind of conference will you hold and how many attendees will you have?

我就是本酒店的会议服务经理。请问会议的类型和会议的规模?

Carter：It's an international teaching seminar. The exact number of delegates hasn't been finalized. It is expected that 300 people will attend the conference.

这是一次国际教学研讨会,到会代表的人数还没有最后确定。预计有 300 人参加这次会议。

Zhao：Our conference center has just been equipped with full simultaneous interpretation facilities. We have two large conference halls. One seats 300 people; the other can seat 500 attendees.

我们的会议中心配置了全套的同声传译设备。我们有两个大会议厅,一个能坐 300 人,另外一个可以坐 500 人。

Carter：Do you have some small meeting rooms and small exhibition rooms? We plan to introduce some advanced teaching equipment to the delegates.

你们还有小会议室和小的展室吗? 我们计划向与会代表介绍一些先进的教学设备。

Zhao：Yes, we do. Besides the largest conference hall, there are five small meeting rooms which can hold 60 people and a small exhibition room.

有,在最大的会议厅旁边有 5 个能容纳 60 人的小会议室,还有一个可用于陈列展品的小展室。

Carter：We'd like to book the largest conference hall, 5 small meeting rooms and an exhibition room.

我们要订那个大的会议厅和 5 个小的会议室,还有一个展室。

Zhao：What about the dates for the conference?

会议定在什么时候?

Carter： From May 20 to 26.

5 月 20 日至 26 日。

Zhao： Would you like some rooms?

还需要一些房间吗?

Carter： Yes, we'd like to reserve 180 standard rooms. Can you give us detailed information about your services and their prices? This is the only way we can make good plans for the conference.

需要,我们预订 180 个标准间。你能给我们提供你们酒店各种服务及服务价目表的详细信息吗? 只有这样,我们才能制订好会议计划。

Zhao： Certainly. Besides the Service Guide and the price list, I'll send you the floor plan of the actual conference center. Now, would you please switch on your fax machine and let me know when you're ready?

当然可以。除了本酒店的服务指南和服务价目单以外,我还给您传一张会议中心的平面图。请您打开您的传真机,给我一个信号好吗?

Carter： OK. I've received them and they're very clear. Thank you. I'll come to your hotel on May 15, to discuss further details with you.

我收到了,非常清楚,谢谢。我 5 月 15 日到你们酒店,就一些细节问题再同你协商。

Zhao： May I have your name? And can I contact you with the fax number?

我能留下您的姓名吗? 我可以用这个传真号与您联系吗?

Carter： My name is Harry Carter and my telephone number is 00492785261.

我叫 Harry Carter,我的联系电话号码是 00492785261。

Zhao： Thank you, Mr. Carter. You've booked a large conference hall, five small meeting rooms, and a small exhibition room for May 20 to 26. You're also reserved 180 rooms. Is that correct?

谢谢,Harry Carter 先生。您订了 5 月 20 日至 26 日的一个大会议厅、5 个小会议室和 1 个小展室,您预订了 180 房间。是这样吗?

Carter： Yes, that's correct. Thanks a lot.

是这样,非常感谢。

Zhao： You're welcome. I look forward to your arrival on May 15.

不用谢。我期盼您 5 月 15 日的到来。

Practice 2　Discussing with the Conference Planner
实训项目 2　与会议策划者商议

Task of Service Practice 实训任务

◆ 350 people will attend the international teaching seminar. They need the largest conference hall and 5 small meeting rooms and a small exhibition room beside them.

350 人将出席国际教学研讨会,他们需要最大的会议厅和它旁边的 5 个小会议室以及 1 个小展室。

◆ There is no discount for the conference reservations this month, but Zhao Jun went to see the General Manager the day before and the General Manager agreed to give them 10% off.

本月会议预订没有折扣,但赵君头一天去找了总经理,他同意给他们 10%的折扣。

◆ Mr. Carter reserves 240 standard rooms, 20 junior suites and 30 deluxe suites for the VIPS in all. He gives Zhao Jun the VIP list so that they can be assigned proper rooms.

Carter 先生订了 240 个标准间,20 个套间,还为 VIP 客人订 30 个豪华套间,他把 VIP 的名单交给赵君,以便为他们安排恰当的房间。

◆ The suppers on the first day and the last day of the conference are banquets. Buffets are for other meals. Mr. Carter chooses American breakfast and Continental breakfast among the three west breakfasts as the breakfast of the conference. Some attendees are overseas Chinese. So Mr. Carter suggests some Chinese breakfast in addition to them.

会议的第一天和最后一天的晚餐为宴会,其余每餐用服务式自助餐。Carter 先生从三种西式早餐中挑选美式早餐和欧式早餐作为本次会议的早餐。有些与会者是华侨,Carter 先生建议,除了这两种早餐外,最好还提供一些中式早餐。

◆ They also need some office support services, such as the secretarial services and 20 laptop computers.

他们还需要秘书办公服务和 20 台笔记本电脑。

Service Practice 服务实训

Now, let's begin the practice according to *Task of Service Practice*.
请按照上述实训任务开始实训。

29 2 Discussing with Conference Planner . mp3

Model of Service Practice 实训对照

Zhao: Zhao Jun, Convention Service Manager.
Carter: Harry Carter, a convention planner.

Zhao: Good morning, sir. Welcome to our hotel. May I help you?
早上好,先生。欢迎来到我们酒店,需要我帮忙吗?

Carter: Good morning. Are you Miss Zhao? I'm Harry Carter.
早上好,您是赵小姐吗? 我是 Harry Carter。

Zhao: Oh, I see. Glad to meet you, Mr. Carter.
是的,我是。见到您很高兴,Carter 先生。

Carter: Glad to meet you, too. I'd like to discuss some details of the conference services with you.
我也很高兴见到您。我想和您协商一下会议服务的一些细节。

Zhao： Have you finalized the number of participants?

已经确定了与会代表的人数吗？

Carter： Yes, we have. 350 people will attend our international teaching seminar. We need the largest conference hall, five small meeting rooms and a small exhibition room beside them.

确定了，350 人将出席我们的国际教学研讨会。我们需要最大的会议厅，和它旁边的 5 个小会议室以及 1 个小展室。

Zhao： What about the rooms?

房间呢？

Carter： Is there any discount for conference reservations this month?

本月会议预订有折扣吗？

Zhao： No. But I went to see the General Manager yesterday, and he agreed to a discount for your conference. We'll give you 10％ off.

没有。但是昨天我去找了总经理，他同意为你们会议打折。我们给您 10％的折扣。

Carter： That's very kind of you. Wait a moment, please. We'll reserve a few deluxe suites for our VIPs. Miss Zhao, we need 240 standard rooms, 20 junior suites and 30 deluxe suites in all.

太好了，请等一会儿。我们想为贵宾订几个豪华套间。赵小姐，我们一共订 240 个标准间、20 个套间、30 个豪华套间。

Zhao： Can you send us a VIP list so that we can assign the proper rooms for them?

请把贵宾的名单交给我，以便为他们安排恰当的房间。

Carter： Here you are.

给您。

Zhao： Thank you. Could you tell me your catering requirements for the conference?

谢谢，请问您对会议的餐饮安排有什么要求？

Carter： The suppers on the first day and last day of the conference are banquets. The other meals are buffets.

会议的第一天和最后一天的晚餐为宴会。其余每餐用服务式自助餐。

Zhao： Mr. Carter, please choose two out of the three western breakfasts as the breakfast for the conference.

Carter 先生，请您从这三种西式早餐中挑选两种作为本次会议的早餐。

Carter： American breakfast and Continental breakfast. Some attendees are overseas Chinese. So I think it would be a good idea to serve some Chinese breakfast in addition.

美式早餐和欧式早餐。有些与会者是华侨，因此，我认为除了这两种早餐外，最好还提供一些中式早餐。

Zhao： Good idea.

好主意。

Carter： From the conference service guide, I know that you can provide advanced conference facilities. Do you offer office support services such as Telex, photocopying and secretarial services? And we need 20 laptop computers as well.

从会议服务指南里，我知道你们能提供非常先进的会议设施。请问能否提供传真、复印和秘书服务？而且我们还需要 20 台笔记本电脑。

Zhao：Certainly, we can. Is there anything else I can do for you?

当然能够，还有其他的事情需要我为您服务吗？

Carter：No, thank you.

没有了，谢谢。

Zhao：We look forward to serving you.

我们期盼着为您服务。

Practice 3　Registering for Conference
实训项目 3　会议报到服务

Task of Service Practice 实训任务

◆ Dr. Peter Moran from Columbia University is coming to register for the conference. He has pre-registered.

来自 Columbia 大学的 Peter Moran 博士前来开会报到，他预先登记过。

◆ Wang Ling handles the registration for Dr. Moran.

王玲为 Moran 博士办理开会登记手续。

◆ Dr. Moran has been arranged in Room 3678. This room is a deluxe suite. Wang Ling gives the key card, the meeting badge and the meeting packet to Dr. Moran.

Moran 博士被安排在 3678 房间，这是一个豪华套间。王玲把钥匙卡、会议证章和会议资料袋交给 Moran 博士。

◆ Wang Ling tells Dr. Moran that Prof. Jack Cooper from Landon University has arrived and he stays in Room 3679, next to his.

王玲告诉 Moran 博士，来自 Landon 大学的 Jack Cooper 教授已经到达，住在 3679 房间，就在他的隔壁。

◆ Li Wei will show Dr. Moran to his room, and he will serve Dr. Moran during the meeting.

李伟将送 Moran 博士到房间，会议期间他将为 Moran 博士服务。

Service Practice 服务实训

Now, let's begin the practice according to *Task of Service Practice*.

请按照上述实训任务开始实训。

29 3 Registering for Conference. mp3

Model of Service Practice 实训对照

Wang：Wang Ling, a clerk.

Moran：Dr. Peter Moran.

Wang：Good morning, sir. Would you like to register for the conference?

上午好，先生。请问您是开会报到吗？

Moran：Yes.

是的。

Wang：Have you pre-registered?

您预先登记过吗？

Moran：Yes, I have.

登记过。

Wang：Your name, please?

请问您尊姓大名？

Moran：Peter Moran.

Peter Moran。

Wang：Wait a moment, please. Which university are you from?

请您等一下。您来自哪个大学？

Moran：I'm from Columbia University.

Columbia 大学。

Wang：Dr. Moran, we've put you in Room 3678. It's a deluxe suite. Here is your key card. And here is your meeting badge and meeting packet.

Moran 博士，您的房号是 3678，这是一个豪华套间。给您房卡，这是您的会议证章和会议资料袋。

Moran：Could you tell me whether Prof. Jack Cooper from Landon University has arrived?

你能告诉我 Landon 大学的 Jack Cooper 教授到了吗？

Wang：He has arrived. His room is 3679, next to yours.

到了。他的房号是 3679，在您隔壁。

Moran：Thank you.

谢谢。

Wang：My pleasure. Li Wei will show you to your room, and he will serve you during the conference. Have a pleasant stay here.

为您服务是我的荣幸。李伟会带您到您的房间，会议期间他将为您服务。祝您入住愉快！

Hotel Knowledge
新酒店人须知

(1) Different from the room reservation, the conference planner(exhibition planner) of the conference reservation (exhibition reservation) will have several discussions something about the conference with the Conference Service Manager before it begins.

与客房预订不同的是,会议(还有展览)预订的会议组织者(办展商)与会议服务经理在会议开始前的一段时间还需要多次会面商谈会议的有关事宜。

(2) Some useful expressions in the conference facilities：

常用会议设备：

photocopying	复印
HP fax machine	HP 传真机
laptop computer	笔记本电脑
laser printer HP	激光打印机
LCD	液晶显示屏
video recorder Sony	录像机
DV shooter Sony	摄像机
microphone	麦克风
loudspeaker	扩音器
earphone	耳机
recorder	录音机
projector	投影仪
slide	幻灯
slide projector	幻灯片投影仪
audiovisual	视听设备

Unit 30
Exhibition Service

技能实训 30　展览服务

Main Services 主要服务

◆ Book an exhibition.
　预订展览。

◆ Discuss something about the exhibition.
　协商展览服务的有关事宜。

◆ Set up the booths.
　布展。

◆ Serve during the exhibition.
　展出服务。

◆ Tear down the booths.
　撤展。

◆ Make the payment.
　结账。

Skill Points 技能要点

◆ Booking the exhibition, we need to get the following information from the exhibition planner.
　预订展览时，我们需要从办展商那里获取下列信息。

　　The size of the exhibition hall.
　　所需展厅的大小。
　　The number of the participants.
　　参展商数。
　　The number of the visitors.
　　看展的人数。
　　What kind of exhibits and special demands for the exhibition hall.
　　展品的类型及展品对展厅的要求。
　　Whether a storehouse is needed or not and what size.

是否需要仓库,要多大的仓库。

The demands for the exhibition.

对展览服务的要求。

The special demands for the clerks who will take part in setting up the exhibition service.

对布展员工的特殊要求。

The time of the conference.

展出的时间。

◆ Introduce the facilities and services of the hotel according to the information above.

根据上述信息向布展商介绍酒店的会议设施和服务。

◆ Get the name of the exhibition planner and his telephone number.

获得布展商的姓名和电话号码。

◆ Setting up the exhibition,We need to pay attention to the following:

布展时,我们要注意:

The surrounding demands for the exhibits,for example,lights.

展品对展览环境的要求,如灯光。

The demands for the stands,for example,an island booth or a peninsula booth.

对展台的要求,如岛形还是半岛形。

Practice 1　Reserving an Exhibition
实训项目 1　预订展览

Task of Service Practice 实训任务

◆ The exhibition planner Harry Smith wants to reserve an exhibition in the hotel from April 25 to 27. The Convention Service Manager Zhao Jun receives Mr. Harry Smith.

办展商 Harry Smith 要向酒店预订展览,时间为 4 月 25 日至 27 日。会议经理赵君接待了他。

◆ They will show some advanced building materials for communication and tools for communicational construction. They need an exhibition hall with an attendance of 800 at a time.

他们展出一些先进的交通建筑材料和交通建设工具。他们需要一次能容纳 800 人的展览大厅。

◆ The hotel has two halls connected,and each has the capacity of 450. And in the East Exhibition Hall,there are two rooms,which can be used as offices. Beside the West Exhibition Hall,there is a storehouse which can contain 25 containers at a time.

酒店有两个相连的展览大厅,每个大厅能容纳 450 人。东大厅有两间可用作办公室的房间,西大厅的旁边有一个一次能容纳 25 个集装箱的仓库。

◆ The suggestion of Zhao Jun is that the exhibits are two different kinds. It will be better to divide them into two parts.

赵君的建议：展出的是两种不同的展品，把它们分成两部分展出可能更好一些。

◆ Special demands for the exhibition：

对展出的特殊要求：

Fifteen containers will be sent here, so they need a big storehouse.

15 个集装箱要运到这里，所以需要一个大仓库。

They will set off the example pictures of building, so they have a special requirement for the lights and the wall.

他们要展示建筑样图，所以对灯光和墙壁有特殊要求。

Every booth of the tools for communicational construction needs a color TV to show the procedure in which the tool is operated, 12 altogether.

交通建设工具展位需要彩色电视机来演示工具的操作过程，共要 12 台。

◆ The clerks of the hotel will begin to set up the exhibition on April 22. The exhibits will be sent to the hotel on April 21. Mr. Harry Smith will come to the hotel to set up the exhibition with the clerks on April 22. His phone number is 00495678912441.

酒店员工 4 月 22 日开始布展，展品 21 日运抵酒店，Harry Smith 先生 4 月 22 日到酒店和员工们一块布展。Smith 先生的电话号码是 00495678912441。

Service Practice 服务实训

Now, let's begin the practice according to *Task of Service Practice*.

请按照上述实训任务开始实训。

30 1 Reserving an Exhibition. mp3

Model of Service Practice 实训对照

Zhao：Zhao Jun, Convention Service Manager.

Smith：Harry Smith, an exhibition planner.

Zhao：Good morning.

上午好。

Smith：Good morning. You're this hotel's Convention Service Manager, aren't you?

上午好。你是酒店会务经理，是吗？

Zhao：Yes, I am. My name is Zhao Jun. How can I help you?

我就是。我叫赵君。需要为您服务吗？

Smith：We'd like to hold an exhibition in your hotel from April 25 to 27.

我们想在贵酒店办展览会，时间为 4 月 25 日至 27 日。

Zhao：What kind of exhibition?

请问什么类型的展览？

Smith：We want to exhibit some advanced building materials and tools for transportation construction. Do you have an exhibition hall that can hold 800 at a time?

我们想展出一些先进的交通建设材料和交通建设工具。贵酒店有一次能容纳 800 人的展览大厅吗?

Zhao：I'm afraid not. But we have two halls connected, and each has a capacity of 450. And in the East Exhibition Hall, there are two rooms, which can be used as offices. You could show two different exhibits, dividing the one exhibit into two parts.

恐怕没有。但我们有两个相连的展览大厅,每个大厅能容纳 450 人。东展厅内还有两间可用作办公室的房间。你们展出的是两种不同的展品,我认为把它们分成两部分来展出可能会更好一些。

Smith：That's a good idea. I'd like to reserve the two halls and the two rooms. Do you have a big storehouse? Our fifteen containers will be sent here.

好主意。我订这两个展览大厅和这两间房。你们有仓库吗? 我们有 15 个集装箱要运到这里。

Zhao：No problem. Our storehouse can hold 25 containers at a time, and it's next to the West Exhibition Hall. Do you have any special requirements for the exhibitions?

没问题。我们的仓库一次能容纳 25 个集装箱,而且就在西展厅的旁边。您对展出还有什么特殊的要求?

Smith：We have a special requirement for lighting the wall. We'll need to illuminate pictures of buildings.

我们对灯光和墙壁有特殊要求,它们需要衬托建筑样图。

Zhao：Anything else?

还有别的要求吗?

Smith：Each booth for construction tools needs a color TV, twelve altogether.

交通建设工具展位需要彩色电视机,共要 12 台。

Zhao：May I know your name and your phone number?

能留下您的姓名和电话号码吗?

Smith：My name is Harry Smith and my phone number is 00495678912441.

我叫 Harry Smith,我的电话号码为 00495678912441。

Zhao：Thank you, Mr. Smith. You have reserved two exhibition halls, two rooms as offices and a storehouse. You need twelve TV sets. Your phone number is 0049 5678912441. The time of the exhibition is April 25 to 27. Is that correct?

谢谢您,Smith 先生。您预订两个展览大厅,两个作办公室的房间,1 个仓库,12 台电视机。您的电话号码是 00495678912441。展出时间为 4 月 25 日至 27 日。是这样吗?

Smith：Yes. When will you begin to set up the exhibition?

是。你们什么时间开始布展?

Zhao：April 22.

4 月 22 日。

Smith：Our exhibits will be sent here on the 21st and I'll come to set up the exhibition with you on April 22. Thank you for your help.

我们的展品 4 月 21 日送抵酒店,我 22 日到这里和你们一块布展。谢谢你们的帮助。

Zhao： We are very happy to be chosen for your exhibition. We'll try our best to make your exhibition successful.

酒店被选为展出之地我们不胜荣幸,为成功地办好此次展览会我们将竭尽全力。

Practice 2　Setting Up an Exhibition
实训项目2　布展

Task of Service Practice 实训任务

◆ How to arrange the exhibition halls：

怎样安排展厅：

The East Exhibition Hall is arranged as the exhibition hall for the building materials of communication.

东展厅用作交通建筑材料展厅。

The tools of the communicational construction are shown in the West Exhibition Hall.

西展厅展出交通建设工具。

The gate of the East Exhibition Hall is decorated as the entrance of the International Exhibition for Building Material and Constructional Stool of Communication.

东展厅大门布置成此次"国际交通建筑材料和建设工具展"的入口。

◆ How to arrange the rooms：

怎样安排房间：

The north room is for the exhibition office.

北边的房间用作展览办公室。

The south one is for the talking room. The trade talks and reaching contracts can be carried out here.

南边的房间用作洽谈室,贸易洽谈、合同签订都在这里进行。

◆ How to set up the stands：

怎样布置展台：

The exhibitors of building materials of communication are more than those of the tools for communicational construction. The material booths are in a peninsula.

交通材料建筑参展商比交通工具的参展商要多。材料展台布置成半岛形。

The stool booths are in the shape of an island.

工具展台布置成岛形。

◆ How about food & beverage：

餐饮安排：

The exhibition planner plans to provide some free snacks and mineral water for the visitors.

布展商计划为参观者提供一些免费的小吃和矿泉水。

Food and beverage service is arranged at the corridor connecting the two halls.

餐饮服务就设在两个大厅的过道上。

◆ The time of examining：

检查时间：

2 o'clock in the afternoon of April 24.

4 月 24 日下午两点。

30 2 Setting Up an
Exhibition. mp3

Service Practice 服务实训

Now，let's begin the practice according to *Task of Service Practice*.

请按照上述实训任务开始实训。

Model of Service Practice 实训对照

Zhao：Zhao Jun，Convention Service Manager.

Smith：Harry Smith，an exhibition planner.

Zhao：I'm glad to see you again，Mr. Smith.

Smith 先生，再次见到您真高兴。

Smith：I'm glad to see you again，too. Miss Zhao，have you begun the work?

再次见到您我也是很高兴。赵小姐，你们开始工作了吗?

Zhao：Yes，we've started the preparations. Let's go to the exhibition halls. This is the East Exhibition Hall and that's the West Exhibition Hall. How should we arrange them?

开始了，我们已做好准备。我们到展厅去吧。这是东展厅，那是西展厅。我们怎样安排展厅?

Smith：The East Exhibition Hall should be for building materials. The West Exhibition Hall should be for construction tools.

东展厅用作交通建筑材料展厅，西展厅展出交通建设工具。东展厅大门布置成此次展会的入口。

Zhao：We have the same idea. It's convenient for us to carry those big tools to the exhibition hall from the storehouse. How should we deal with the two rooms?

我们的想法也一样。从仓库搬那些大型的工具也方便。这两间房怎样布置?

Smith：The north room will be our exhibition office，and the south one is for negotiations. The trade talks and contract discussions can be carried out there.

北边的房间用作我们的展览办公室，南边的房间用作洽谈室，贸易洽谈、签合同都在这里进行。

Zhao：How about setting up the booths? There are more exhibitors of building materials than construction tools.

怎样布展台? 交通材料建筑参展商比交通工具的参展商要多。

Smith：The material booths should be arranged in a peninsula，while the tool booths should be set up in the shape of an island.

材料展台布置成半岛形,工具展台成岛形。

Zhao： Would you like some flowers and plants to decorate the booths and the halls?

展台和大厅需要用鲜花和绿色植物来装饰吗?

Smith： Certainly.

当然需要。

Zhao： Will you provide some snacks and refreshments for the visitors?

为参观者提供小吃和饮料吗?

Smith： Yes, we plan to provide some free snacks and mineral water for the visitors.

提供,我们计划为参见者提供一些免费的小吃和矿泉水。

Zhao： Food and beverage service will be in the corridor connecting the two halls.

餐饮服务就设在两个大厅的过道上。

Smith： That's a good idea.

好主意。

Zhao： Do you have any other suggestions or requirements for us?

对我们的工作还有什么建议或要求吗?

Smith： No.

没有了。

Zhao： Could you come to inspect our work at 2 o'clock on the afternoon of April 24?

4 月 24 日下午 2 点您能过来检查我们的工作吗?

Smith： Yes, I will. See you the day after tomorrow.

能,我会来的。后天见。

Zhao： See you the day after tomorrow.

后天见。

Hotel Knowledge
新酒店人须知

Martin W. B. once pointed out that the ability of building up the sound and friendly relationship between the clerk and the guest contains the following 9 points.

Martin W. B. 指出,服务人员与客人建立良好而友善的关系的能力包括以下九个要点。

attitude	友善的态度
attentiveness	无微不至的关照
tone of voice	悦耳的声音
body language	得体的肢体语言
naming names	叫出客人的姓名
guidance	准确的指引
suggestion selling	建议性销售
problem solving	解决问题

tact   灵活机智

Case and Improvement：Meeting the Guest's Urgent Needs
案例与提高：满足客人急需

After six months of practice in the hotel, Zhao Tong was pointed by the Convention Service Manager Zhao Jun to be responsible for the work of the International Exhibition for Building Material and Constructional Stool of Communication.

在酒店实训 6 个月后,赵童被会议服务经理赵君指定负责此次国际交通建筑材料和建设工具展出的工作。

The exhibition was planned to open at 9 in the morning of April 25. At 8：10, everything is ready. But at that time, the exhibition planner Mr. Harry Smith came to her office in a hurry with two exhibitors. The following was the conversation between them.

展出计划 4 月 25 日上午 9 点开幕,8：10 分一切就绪。这时,展出商 Harry Smith 先生和两个参展商匆忙来到赵童的办公室。下面是他们的对话。

Smith： These exhibitors didn't know about the exhibition until yesterday, and they couldn't get in touch with us, so they came here with their exhibits directly. Could you please arrange booths for them to exhibit?

他们昨天才知道开展览会的消息,他们也没有和我们联系上,就直接带着展品来到这儿。请你给他们安排展位展出好吗?

30 C&I Meeting the Guest's Urgent Needs. mp3

Zhao Tong： The two exhibition halls are full. Let me think. We have no place for you. Would you mind using our office as your exhibition hall? As you see, visitors going to the two exhibition halls will pass by the office door.

两个展览大厅都已安排满了,让我想想,我们没有地方给你们。把我们的办公室做你们的展厅,你们介意吗? 正如你们所见到的,两个大厅的参观者都需要从我们办公室的门口通过。

Exhibitors： It's a good place for us. It's very kind of you.

对我们来讲这是个好地方,你太好了。

Zhao Tong： I'm very happy to serve you. Please fetch your exhibits at once. We'll set up booths for you. We can open our exhibition on time.

为你们服务我很高兴。请把你们的展品马上拿来,我们为你们布展台。我们的展览可以按时开幕。

The exhibition was closed at 5 in the evening of April 27. The clerks had been busy with tearing down for three hours. Some tools had been loaded into the containers. Mr. Smith found out Zhao Tong in the West exhibition Hall.

4月27日下午5点展览会闭幕。员工们忙于拆展已经三小时了,一些工具都已被打包装进集装箱。Smith先生在西展厅找到赵童。

Smith: Miss Zhao, we're in urgent need for your help.

赵小姐,我们急需你的帮助。

Zhao Tong: What can I do for you?

需要我做什么?

Smith: Many visitors are asking us to prolong the exhibition for one more day. Some of them have new construction plans and they want to use new materials and advanced tools, so they want the people involved to visit. Can you help us?

一些参观者要求我们把展览会延长一天。他们当中有一些人有新的建设计划,他们想用新的建筑材料和先进的交通建设工具,所以他们想组织有关的人员来参观。你能帮我们吗?

Zhao Tong: Certainly. Our clerks will reset up the booths for you tonight. We'll charge the extra expenses to your account.

当然可以。我们的员工将连夜为你们重新布置展台。但是我们得把额外的费用和员工的加班工资加到你们的账上。

Smith: No problem. Thanks for your help.

没问题,谢谢你的帮助。

Zhao Tong: You're welcome.

不用谢。

Case Topic 案例话题

(1) My opinion about Zhao Tong in the case.

我对赵童所做工作的看法。

(2) My experience in meeting the guest's need.

我在满足客人需求方面的经验。

> **Hotel Manager's Comments**
> **酒店经理点评**

怎样才能做好会展服务工作? 我在这里谈两点。

(1) 会展服务工作人员需具有较高的沟通能力、协调合作能力和一定的组织策划领导能力。

与酒店其他岗位服务相比,会展服务是一种综合性的服务。会展工作人员直接提供的服务,包括会展活动策划、会展设备配置、布展、会议大厅布置、会展中服务、宴会装饰、舞台表演、印刷宣传品;国际会议还有同声传译、文件翻译等。这些是计划好、安排好的服务。会展中,客人经常会有一些临时的要求要满足;他们随时会遇到问题,需要我们帮他们排忧解难。会展人员还要与酒店其他部门——前台、客房、餐饮、维修安装、娱乐中心等部门沟通协调,共同合作才能完成会展服务。会展工作人员还有一项特别的工作,处理好其他部门在为客人服务中所产生的投诉。所以,会展服务工作人员除了一专多能外,还要具有较强的沟通能力、协调合作能力和一定的组织策划与领导能力。

(2) 会展服务中要灵活机智。

首先,解决客人难题时要多动脑、多动手、会说话、灵活机智。

案例中,临时来的参展商没地方设展台的,赵童把他的办公室用来布置他们的展台,还说了这么一段话 Could you mind using our office as your exhibition hall? As you see, the visitor of the two halls will pass by the door of our office. (把我们的办公室做你们的展厅,你们介意吗? 正如你们所见到的,两个大厅的参观者都需要从我们办公室的门口通过。)参展商不会有这样的感觉:没有地方,由我们随意安排。参展商现在的感觉是:我们虽来晚了,但他们还给我们安排了一个参观者来去的必经之地,非常高兴,所以 It's a good place for us. It's very kind of you. (对我们来讲这是个好地方,你太好了。)

其次,在为客人服务时正当、合理地提出我们的要求。我们要热情周到地为客人服务,满足客人的需求,为客人排忧解难。我们也需要合理地提出我们正当的要求,为酒店创造利润。案例中,赵童答应:"Our clerks will reset up the booths for you tonight. We'll charge the extra expense to your account." (我们的员工将连夜为你们重新布置展台。但我们得把额外的费用和员工的加班工资加到你们的账上。)赵童灵活机智地为酒店争取了应得的利益。

最后,提出合理的销售建议,灵活机智地争取订单。

大家知道,会展服务不仅增加会展中心的收入,还会保证酒店连续数天的入住率,增加酒店许多部门的收入。酒店的设施是固定的,会展的要求各不相同,会展举办人需要挑选合乎自己要求的酒店。这就要求我们提出合理的销售建议,灵活机智地争取订单。Practice 1 中,布展商 Smith 先生需要一个一次能容纳 800 人的展厅,但酒店没有。赵君回答不是"I'm terribly sorry that we haven't such a large exhibition hall for you." (非常抱歉,我们没有您所需要的这么大的展览大厅。)"礼貌地"放走一笔大订单。她回答的是:"I'm afraid not. But we have two halls connected, and each has a capacity of 450. And in the East Exhibition Hall, there are two rooms, which can be used as offices. You could show two different exhibits, dividing the one exhibit into two parts." (恐怕没有。但我们有两个相连的展览大厅,每个大厅能容纳 450 人。东展厅内还有两间可用作办公室的房间。你们展出的是两种不同的展品,我认为把它们分成两部分来展出可能会更好一些。)这段话给布展商的感觉:两种不同的展品在两个相连的展厅展出效果会更好。参观人数增加,厅大不用愁。还有两个房间可作办公室,方便。如果你是布展商 Smith 先生,你会走吗? 对,不会。赵君灵活机智地为酒店留下了这份大订单。

Chapter Thirteen   Shopping Service

实训模块十三   购物服务

Shopping（Ⅰ）

技能实训 31　购物（一）

Service Procedure 服务流程

◆ Greet the guest.
使用礼貌用语招呼顾客。
◆ Find out what the guest wants.
弄清顾客的购买意图。
◆ Recommend or introduce to the guest.
向顾客作推荐或介绍。
◆ Praise the article that the guest chooses.
向顾客夸赞所选的商品。
◆ Tell the guest where and how to pay.
告知顾客付款地点和付款方式。
◆ See a guest off.
使用礼貌用语与顾客道别。

Skill Points 技能要点

◆ The guests shopping in the hotel shop generally pay much attention to the brand, quality and design of articles. The price is also considered, but the shop assistant shouldn't emphasize it too much.
在酒店购物的客人，一般会注重商品的品牌、质量、设计等因素。虽然价格也是他们考虑的要素之一，但不宜过分强调。
◆ You can use the following to greet the guest.
招呼顾客可以用下列几种方式。
Excuse me. Can/May I help you?
Good morning, sir. What can I do for you?
Hello. Are you being attended to?
Can I be of some assistance for you?

Could I be of service to you?

◆ If the guest says: "I'm just looking." This means they want to choose the articles they prefer in no hurry without being interfered.

如果客人说:"我只是看看。"说明他们不想被关注,希望自己慢慢挑选合意的商品。

◆ You can use the following to ask what the guest wants and give your recommendations.

询问顾客意愿并推荐商品可用以下方式。

What kind of... would you like?

How about this one?

What style do you prefer?

Do you like this design?

What color and size do you want?

◆ If the articles which the guest has bought are antiques and valuables, the shop assistant still needs to remind him to keep the receipt or invoice well in case it is inspected by the guests.

如果客人购买的是古玩或特别贵重的物品,还需要提醒客人保存好收据或发票,以备海关查验。

◆ You can use the following to praise the article that fits the guest well.

夸赞商品很适合其本人可用以下方式。

I think it looks terrific on you.

This latest style is very popular nowadays and it goes really well with you.

This dress looks good on you, Miss. I think it's a perfect fit.

I think the color and style make you much younger.

You've made a great/good choice.

◆ Seeing a guest off.

送别客人。

You are welcome.

Please come again.

Have a good day.

Practice 1 At the Jewelry and Crafts Shop
实训项目 1 在珠宝工艺品部

Task of Service Practice 实训任务

◆ Mr. Smith wants to buy something for his wife as the birthday gift. But he doesn't decide what to choose.

Smith 先生想给他的妻子买一个生日礼物。但是他很犹豫,不知道该买什么合适。

◆ Wang Juan, a shop assistant in the hotel shop arcade, recommends a pair of pearl earrings to Mr. Smith. And she introduces much to him patiently. Mr. Smith is quite satisfied with her service and decides to take it finally.

王娟是商场部的售货员,她向 Smith 先生推荐了一副珍珠耳环。还很耐心地作了详细的介绍。Smith 先生非常满意王娟的服务并最终决定购买。

Service Practice 服务实训

Now, let's begin the practice according to *Task of Service Practice*.
请按照上述实训任务开始实训。

Model of Service Practice 实训对照

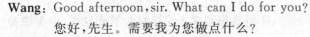

31 1 At the Jewelry
and Crafts Shop. mp3

Wang:Wang Juan, a shop assistant.
Smith:Mr. Smith, a guest.

Wang:Good afternoon, sir. What can I do for you?
您好,先生。需要我为您做点什么?

Smith:I'd like to buy something special for my wife.
我想给我妻子买一点独特的东西。

Wang:OK. We have various selections. Let me show you some. How do you like this pair of pearl earrings?
好的,我们有多种商品可供选择。让我带您看看。您觉得这副珍珠耳环怎么样?

Smith:They look very beautiful. But are they really genuine? I want to send them to my wife for her birthday.
哦,看上去很漂亮。可这珍珠耳环是真品吗? 我想送给我的妻子作生日礼物。

Wang:Certainly, sir. Everything sold here is real. And we have a very good reputation in this business.
当然了,先生。这里出售的都是真珠宝。我们在这个行业享有盛名。

Smith:Can you show me other styles of pearl earrings?
你能再给我看看这款的其他样式吗?

Wang:OK, how about this one? It is made of natural pearls and the luster will never fade. Also, this latest style is very popular nowadays and your wife will really like them.
好的。您觉得这副如何? 它是由天然珍珠做成的,而且光泽永远不会褪。并且这是最新款,现在很流行,您的妻子应该会非常喜欢的。

Smith:Sure. Those are better. How much do they cost?
嗯,这一对比较好。请问多少钱?

Wang:They cost 300 RMB.
300 元。

Smith:OK, I'll take them.
好吧,我买了。

Wang：All right, I'll wrap them up for you. Would you please go to the cashier to pay for them?

我来帮您包好。麻烦您到收银台付款。

Smith：That will be fine. Thank you.

好的,谢谢。

Wang：You're welcome.

欢迎下次光临。

Practice 2   At the Textiles and Knitwear Shop
实训项目 2   在丝绸纺织品部

Task of Service Practice 实训任务

◆ Mrs. Grace wants to buy a dress closely related to Chinese culture. So Li Yang, a shop assistant in the hotel shopping arcade, recommends qipao to her and offers her many to choose.

Grace 太太到酒店商场部想要买一件具有中国文化特色的裙子。李阳是商场部的售货员,她向 Grace 太太推荐了中国的旗袍并帮助她挑选。

◆ Mrs. Grace knows little about Chinese silk. Li Yang gives her such detailed explanations that Mrs. Grace is quite pleased to take it.

Grace 太太对中国的丝绸了解甚少,李阳给她作了很详细的介绍。Grace 太太非常满意李阳的服务并最终决定购买。

Service Practice 服务实训

Now, let's begin the practice according to *Task of Service Practice*.

请按照上述实训任务开始实训。

31 2 At the Textiles and Knitwear Shop. mp3

Model of Service Practice 实训对照

Li：   Li Yang, a shop assistant.

Grace：Mrs. Grace, a guest.

Li：Welcome to our shop. Can I help you, ma'am?

欢迎光临,请问您需要点什么,夫人?

Grace：I'd like to buy a traditional-style Chinese dress as memento of my trip to China. What do you think would be most suitable for me?

我想买一件具有中国文化特色的衣服,作为我中国之行的留念。你觉得什么样的比较合适呢?

Li： Well, ma'am. You're so graceful and slim. Would you like to have a Chinese qipao? It is very popular with young ladies in China nowadays.

夫人,您的身材苗条,气质高雅。您想试一试旗袍吗? 在中国,现在的年轻女性很流行穿旗袍。

Grace： Qipao? May I see it, please?

旗袍? 我能看一看吗?

Li： Sure. How do you like this one? It's made of pure Chinese silk. It's velvety and the color is brilliant.

当然可以。您喜欢这件吗? 这件旗袍是真丝做的,质地柔软而且颜色亮丽。

Grace： Ah, that's my favorite color. Can I try it on?

那是我最喜欢的颜色。我能试穿吗?

Li： Yes, of course. The dressing room is over there.

可以,试衣间就在那边。

Grace： I like the style very much and it fits me nicely. Do you think so?

我非常喜欢这种样式而且大小也很合适,你觉得呢?

Li： I think it looks terrific on you.

我也认为您穿上真的太漂亮了。

Grace： OK, I'll take it. But I wonder if the color won't come out in the laundry.

好的,那我就买了。但不知道这种颜色在洗的时候会不会褪色。

Li： As a matter of fact, all the dresses here are colorfast. By the way, silk shouldn't be hung out in the sunshine.

事实上,我们这里出售的衣服都不会褪色。顺便提醒您,真丝不能放在阳光下曝晒。

Grace： Well, I see. How much do you charge for this?

好的,我明白了。这件旗袍多少钱?

Li： 1 200 RMB.

1 200 元。

Grace： All right. May I use my credit card here?

好的。这儿付款能使用信用卡吗?

Li： Sure.

可以。

Unit 32

Shopping（Ⅱ）

技能实训 32　购物（二）

Practice 1　At the Chinese Arts and Stationery Shop
实训项目 1　在中国书画部

Task of Service Practice 实训任务

◆ Mr. White wants to buy a jade seal in the hotel shopping arcade. Having known what he wants, the shop assistant helps him to choose.

White 先生来到酒店商场部想要买一枚玉章。知道他的需求后,售货员帮助他挑选。

◆ Mr. White also wants to buy something as a gift to his wife who is interested in Chinese calligraphy. The shop assistant suggests a set of the Four Treasures of the Study to him. Mr. White is pleased to accept it.

White 先生还想给他的妻子买一样礼物,他妻子对中国的书法很感兴趣。售货员给他推荐了中国的"文房四宝"。White 先生很高兴地接受了。

Service Practice 服务实训

Now, let's begin the practice according to *Task of Service Practice*.
请按照上述实训任务开始实训。

32 1 At the Chinese Arts and Stationary Shop. mp3

Model of Service Practice 实训对照

White： Mr. White，a guest.

SA： a shop assistant in the shopping arcade.

White： Excuse me.
对不起,打扰了。

SA： Yes. What can I do for you?
您想买点什么?

White：I would like to have a look at jade seals.

我想看看您这儿有没有玉章卖。

SA：You've come to the right store. We've got a wide selection of seals for you to choose from.

您算是来对地方了。我们这儿有多种印章供您挑选。

White：Well, I'd like to see a medium-sized one with traditional patterns on it.

太好了,我想看看印章上刻有传统图案的那种,中等大小就可以。

SA：How do you like this one with a dragon on it? In China, the dragon seal is especially for gentlemen.

您觉得这个刻有龙图案的玉章怎么样? 在中国,龙印代表男士。

White：Oh, I guess it looks quite Chinese. I'll take it.

哦,看上去很有中国味,我买了。

SA：I'm glad you like it.

很高兴您能喜欢。

White：Also, I'd like to buy something for my wife. She's getting interested in Chinese calligraphy these days. What do you recommend?

我还想给我的妻子买点东西。她最近对中国的书法感兴趣。你能给我点建议吗?

SA：How about a set of the Four Treasures of the Study?

您觉得中国的"文房四宝"如何?

White：What is that?

"文房四宝"是什么?

SA：It's a kit with Xuan paper, a writing brush, an ink slab and an ink stick. She will like it.

它们是中国的宣纸、毛笔、砚台和墨。您妻子会喜欢的。

White：I hope so. OK, how much are they altogether?

我希望是,这些东西总共多少钱?

SA：They come to 890 yuan. Please wait a moment. I'll wrap them up for you.

加起来总共890元。请稍等,我给您包一下。

Practice 2   At the Chinese Tea Counter
实训项目2 在中国茶品部

Task of Service Practice 实训任务

◆ Mr. Colin wants to buy some Chinese Wulong tea, but he knows little about it.

Colin 先生想买中国的乌龙茶,但是他对乌龙茶了解得很少。

◆ Having known what he wants, Sun Jing, a shop assistant in the hotel shopping arcade, gives him detailed explanations of the tea and tells him it also has a weight reducing effect. Mr. Colin is pleased to take it.

孙婧是该酒店茶品部的售货员。在知道了客人的需求后，向他讲解了乌龙茶，并告诉他此茶有减肥的效果。Colin 先生很高兴地买了。

Service Practice 服务实训

Now, let's begin the practice according to *Task of Service Practice*.

请按照上述实训任务开始实训。

Model of Service Practice 实训对照

32 2 At the Chinese Tea Counter. mp3

Sun：　Sun Jing, a shop assistant.

Colin：　Mr. Colin, a guest.

Sun：　Good afternoon, sir. What can I do for you?

您好，先生。需要我为您做点什么？

Colin：　I'd like to have a look at Chinese tea.

我想看看中国的茶叶。

Sun：　We have Wulong Tea, Dragon Well Tea, Anxi Tieguanyin and so on. Which do you prefer?

我们有乌龙、龙井、安溪铁观音等。您想要哪一种？

Colin：　I was told there's a kind of Chinese tea that's called "Vigorous and Graceful Tea". Is that so?

我听说中国有一种茶叫"健美茶"，有这种茶吗？

Sun：　Ah, that's Wulong Tea. It's a high quality green tea mixed with dried jasmine flowers. This kind of tea is fine both in appearance and in taste, and it also has a weight reducing effect.

哦，那叫乌龙茶。这种绿茶质量高，里面有晒干的茉莉花。无论是外形还是味道都很不错，而且它具有减肥效果。

Colin：　Does it really have any special effect?

它确实有此效果吗？

Sun：　Yes, of course. That's why many foreign visitors, especially ladies, come to buy Wulong Tea in order to keep fit.

当然了，这就是为什么很多的外国游客，尤其是女士们来买乌龙茶的原因，为的是保持身材。

Colin：　Wonderful. My wife has been gaining weight these days. She is quite annoyed at her figure now.

太好了，我的妻子最近发胖了，她正为此事而苦恼呢。

Sun：　It's necessary for her to exercise. But I suggest she also take some Chinese green tea as a must for her daily diet. It's quite effective.

加强锻炼是有必要的。但是我也建议她把中国的绿茶当成每日饮食的必需品,这还是很有效果的。

Colin：Thank you. I'll take six boxes then.

谢谢你,那我要 6 盒吧。

Sun：All right, I'll wrap them up for you. Would you please go to the cashier to pay for them?

好的,我来帮您包好。麻烦您到收银台付款吧?

Colin：That will be fine. Thank you.

好,谢谢。

Sun：You're welcome.

欢迎下次光临。

Hotel Knowledge
新酒店人须知

Useful Expressions：
常用词汇：

green tea	绿茶	scented tea	花茶
black tea	红茶	brick tea	砖茶
malt tea	麦芽茶	lemon tea	柠檬茶
Tie Guan Yin	铁观音	pekoe	白毫
gonfou tea	工夫茶	ginseng tea	人参茶
narcissus tea	水仙茶	almond tea	杏仁茶
jasmine tea	茉莉花茶	pu'er tea	普洱茶
Longjin Tea(Dragon Well tea)	龙井茶	Wulong Tea(oolong tea)	乌龙茶
chrysanthemum tea	菊花茶	strong tea	浓茶
weak tea	淡茶	tea bags	袋茶
tea set	茶具	tea pot	茶壶

Chapter Fourteen   Other Services

实训模块十四   其他服务

Unit 33

Lost and Found Service

技能实训 33　失物招领服务

Main Services 主要服务

◆ Putting numbered tags on the items found.
为拾到物品编号。

◆ Assisting the guest to fill in the lost report.
协助客人填写报失单。

◆ Keeping the lost and found log.
完成失物招领日志。

◆ Assisting the guest to fill in the request slip.
协助客人填写取物单。

◆ Asking the guest for his/ her proof of identity.
要求客人出示身份证明。

Skill Points 技能要点

◆ When the guest reports a loss, the attendant should show his/her sympathy and try to comfort the guest by saying.
当客人报失时,服务人员应表示理解同情,可用如下表达。

　Don't worry, sir/ma'am, we'll see to it immediately.
　请您不要担心,我们会立刻处理。

　I am really sorry to hear this, but we will try to help you with it.
　很抱歉听到这个消息,但我们会尽力帮助您。

◆ You can use the following expressions to ask for the details of the item.
可以使用如下表达询问丢失物品信息。

　What is the make of your watch/phone/wallet?
　您的手表/手机/钱包是什么牌子的?

　What color is it?
　那是什么颜色的?

Is it brand new?

是崭新的吗？

◆ You can use the following expressions to respond to the guests' request.

可以使用如下表达答复客人。

We will see to it immediately.

我们立刻处理此事。

I am sorry, it has not been found yet.

很抱歉，还没有找到。

◆ You can use the following expressions to ask for the guest's personal information.

可以使用如下表达询问客人个人信息。

May I have your name/room number/address?

能留下您的姓名/房号/地址吗？

Could you show me your ID card?

能否出示您的身份证明？

Would you mind leaving your name/address here?

可否留下您的姓名/住址？

◆ You can use the following to require the guest to fill out the relevant forms.

可以使用如下表达要求客人填写相应表格。

Could you fill in the lost report?

您能填写报失单吗？

Would you mind finishing this request slip?

您能填写领物单吗？

◆ Do ask the guests about the time they last saw their lost items and the places they had been.

为寻找方便，一定要询问客人最后见到失物的时间地点。

Do you remember the last time you had it?

您记得最后看见它是什么时候吗？

Where have you been this morning/afternoon?

今天早晨您都去过哪里？

Practice 1 Reporting the Lost Property
实训项目 1 报失

Task of Service Practice 实训任务

◆ Mr. Macleod has just lost his mobile phone.

Macleod 先生刚刚丢了自己的手机。

◆ The phone is a Nokia make flip phone. It is black.

这是一部诺基亚黑色翻盖手机。

◆ All his contacts are inside of it.
所有的联系电话都在里面。

◆ He has been to the souvenir shop, the café, and the barber's.
他去过纪念品商店、咖啡厅和理发店。

◆ He leaves his name and room number in the lost report.
他留下了姓名和房间号。

Service Practice 服务实训

Now, let's begin the practice according to *Task of Service Practice*.
请按照上述实训任务开始实训。

Model of Service Practice 实训对照

33 1 Reporting the
Lost Property. mp3

Wu： Wu Xi, a receptionist.
Macleod：Mr. Macleod, a guest.

Wu： Good morning, sir, what can I do for you?
早上好,先生,能为您做点什么?

Macleod：Well, today is really a terrible day. I just lost my mobile phone. All my contacts are in it, including business partners. It's really important to me!
今天真不走运。我刚刚丢了自己的手机。所有的通讯录都在里面,包括生意伙伴的,它对我太重要了!

Wu： I can understand how you feel, sir. Don't worry. We'll try our best to help you. Do you remember the last time you used it or saw it? Where was it?
我能理解您的心情。不要担心,我们会尽力帮助您。您记得最后一次看见手机是什么时候吗? 在哪里?

Macleod：This morning. I got a call from my wife, and then I left the room, with the phone on me.
今天早晨。我接了妻子打来的电话,然后我就离开房间了,手机在我身上。

Wu： Where did you go after that?
之后您都去了哪里?

Macleod：A lot of places, the souvenir shop, the café, and the barber's. I think the mobile phone is still in the building.
很多地方。纪念品店、咖啡厅、理发店。我觉得手机肯定还在这个楼里。

Wu： Could you leave your name and room number here on this form?
您能否留下您的姓名和房间号?

Macleod：Sure.
当然。

Wu：   What is the make and model of your phone? And what's the color?

您的手机是什么牌子的？什么颜色？

Macleod： It is a Nokia phone，a flip one，and it's black.

诺基亚黑色的翻盖手机。

Wu：   We will arrange a search for it as soon as possible. If we can find it，we'll let you know immediately.

我们会安排人尽快查找。如果能找到的话，我们会马上通知您。

Macleod： I hope you can. Thank you for your help.

希望你们能找到。谢谢你。

Wu：   You're welcome.

不用谢。

Practice 2   Claiming the Property
实训项目2   失物认领

Task of Service Practice 实训任务

◆ The receptionist at the Lost and Found Office gets a phone call from Mr. Frank in the morning.

早上，失物招领处的工作人员接到 Frank 先生打来的电话。

◆ Mr. Frank has checked out，but he has left his coat in the room.

Frank 先生已经退房，却把大衣忘在了房间里。

◆ The room attendant will take the coat to the Lost and Found Office.

房间服务员将大衣送到失物招领处。

◆ Mr. Frank will come to claim it.

Frank 先生来取走大衣。

Service Practice 服务实训

Now，let's begin the practice according to *Task of Service Practice*.

请按照上述实训任务开始实训。

Model of Service Practice 实训对照

33 2 Claiming the
Property. mp3

Wu：   Wu Xi，a receptionist.

Frank： Mr. Frank，a guest.

Wu：   Good morning. Sun Glory Hotel，Lost and Found Office，can I help you?

早上好，朝辉酒店失物招领处。

Frank: Hello, this is Mr. Frank.

你好, 我是 Frank 先生。

Wu: Mr. Frank, what can I do for you?

您好, 有什么可以为您效劳的吗?

Frank: I just checked out half an hour ago, but I'm afraid I left my coat in the wardrobe in my room.

我半小时前退房了, 但我想我把大衣落在衣柜里了。

Wu: May I have your room number please?

请问您的房间号是多少?

Frank: Room 1302.

1302 房间。

Wu: What is the coat like?

您的大衣是什么样子的?

Frank: It is a long black one.

黑色长款。

Wu: All right, we will send the room attendant for the coat right away. We will see you at the Lost and Found Office.

好的, 我们会让客房服务员立刻查看。我们在失物招领处等您。

Frank: Thank you very much.

非常感谢。

(One hour later)

(一小时后)

Frank: Hi, I'm here to claim my coat. Sorry about that.

我来拿大衣, 抱歉麻烦你们了。

Wu: Don't mention it. Can I see your ID?

没关系。能看一下您的身份证吗?

Frank: Sure, here you are.

当然, 给你。

Wu: Could you fill in this request slip?

请您填写这张领物单。

Frank: OK.

好的。

Wu: Here is your coat, sir.

这是您的大衣, 先生。

Frank: Thank you very much.

非常感谢。

Wu: You're welcome. Have a nice day.

不客气, 祝您愉快。

Practice 3 Mailing the Property
实训项目3 失物邮递

Task of Service Practice 实训任务

◆ The receptionist at the Lost and Found Office gets a phone call from Ms. Douglas.
失物招领处的工作人员接到 Douglas 女士打来的电话。

◆ Her family stayed in the Sun Glory Hotel last week, and now they have been back to Los Angeles.
她一家人上周住在朝辉酒店,现在已经回到了洛杉矶的家中。

◆ Her daughter left her necklace in the hotel. It is a gold one with a dolphin pendant.
她的女儿把项链丢在了酒店。项链是纯金的,有一个海豚吊坠。

◆ Ms. Douglas hopes the staff here could mail the necklace to her if they could find it. Her address is 2 Stewart Street, Los Angeles, California, 90013.
如果找到的话,Douglas 女士希望酒店工作人员能把项链邮寄给她。地址是加利福尼亚州,洛杉矶,Stewart 街 2 号,邮编是 90013。

Service Practice 服务实训

Now, let's begin the practice according to *Task of Service Practice*.
请按照上述实训任务开始实训。

33 3 Mailing the Property. mp3

Model of Service Practice 实训对照

Li: Li Lin, a receptionist.
Douglas: Ms. Douglas, a guest.

Li: Sun Glory Hotel, Lost and Found Office, can I help you?
朝辉酒店失物招领处,有什么可以效劳的吗?

Douglas: This is Ms. Douglas calling from Los Angeles.
我是洛杉矶的 Douglas 夫人。

Li: Good morning, Ms. Douglas, what can I do for you?
您好,您有什么需要?

Douglas: My daughter and I stayed in your hotel two days ago. After we got back, she found that she had lost her necklace. It was her favorite birthday gift. But she is not sure where she lost it. I'm just calling to see whether you have picked it up or not.
我和我女儿两天前住在你们酒店。回来后,她发现项链丢了。那条项链是她最喜欢的生日礼物,但是她不确定丢在哪里。我想问问你们捡到没有。

Li: Hold on for a moment, let me check the lost and found log. Ms. Douglas, what is

273

the necklace like?

请稍等,我查一下我们的日志。夫人,请问项链是什么样子的?

Douglas: It is a thin, gold one, with a dolphin pendant.

很细,黄金的,有一个海豚吊坠。

Li: You are really lucky, Ms. Douglas, our staff found one in the hallway yesterday. I think it belongs to your daughter.

您真幸运。昨天我们的工作人员在走廊捡到一条。我想是您女儿丢的。

Douglas: Fantastic! Thank you so much.

太好了! 非常感谢。

Li: You're welcome, ma'am. Can I have your address? We'll send it to you by EMS.

不客气。能留下您的地址吗? 我们为您快递过去。

Douglas: My address is 2 Stewart Street, Los Angeles, California, 90013.

我的地址是 2 Stewart Street, Los Angeles, California 州,邮编是 90013。

Li: 2 Stewart Street, Los Angeles, California, 90013.

Stewart 街 2 号,Los Angeles,California 州,邮编是 90013。

Douglas: Right.

没错。

Li: Thank you ma'am. Have a nice day!

谢谢您夫人,祝您愉快。

Douglas: You too.

你也是。

Hotel Knowledge
新酒店人须知

Lost and Found Service

The room attendant should check the room thoroughly after the guest checks out. Should the guest leave his/her belongings in the room, the room attendant should inform the Front Desk immediately and record the information in the lost and found log with details including the room number, the guest's name, time, item name and the finder's name. The term for keeping the belongings is one year.

失物招领服务

客人离店后,服务员要仔细检查客房,如发现有客人遗留物品,应立即通知总台。如此时客人已离去,则将客人遗留物品记录于《失物招领登记表》,其上注明房号、客人的姓名、时间、物品名称、拾物者姓名。失物一般保存一年。

Unit 34
Safekeeping Service

技能实训 34　寄存服务

Service Procedure 服务流程

◆ Assisting the guest to finish the Valuables Deposit Form.

协助客人填写贵重物品寄存表。

◆ Giving the guest a tag for withdrawing.

收到物品时给客人取物牌。

◆ Explaining the cost of the service.

向客人提供服务收费标准。

Skill Points 技能要点

◆ When the guest comes to the desk, you can greet him/ her by saying.

当客人来到服务台时，你可以用如下表达问候客人。

Good morning/ afternoon, would you like to deposit or withdraw something?

早上好/下午好，您要存取什么吗？

May I help you?

能为您效劳吗？

◆ If the guest needs a safety deposit box to store valuables, remind the guest to:

如果客人需要保险箱寄存贵重物品，提醒客人：

Keep the key carefully.

小心保存钥匙。

Fill out the application form.

填写申请表。

Sign his/ her name.

签名。

Keep the tag in a safe place.

保存好取物牌。

◆ Inform the guest of the price with the following expressions.

用下列表达告知客人收费标准。

The service costs you xx yuan per bag per day.

行李寄存需要支付每件每天××元。

The safety box service is free.

保险箱寄存服务是免费的。

Practice 1 Depositing the Luggage
实训项目 1 寄存行李

Task of Service Practice 实训任务

◆ A guest wants to store his luggage in the hotel after checking out, because he will be taking several days' trip.

一位客人想在退房后寄存自己的行李,因为他有出游的计划。

◆ He will be checking out at 11:30 this morning, and will claim his luggage a week later.

他将在中午 11 点半退房,一周后取行李。

◆ The charge for the service is 5 yuan per bag per day.

寄存收费为每件每天 5 元。

◆ His room number is 1012.

他的房间号是 1012。

Service Practice 服务实训

Now, let's begin the practice according to *Task of Service Practice*.

请按照上述实训任务开始实训。

34 1 Depositing the
Luggage. mp3

Model of Service Practice 实训对照

Green：Mr. Green, a guest.

Wang：Wang Li, an attendant.

Green：Excuse me. I'll be checking out later. I wonder it I could leave my luggage here after I check out.

您好。我中午要退房。我想问一下退房后能否在这里寄存行李?

Wang：Yes, sure. We do provide luggage storage service. When will you collect them?

当然,我们有寄存服务。您想什么时候提行李?

Green：In a week.

一周后。

Wang：I see. When will you be checking out?

好的,您几点退房?

Green：About 11:30.

大约 11:30。

Wang：Then shall we arrange the bellman to pick up your luggage at 11?

行李员 11 点为您提行李可以吗？

Green：Sure.

好的。

Wang：May I have your room number please?

请问您的房间号？

Green：Room 1210.

1210 房间。

Wang：Room 1210. We will collect your luggage at 11 in the morning. Would you come to the service desk to get your storage receipt after that?

1210 房间。我们会在 11 点钟为您提取行李。然后请您来服务台领行李单好吗？

Green：Sure. By the way, may I ask the rate per day for depositing my luggage?

好的。请问每天的收费是多少？

Wang：It is 5 yuan per bag per day.

每天每件 5 元。

Green：I see. Thanks a lot.

好的，谢谢。

Wang：You're welcome.

不客气。

Practice 2　Depositing the Valuables
实训项目 2　寄存贵重物品

Task of Service Practice 实训任务

◆ Mr. Green wants to use a safety deposit box.

Green 先生想使用保险箱储存贵重物品。

◆ Liu Yuan asks him to fill out a form and sign his name.

刘媛让客人填写存物单并签字。

◆ Liu Yuan tells Mr. Green to keep the tag carefully.

刘媛让 Green 先生保存好寄存单。

Service Practice 服务实训

Now, let's begin the practice according to *Task of Service Practice*.

请按照上述实训任务开始实训。

Model of Service Practice 实训对照

34 2 Depositing the
Valuables. mp3

Liu： Liu Yuan, an attendant.

Green： Mr. Green, a guest.

Liu： Good evening, sir, may I help you?

晚上好，先生。您需要什么帮助？

Green： Yes. I would like to use a safe deposit box. Will this fit into one?

我想使用一个保险箱。这个东西放得下吗？

Liu： Let me see. I think it's all right.

我看看。我想应该可以。

Liu： Could you fill out this form and sign at the bottom, please?

请您填写这份表格并在下面签字好吗？

Green： Here you are.

给您。

Liu： Please put your items in this bag, and we'll seal it.

请您把东西放在这个袋子里，我们会密封它。

Green： OK.

好的。

Liu： Thank you. Here is your tag.

谢谢。这是您的取物牌。

If you would like to use the items while we're storing them, please come here in person with the tag. After confirming your signature, we'll open the box.

如果在寄存期间您要领取物品，请您亲自过来，出示取物牌。我们核对签字后会为您打开保险箱。

Green： I see. Thank you.

好的，谢谢。

Liu： You're welcome.

不客气。

Unit 35
Introducing Tourism Information

技能实训 35　介绍旅游信息

Skill Points 技能要点

◆ You can use the following expressions to show the directions.

你可以用以下方式表达方位。

The Yong He Lama Temple is located on...road.

雍和宫位于……路。

You can take bus No. 1, and then change to bus No. 2 at...

您先坐 1 路,然后在……站换乘 2 路。

Cross the road, go down three blocks and you will see the gallery.

穿过这条路,向前走三个街区就能看到美术馆了。

Please go straight and then turn right at the traffic lights.

直走,在红绿灯处向右拐。

◆ You can use the following expressions to give traveling advice.

你可以用以下句型给予旅游建议。

I suggest you go to the Summer Palace.

我建议您去颐和园。

If I were you, I would go to the Summer Palace.

如果是我,我会去颐和园。

Why not go to the Summer Palace?

您为什么不去颐和园呢?

Well, the Summer Palace is a very nice place to go.

颐和园是一个很好玩的地方。

Practice 1　Recommending Tourism Spots
实训项目 1　推荐景点

Task of Service Practice 实训任务

◆ A guest is asking about traveling information in Beijing at the Reception Desk.

一位客人在服务台咨询北京旅游信息。

◆ He just arrives in Beijing and asks the receptionist to recommend some sites.

他刚刚到北京，希望服务员推荐一些景点。

◆ The receptionist recommends him both historic sites and modern attractions, including the Forbidden City, the Summer Palace, the Temple of Heaven, the International Trade Center zone, the Financial Street and Zhong Guan Village.

前台人员向他推荐了历史古迹和现代商务中心，包括紫禁城、颐和园、天坛、国贸商圈、金融街和中关村。

◆ The receptionist tells the guest to take subway and transfer to buses to reach those sites.

前台人员告诉客人乘坐地铁并转公交车到达上述景点。

Service Practice 服务实训

Now, let's begin the practice according to *Task of Service Practice*.

请按照上述实训任务开始实训。

35 1 Recommending Tourism Spots. mp3

Model of Service Practice 实训对照

Deng: Deng Juan, a receptionist.

Young: Young Smith, a guest.

Deng: Good morning, sir, may I help you?

早上好，先生，有什么可以为您做的吗？

Young: Good morning. I've just arrived. I don't know much about Beijing. Could you suggest some places to visit?

早上好。我今天刚到，还不熟悉北京这座城市。你能给我介绍一些值得游览的地方吗？

Deng: Certainly. I suggest you first visit some historic sites like the Forbidden City, the Summer Palace and the Temple of Heaven. They all represent the history of the city.

当然可以。我建议您去看看历史古迹，如故宫、颐和园和天坛。他们代表了这座城市的历史。

Young: That sounds great. Is the transportation convenient?

听上去不错。交通方便吗？

Deng: Yes, of course. The subway will take you directly to the Forbidden City. For the other two, you just need to take a bus or a taxi after getting off the train. Or, you could book a day tour and take a guided trip.

交通很方便。乘坐地铁就可以到达故宫。其他两个景点只需要下地铁后再倒一次公交或是乘坐出租车。或者您也可以预订随团游，有导游讲解。

Young: That's nice. What about other places of interest?

太好了。还有其他有意思的地方吗？

Deng： If you're interested in seeing the modern side of the city, you could have a look at the Central Business Districts and do some pleasant shopping. You can go to the International Trade Center zone, the Financial Street or Zhong Guan Village for digital products. They're all located near subway stations.

如果您对这座城市现代化的一面感兴趣，可以看看中央商务区一带，体验购物乐趣。您可以去国贸商圈、金融街。如果您想买数码产品，可以去中关村。这些地方就在地铁站附近。

Young： Fantastic. I think I really need to plan my trips in this large city. There are so many places to go.

太棒了。我想我需要好好计划一下在这座大城市里的游览。有这么多可去的地方。

Deng： Yes. Why don't you take a free travel brochure here? It can give you a lot of useful information, including restaurant lists.

是啊。您从这里取一份免费的旅游指南吧，里面有很多有用的信息，还有餐馆名录。

Young： Oh, that's good. Thank you very much for your help.

太好了。非常感谢你的帮助。

Deng： You're welcome. Have a good day!

不客气。祝您愉快！

Practice 2 Showing the Way
实训项目 2 指路

Task of Service Practice 实训任务

◆ The Bellows are asking the way at the Reception Desk.
Bellow 一家在前台问路。
◆ They want to travel to Yong He Lama Temple by subway.
他们想乘地铁去雍和宫。
◆ The entrance fee for Yong He lama temple is 30 yuan per adult.
雍和宫的成人票是每人 30 元。

Service Practice 服务实训

Now, let's begin the practice according to *Task of Service Practice*.
请按照上述实训任务开始实训。

Model of Service Practice 实训对照

35 2 Showing the Way. mp3

Deng： Deng Juan, a receptionist.

Bellow：Mr. /Ms. Bellow，the guests.

Deng：Good morning，sir.

早上好，先生。

Bellow：Good morning. I was told that there is a famous temple in the city center. Could you tell me where it is?

早上好。别人告诉我在市区有一座非常著名的庙宇，您能告诉我在哪儿吗？

Deng：Certainly，sir. I guess you mean Yong He Temple. It is not far from here. You could go either by subway or by taxi. I'd be pleased to arrange a taxi for you if you like.

当然可以，先生。我想您说的是雍和宫，距离这里不远。您可以坐地铁或者乘的士去，如果您需要，我可以为您安排酒店的出租车。

Bellow：I prefer to go by subway. Could you show me the way?

我想坐地铁去。您能告诉我路线吗？

Deng：Yes，sir. Just take the subway to Jian Guo Men Station and transfer to Line 2. Follow the directions to Chao Yang Men. It is just a few stops after that. There are very clear directions at the subway station.

好的。您坐地铁到建国门站，换乘2号线，去往朝阳门方向。几站就到了。站台里有非常清楚的方位信息。

Bellow：Thank you very much. By the way，do you know the price of admission?

非常感谢。对了，你知道门票多少钱吗？

Deng：It should be around 30 yuan.

应该是30元左右。

Bellow：OK，I see. Thank you.

好的，谢谢你。

Deng：Enjoy your trip!

旅途愉快！

Hotel Knowledge
新酒店人须知

Useful Expressions：
常用词汇：

Tian'anmen Square	天安门广场
The Palace Museum	故宫
The Temple of Heaven	天坛
The Summer Palace	颐和园
The Great Wall	长城
The Ming Tombs	明十三陵

Bei Hai Park	北海公园
The White Cloud Taoist Temple	雍和宫
Yong He Lama Temple	白云观

Bei Hai Park　　　　　　　　　　　北海公园

Yong He Lama Temple　　　　　　　雍和宫

The White Cloud Taoist Temple　　白云观

Beijing Confucius Temple　　　　　北京孔庙

The Imperial College　　　　　　　国子监

Tan Zhe Temple　　　　　　　　　潭柘寺

The Ruins of Yuan Ming Yuan　　　圆明园

Peking Man Site　　　　　　　　　北京猿人遗址

China Ethnic Culture Park　　　　　中华民族园

Beijing World Park　　　　　　　　世界公园

Case and Improvement：A Lost Purse
案例与提高：丢失的皮夹

Wang Li just takes his shift at the lost and found desk when a lady makes her way to the desk and talks to him in an upset voice.

王力刚刚在失物招领处接班，这时，一位女士走过来，很不耐烦地和他讲话。

35 C&I A Lost Purse. mp3

Adams： I've lost my purse. Your staff promised to look for it right away. Now, two hours have passed and I still haven't heard from you. What's the problem?

我的皮夹丢了。你们的员工向我保证马上帮助我找，现在两个小时过去了，我没有收到任何答复。怎么回事？

Wang： We're sorry to have kept you waiting. May I have your name and room number please?

很抱歉让您久等了。请问您的姓名和房间号？

Adams： Ms. Adams, Room 708.

Adams 女士，708 号房。

Wang： Thank you. Let me check the lost and found log. Oh, your report is here, but the purse has not been reported found yet. Do you remember where you last saw it?

谢谢您。我看看日志上有没有记录。您看，您的报失单在这里，但是还没有皮夹找到的记录。您记得最后一次看见皮夹是在哪里吗？

Adams： The purse was always on me. I found it was lost after I checked out. I think it was still in my room at that moment, but the room attendant said it was not. I doubt it, to be frank.

那个皮夹我一直带在身上。但是退房时我发现不见了。那时候皮夹肯定是落在房间里了，但是服务员说没有。说实话，我有点怀疑。

Wang Li realizes the guest suspects the room attendant is telling lies and seems not to trust their work. He tries to comfort her and seeks ways to solve the problem.

王力意识到这位女士怀疑客房服务员在说谎,她不信任这里的工作人员。王力尽力安慰客人,并且积极寻找解决问题的办法。

Wang: I understand how important the purse is to you, Ms Adams. I will call the Chamber Department to make sure they're still working on it.

我明白这个皮夹对您很重要,Adams 女士。我现在就给客房部打电话,确认他们还在继续帮您寻找。

At the same time, Wang Li also makes a call to the checkroom of the hotel, asking her colleague to double check whether Ms. Adams checked in any items there. The answer is yes.

同时,王力给酒店寄存部打电话,让那里的工作人员再检查 Adams 女士是否寄存过任何东西。果然,她把皮夹寄存了。

Wang: Ms. Adams, sorry to keep you waiting. I think you actually checked your purse and one of our staff found it in the checkroom. She'll bring it here soon.

让您久等了。您可能忘记了您寄存过皮夹,我们的工作人员会马上送过来。

Adams: Oh, I'm so sorry. Yes, I checked it because it's very precious. But I forgot that. I'm terribly sorry for the mistake.

真抱歉。我想起来了,我的确寄存了,因为这个皮夹很贵重。但是我忘了。实在抱歉。

Wang: That's all right, ma'am. I am glad I can help you.

没关系。很高兴帮您解决了问题。

Adams: I really appreciate that.

非常感谢。

Wang: You're welcome.

不客气。

Case Topic 案例话题

My opinion about Wang Li's service in the case.
我对案例中王力服务的看法。

Hotel Manager's Comments
酒店经理点评

(1) 本案例中王力的做法,是冷静处理问题的体现。失物招领部门经常需要面对因丢失物品而恼怒的客人,甚至需要面对客人的牢骚和怀疑。当客人心存疑虑的时候,争辩不能解决任何问题。一定要保持冷静的心态,设法圆满地解决问题。尽量不要和客人理论,如果客人坚持己见,理论只能使矛盾升级。本案例中王力首先给客房部打电话以确认工作人员还在寻找丢失的皮夹,来安慰客人,让他知道酒店正在全力帮助她。继而根据自己的经验查询客人是否寄存了贵重物品,非常灵活地处理了问题,并最终圆满解决,体现了他很高的服务水平。

（2）在酒店失物招领部门工作是充满挑战的，随时要面对各种层次的客人，面对不同价值的物品丢失与认领，工作人员肩负着整个酒店的形象和声誉。服务员应把"服务至上，宾客至上"作为工作的纲领，不论在什么情况下，从客人的角度考虑问题，为他们提供细致耐心的服务，为自己的酒店树立良好的形象，展现其文明程度。

Appendix 1
附录 1

World Famous Hotel Groups
国际著名的酒店集团

InterContinental Hotels Group	England
洲际酒店集团	英国
Cendant Corporation	America
圣达特国际集团/胜腾集团	美国
Marriott International/	
Marriott International Inc.	America
万豪国际酒店集团	美国
Accor	France
雅高国际酒店集团/雅高集团	法国
Wyndham Hotel Group	
Wyndham International	America
温德姆酒店集团	美国
Choice Hotels International	America
精选酒店国际	美国
Hilton Hotels Corp.	America
希尔顿酒店集团	美国
Best Western International	America
最佳西方酒店国际集团	美国
Starwood Hotels & Resorts Worldwide	America
喜达屋国际酒店集团	美国
Home Inns & Hotels Management	China
如家酒店集团	中国
Shanghai Jin Jiang International Group	China
上海锦江国际酒店集团	中国
Global Hyatt Corp.	America
凯悦国际酒店集团/全球凯悦国际酒店集团	美国
7 Days Inn Group	China
七天酒店集团	中国
Carlson Hospitality Worldwide	America
卡尔森国际酒店集团	美国
Hilton Hotels Corporation	
Hilton Worldwide	England

希尔顿酒店集团公司	英国
TUI AG/TUI Hotels & Resorts	Germany
途易酒店与度假村集团	德国
Sol Melia SA	Spain
索尔·梅丽亚集团	西班牙
Extended Stay Hotels	America
超时延住酒店集团	美国
Interstate Hotels & Resorts	America
洲际酒店与度假村集团	美国
Kempinski Hotel	Germany
凯宾斯基国际酒店集团	德国

Appendix 2
附录 2

The Chinese and English of the Indicating Fascias in the Hotel
酒店指示标识的中英文

停车场	parking/parking lot
出租车乘车处	taxi loading
出租车站	taxi station
内部停车场	staff parking/private parking
专用停车场	reserved parking
酒店专车乘车处	hotel bus loading
问讯处	information
接待处	Reception
电话间	telephone booth/telephone
购物中心	shopping center
盥洗室	toilet/washroom
淋浴间	shower(room)
厕所	toilet/W. C. /lav/lavatory
男性	male
女性	female
男厕所	men's/gentlemen's/men/gentlemen
女厕所	women's/ladies'/women/ladies
康乐中心	recreation center
健身房	gymnasium
健身俱乐部	health club
健身中心	fitness center
美容室	beauty parlor/beauty salon
美发厅	hairdresser/hair salon
餐厅	restaurant
酒吧	bar
咖啡厅	coffee shop/cafe
礼品店	gift shop
留言板	message board
旅行代办处	travel counter
商务中心	business center
收银台	cashier
外币兑换	foreign exchange

问询处	information
无烟楼层	non-smoking floor
小卖部	shopping arcade
行政楼层	executive floor
衣帽间	cloakroom
银行	bank
值班经理	duty manager
总服务台	reception
总经理室	general manager's office
行李寄存	left luggage
方向	direction
安全出口	emergency exit
入口	way in
出口	way out
上楼梯	stairs up
下楼梯	stairs down
会议室	conference room
废物箱	rubbish receptacle

参 考 文 献

[1] 肖璇. 现代酒店英语实务教程[M]. 北京:世界图书公司,2006.

[2] 郭兆康. 饭店英语[M]. 北京:旅游教育出版社,2003.

[3] 李红. 敢说饭店服务英语[M]. 北京:机械工业出版社,2005.

[4] 陈昕. 酒吧服务训练手册[M]. 北京:旅游教育出版社,2006.

[5] 刘友道. 饭店管理实用英语[M]. 北京:外文出版社,2006.

[6] 程中锐. 饭店工作英语[M]. 北京:中国旅游出版社,2002.

[7] 张伟. 饭店英语[M]. 天津:南开大学出版社,2008.

[8] 胡扬政. 现代酒店服务英语[M]. 2版. 北京:清华大学出版社,2013.

[9] 夏伟华. 酒店英语[M]. 上海:复旦大学出版社,2015.

[10] 胡扬政. 高职酒店英语课程改革探索与研究[J]. 中国科教创新导刊,2008(29):189-190.

[11] 全国旅游星级饭店评定委员会办公室. 星级饭店经典服务案例及点评[M]. 北京:中国旅游出版社,2008.

[12] http://en.wikipedia.org/wiki/Mahjong.

[13] http://en.wikipedia.org/wiki/Board games.

[14] http://www.ehow.com/list_6459495_pool-emergency-procedures.html.